Radio Goes to War

Radio Goes to War

The Cultural Politics of Propaganda
during World War II

Gerd Horten

UNIVERSITY OF CALIFORNIA PRESS

Berkeley / Los Angeles / London

University of California Press
Berkeley and Los Angeles, California

University of California Press, Ltd.
London, England

First paperback printing 2003

Library of Congress Cataloging-in-Publication Data

Horten, Gerd
    Radio goes to war : the cultural politics of propaganda during World
War II / Gerd Horten.
        p.   cm.
    Includes bibliographical references and index.
    ISBN 0-520-24061-8 (pbk : alk. paper)
    1. Radio broadcasting — Political aspects— United States.   2. Radio
in propaganda — United States — History — 20th century.   3. Radio
broadcasting — United States — History — 20th century.   I. Title.
    HE8697.85.U6 H67 2002
    940.54'88973 — dc21   2001005279

Manufactured in the United States of America

11   10   09   08   07   06   05   04   03
10   9   8   7   6   5   4   3   2   1

The paper used in this publication is both acid-free and totally chlorine-free
(TCF). It meets the minimum requirements of ANSI/NISO Z39.48-1992
(R 1997) (*Permanence of Paper*). ∞

To Anette, Max, Ben, Hannah, and Maya

Contents

Illustrations follow page 86

Acknowledgments

I feel an overwhelming sense of debt and gratitude to the many people and institutions that have aided me these past ten years and made this book possible. The first to be singled out for thanks are Larry Levine and the members of his dissertation group at Berkeley, which provided an ongoing and incisive forum for discussion and criticism of my work in the early stages of this project. This merry group provided an invaluable support network and sense of camaraderie. I am indebted to all of them for their close readings of various chapters: Eric Avila, Leif Brown, Francis Cadogan, John Cheng, Larry Glickman, Sara Nicols, Cecilia O'Leary, Lisa Rubens, Cornelia Sears, Philip Soffer, and Michael Thompson. For four years, this group kept me on track. My friend and mentor, Larry Levine, has stuck with me for the duration. His continuous support and words of advice have been invaluable and have made this a much better book.

I would like to thank the many archivists and librarians who provided me with both professional guidance and valuable leads since my first research trip in 1990. The most important research libraries for my project were the National Archives and the Library of Congress, especially its Manuscript Division as well as its Division for Recorded Sound, in Washington, D.C.; the Mass Communications Center at the State Historical Society in Madison, Wisconsin; and the UCLA Department of Special Collections. I have also greatly benefited from the collections at the Franklin D. Roosevelt Library, the Columbia University Rare Book and Manuscript Division, the J. Walter Thompson Archives at

Duke University, and the Advertising Council Archives at the University of Illinois.

My research at a number of other institutions helped expand my knowledge of the field and develop my focus: the Pioneer Broadcast Museum in Washington, D.C.; the Museum of Broadcasting in New York City; the Department of Special Collections at the Doherty Library at the University of Southern California; and the Library of the Pacific Pioneer Broadcasters in Los Angeles. Finally, I want to thank the many "radio buffs" whom I met along the way and whose infectious enthusiasm helped me stay the course. They also provided me with a number of tapes of original broadcasts that are unavailable at the research libraries.

I am equally grateful to the institutions that helped fund my many research trips and periods of writing. My thanks go to the University of California at Berkeley for a Humanities Research Grant and a yearlong grant from the Mellon Foundation, as well as the H. V. Kaltenborn Foundation, the Roosevelt Library, and the Rockefeller Library for summer research grants. I want to express my gratitude to Menlo School, my employer for four years, which generously awarded me two grants that allowed me to finish the last chapter of the study and revise my whole manuscript over two consecutive summers. Without this help, the project would have lain dormant even longer. Finally, I wish to thank Concordia University for technical support in the last stage of finishing up this manuscript.

I have incurred more debts than I will be able to recall. At conferences, participants, commentators, and fellow panelists helped me sharpen my arguments and deepen my understanding of the larger context of my project. The same applies to the reviewers of my articles. Several scholars deserve particular mention in this respect: Todd Gitlin, Jim Gregory, Michelle Hilmes, the late Roland Marchand, Lary May, and Charles McGovern. They all read parts or all of the manuscript— sometimes more than once—and, together with Larry Levine, provided role models for collegiality through their constructive criticisms and unstinting support. I also wish to thank several of my colleagues and friends at Concordia University whose advice and suggestions helped to clarify and strengthen my arguments: Lynell Edwards, Dick Hill, and Mark Ruff.

My editor, Monica McCormick, and my copy editor, Susan Ecklund, have worked hard on the manuscript and improved it immeasurably. I thank them, as well as Jean McAneny, David Gill, and others at the

University of California Press who helped bring this project to conclusion.

A vast measure of thanks, finally, goes to my family. This study, quite literally, would not have been possible without the help of Anette Horten. Her companionship, editorial skills, and abiding support helped sustain this project over the past decade. I dedicate this book to her and our children. The fact that our children were all born between the inception and completion of the book makes this dedication even more fitting and poignant.

Abbreviations

AAAA   American Association of Advertising Agencies

ABC   American Broadcasting Corporation

ANA   Association of National Advertisers

BBC   British Broadcasting Corporation

CBS   Columbia Broadcasting System

CPI   Committee on Public Information

FCC   Federal Communications Commission

MBS   Mutual Broadcasting System

NAB   National Association of Broadcasters

NAM   National Association of Manufacturers

NAP   National Allocation Plan

NBC   National Broadcasting Company

NRA   National Recovery Administration

OEM   Office of Emergency Management

OFF   Office of Facts and Figures

OPA   Office of Price Administration

OWI   Office of War Information

USO   United Service Organizations

WAC   War Advertising Council

WPB   War Production Board

Radio and the Privatization of War

Within historical writing, radio is finally beginning to gain the recognition it deserves. "Radio" here refers to old-time radio, the "golden age" of broadcasting of the 1920s, 1930s, and 1940s. As a number of media historians have pointed out, this development is long overdue, since radio established the basic structure of broadcasting within which television is still operating. Moreover, most cultural genres offered on television nowadays were pioneered during the radio age. Americans were acculturated to national broadcasting and around-the-clock commercial programming during this same period. As we are beginning to realize, this increased interest in radio history not only tells us about the central importance of radio but also helps us discover new and intriguing aspects of the broader American story.[1]

In general, what is becoming apparent is that we cannot fully understand American society from the 1920s to the late 1940s until there are more studies on radio's impact and its interaction with the society and culture at large. For one thing, no other medium changed the everyday lives of Americans as quickly and irrevocably as radio. By the early 1940s, radio fulfilled more tasks than any other medium. It entertained large national audiences while selling the products of commercial sponsors. It provided national and international news coverage, and during World War II it made Americans—as a people—as well informed as they ever had been. In addition, it provided both national and local programs for special interest groups, foreign-language broadcasts for immigrants, programs by minority civic groups, crop prices and weather forecasts for farmers, sports broadcasting, adventure stories for children, and music for all tastes and ages. We certainly cannot imagine what post–World War II America would look like without television. For too long, we have assumed that we know what the United States from the mid-1920s to the late 1940s was like without having an in-depth knowledge of radio.

No period better reflects historians' neglect of radio broadcasting than World War II. Thus far only two areas of domestic wartime radio have received serious scholarly attention: radio news programs and non-commercial black public affairs broadcasts. While there are numerous studies on Hollywood's involvement in the war effort, no one has written a broad-based study of the role of domestic American radio during the war years.[2] Curiously enough, even international American broadcasting during World War II has attracted more scholarly attention than its domestic counterpart.[3] While this book is not comprehensive, it will fill part of the vast gap.

The lack of scholarly attention to radio is all the more surprising because we know from contemporary testimony and opinion polls how dear radio was to Americans in the 1930s and 1940s. During the Great Depression, as numerous social workers reported, families who had to give up their furniture and other items of comfort clung to their radio as their most treasured possession. In November 1939, *Fortune* conducted a survey asking Americans which, if forced to choose, they would rather give up: going to the movies or listening to the radio. Close to 80 percent of respondents said they would give up going to the movies; only 14 percent were willing to live without their radios. In November 1945, twenty-five hundred Americans were asked by the National Opinion Research Center at the University of Denver: "Taking everything into consideration, which one of these do you think did the best job of serving the public during the war—magazines, newspapers, moving pictures or radio broadcasting?" A full two-thirds (67 percent) of the respondents put radio on the top of their list, followed by newspapers (17 percent), movies (4 percent), and magazines (3 percent).[4]

Radio was the primary medium for Americans during World War II because 90 percent of American families owned at least one radio set and listened to an average of three to four hours of broadcasting a day.[5] Radio was a daily companion, a window onto the outside world, a trusted provider of news and information, and last, though certainly not least, a welcome distraction and entertainment medium. Americans of the 1930s and 1940s could not imagine their lives without their radio sets any more than later generations could imagine theirs without television.

One aim of this study is to demonstrate the importance of radio during the war years and its significance for the wartime propaganda effort. Like the other media, radio was an early recruit to this campaign. It willingly disseminated government propaganda and successfully united much of the American public behind the war effort. In fact, because radio was accessible and nearly omnipresent, it saturated popular culture more quickly and completely than any other medium and played a crucial part in transforming the public and cultural arena into a wartime culture. Driven both by a contagious patriotism and by a desire for profits, radio combined its efforts with those of other media to highlight the stakes of the fight and to exhort Americans to make the necessary sacrifices.

In the process, the media created an increasingly narrow consensus that dominated the cultural sphere. Up to the late 1940s radio, in particular, worked primarily as a centrifugal force in American life. Borrowing a term from Benedict Anderson, Michele Hilmes has argued that radio was particularly suited for the creation of an "imagined [national] community" between the early 1920s and the late 1940s. Even though this nationalization project was fraught with racial and ethnic delimitations and contained a penchant for gender bias, providing a sense of national community was one of radio's key functions: "Physically, culturally, in a common language and through national semipublic institutions, radio spoke to, and about, a nation."[6] During the wartime crisis, this tendency became even more pronounced.

This tendency of national broadcasting leads to the second level of analysis: the cultural politics of radio propaganda, meaning the political and cultural environment in which wartime propaganda was organized, executed, and contested. The phrase "cultural politics" draws special attention to the dynamic interaction between such diverse fields as politics, the political economy, and commercial culture. Indeed, it implies that we cannot and should not draw neat distinctions between these sectors. The real importance of the cultural politics of radio propaganda becomes apparent only when it is contextualized within the broader political, social, and economic developments of the war years, because it spoke to and facilitated changes far beyond the field of broadcasting.

The key transformation discussed in this book is the reaffirmation of corporate dominance over the civic sphere, which was one of the most significant and long-lasting effects of the execution of wartime radio propaganda. In the civic and cultural sphere, business and its priorities were relegitimized and affirmed. After the devastating era of the Great

Depression, which undermined Americans' trust in the free enterprise system, business and advertising were back in the saddle by the early 1940s, ready and eager to impose their order and vision on a strengthened nation. This pro-business mobilization, which began in the late thirties and continued into the postwar period, was not "partially adjourned" during the war, as some historians have argued.[7] Instead, this reversal was at the heart of the cultural and political realignments of the war period. An understanding of this critical transformation is especially important if we seek to explain why the powerful challenges to the corporate order in the postwar period overwhelmingly failed.

The crucial development of these years was the expansion of a corporate-led, consumer-oriented ideology and the construction of a new— and increasingly privatized—public sphere. This reversal originated during the war and built up even more steam in the immediate postwar years. Within this period, the terrain of the American political, social, and cultural landscape was reconfigured through a complex, multifaceted process, led by a ferocious battle on the part of business and advertisers to relegitimize their vision of a privatized, consumer-oriented ideology. The focus of my analysis lies with the early part of this period—the war years—and the way in which commercial radio and wartime propaganda interacted with and shaped this decisive transition.[8]

Radio, the medium most closely and intimately aligned with corporate America, provided an invaluable and indispensable linchpin for this pivotal change during the war. Therefore, an analysis of American radio during World War II is significant not just as a way to understand how radio participated in the war effort, although this is a story that needs telling and has been ignored far too long. It is also significant because a clearer comprehension of American wartime radio and propaganda helps us understand the huge divergence between the eras that preceded and succeeded World War II. In the 1930s, the public sphere was a much more contested arena, in which both the state's influence and alternative cultural and political visions were on the rise. In the postwar period, visions other than corporate ones were increasingly relegated to the niches of culture and politics. This study attempts to explain how things changed so quickly and dramatically.

It is worth emphasizing here that commercial radio never spoke with just one voice, nor was any single group ever able to establish a monopoly over the medium. As a number of revisionist historians have argued, even during the war, the much-prized national unity was a fragile construct; the same is true for the postwar consumerist consensus.

Wartime radio culture provides numerous examples of oppositional trends that undermined mainstream ideas and assumptions. Radio was always shaped by a number of different, and often conflicting, impulses. Even during the wartime crisis, neither popular culture nor politics ever became one-dimensional. What we see, then, is the resurgence of a dominant trend, the powerful reinforcement of a master narrative of corporate hegemony, which was consolidated during the war and spilled over into the postwar period.[9]

This book is divided into two parts, each consisting of three chapters. Part I focuses on radio news and noncommercial government radio propaganda from the late 1930s to the early 1940s, highlighting the role of radio within the politics of the time. At the end of the 1930s, American politics was undergoing a tremendous political transformation, and by the early 1940s a decidedly more conservative political climate had settled over the country. The waning of the New Deal expressed itself in a number of ways. In 1942 and 1943, three of the New Deal's most popular programs—the Civilian Conservation Corps, the Works Progress Administration, and the National Youth Administration—were eliminated in rapid succession by Congress. The demise of these programs can be explained in part by the war and the development of a full-employment economy, but the other main reason was that conservative politicians wanted to halt and, if possible, reverse the New Deal legacy. Ever attuned to the shifting winds of the political culture, Franklin Delano Roosevelt expressed this sea change in December 1943 when he remarked that "Dr. Win-the-War" had replaced "Dr. New Deal." This was a tremendously significant reversal, even though it did not mean a return to the 1920s. To be sure, many of the New Deal's policies survived well past the end of World War II—indeed, they became an integral part of the postwar political and economic order. The two most important legacies were the acceptance of Keynesian economics and a commitment to retain and expand the welfare state. Yet, by the end of the war, New Deal liberals set their sights considerably lower and espoused a new kind of politics—"a liberalism less inclined to challenge corporate behavior," as Alan Brinkley put it, "a liberalism more reconciled to the existing structure of the economy."[10]

The first three chapters all speak to this changing political climate. Chapter 1 explores two of the most important radio issues of the time—radio news and government radio propaganda—and analyzes their respective influence on the politics and political culture at the turn of the decade. This chapter sets the stage for the rest of the discussion by high-lighting the ways in which FDR and his administration used radio both to sell his New Deal policies during the 1930s and to channel American public opinion into a more international and interventionist direction.

Chapters 2 and 3 focus on the respective successes and failures of government-run radio propaganda after America's entry into World War II. These two chapters explain why state-sponsored radio propaganda had only a limited reach and lifetime in the United States and why it failed to define radio's overall participation in the war propaganda effort on the home front. In 1942 and 1943, the Office of War Information (OWI)—the central government agency during the war—launched a number of long-running propaganda series. Yet because these ran as public affairs programs—noncommercial shows often in competition with established popular, commercial radio programs—they always faced an uphill battle. Chapter 3 extends this discussion to include a little-explored aspect of radio, foreign-language broadcasting. The government's intention was to use these programs to celebrate cultural pluralism and unite all Americans behind the war effort. But its well-intentioned and broad-minded approach quickly ran aground, both because of internal conflicts and because it was complicated by the conservative political crosswinds that were sweeping the country. By mid-1943, government-run radio propaganda and the FDR administration's primary influence over the content of radio war messages had effectively ended.

Along with this moderation of New Deal liberalism and the end of government-supervised radio propaganda emerged the second defining shift of these early war years: the close relationship and intimacy between free enterprise and the government. As Karl Barry has succinctly put it, "They entered World War II as adversaries and ended as partners." The key question, however, was who would control the "administrative state" that had been created during the 1930s. The answer was that the government would remain a key player, but that more and more of the state's newfound power would be turned over to business during the economic war mobilization. Alan Brinkley has been more blunt in his assessment of this wartime collaboration. For him the defining aspect of the cooperation between the private economic sector and the U.S. government was the pursuit of a conciliatory approach by the FDR administration and, in the process, "the abdication of power to corporate figures." Strong regulatory powers did not remain in the hands of government agencies like the War Production Board (WPB); rather, the WPB became the primary example of the "corporate 'capture' of state institutions" during World War II. In short, the American wartime mobilization was privatized, which allowed business the opportunity to turn it to its own advantage.[11]

This development in the political economy was paralleled by a concomitant response in cultural politics and propaganda. To the same degree that the "dollar-a-year men"—business leaders recruited for government work during World War II—had taken over the WPB and other economic agencies, they had also captured the propaganda apparatus by 1943. Just as the economic mobilization had become privatized, the propaganda effort became privatized as well. The OWI was officially depoliticized, no longer disseminating high-minded political appeals that might favor specific political ideals or emphasize democratic obligations and civic duties. It was now in the hands of advertisers and their corporate clients, who could inscribe this propaganda with private, commercial, and—supposedly—apolitical appeals.

As World War II progressed, Americans' warrior spirit was increasingly aroused by appeals to private, rather than public and civic, motivations and obligations. Robert Westbrook has described the government-sponsored dissemination of wartime pinups as an appeal to American soldiers "to defend private interests and discharge private obligations." Of course, the pinups' sex appeal was the main draw for sex-starved GIs, but there was more to it, as the elevation of Betty Grable as the quintessential pinup demonstrated. What accounted for Grable's appeal was the fact that she best typified most white soldiers' "image of American womanhood"—the "model girlfriend, wife, and finally mother."[12]

A similar approach permeated every aspect of American wartime propaganda. Frank Fox was the first to analyze the privatized propaganda campaign of World War II America, in which the dollar-a-year men used their control of the propaganda operations to fight two wars: one against Hitler and America's international foes, the other against the domestic enemies of business and the advertising industry. The selling of the "U.S. system of free enterprise" became an integral part of the propaganda messages. Mark Leff has studied another key layer of the discourse of wartime politics, which centered on the appeal to sacrifice. As he has charged, the sacrifices of World War II were not equally shared. In addition, in the hands of the advertising industry, the discourse of sacrifice was translated into private, often consumerist deprivations. It neatly intertwined the politics of wartime sacrifice with the self-interest of American business, as the free enterprise system promised to make up for these deprivations in the postwar era.[13]

Part II of my study analyzes the nature of this increasingly commercial and privatized political culture that defined wartime America. Chapter 4 highlights the collaboration between the radio industry and the War Advertising Council (WAC), which was created by the advertising industry as a liaison between the media and government agencies but increasingly emerged as the central clearinghouse for America's propaganda effort. Because radio was so ideally situated to advance the legitimation of consumer capitalism, the cultural politics of wartime radio propaganda held distinctive advantages for radio's commercial clients and business at large. Like no other medium, it could prop up the corporate image and make it shine brighter than it had in a long time.

Chapter 5 demonstrates that this was achieved largely through the ingenious and seamless incorporation of propaganda into established radio entertainment programs. An analysis of *Fibber McGee and Molly* as well as the comedy shows of Jack Benny and Bob Hope reveals radio's superb execution of its propaganda war, yet it also lays bare the mixture of frictions, unease, and popular resentment that characterized Americans' responses toward the war crisis. Chapter 6 deals with wartime soap operas and their participation in radio's propaganda plan, highlighting the complex negotiations radio writers faced when they were confronted with conflicting agendas and impulses.

Another interesting element of this increasingly privatized discourse of wartime propaganda is the film and visual propaganda of World War II. By early 1943, Hollywood, for one, registered increasing signs that the war-related films of the early war years were losing out at the box office to largely escapist movies. As the *Motion Picture Herald* noted in May 1943: "Overwhelmingly preponderant exhibitor opinion holds that the theater is vastly overfed with war pictures and themes of stress and strife. The preponderant demand is for entertainment and entertainment of the sort that puts aside the cares of these war worn days." Thomas Doherty has suggested that this shift eventually convinced all studios to put "the brakes on war films" in 1943. This led to an increase in the production of comedies and films unrelated to the war and shifted the publicity departments of the studios into high gear as they tried "to disguise the militarist content" of the backlog of war movies.[14]

This increasing public resentment of a heavy-handed propaganda approach dovetails with the dominant trend of wartime radio. Overt political propaganda appeals increasingly took a backseat by 1943. Yet the question then became: How do you motivate a people in the midst of a war, with the promised consumerist vision still several years away? Even though the tide of war had turned, the enemies were not yet defeated, and they showed no signs of letting up. The question of how to maintain national morale at the fever pitch necessary to win a total war became a central concern for officials both in the OWI and in the Roosevelt administration, since they warily agreed that the "over-the-hump psychology" was spreading in 1943. Alongside this overconfidence on the part of the American people, they also identified a growing "selfishness," which expressed itself in rampant violations of the wartime rationing measures and boom times for the black market. Yet since they argued that a return to the political campaigns of the early war years was impossible, they embarked on a new visual and discursive strategy: as George Roeder put it, they started "playing the death card."[15]

Roeder employed this phrase to capture a significant reversal in the censorship rules for wartime photographs. Beginning in September 1943, the government allowed and indeed encouraged increasingly graphic pictures of the brutality and horrors of war and death. Pictures that had been locked up in what was known as the "Chamber of Horrors" in War Department circles were reexamined, and dozens were cleared for release. Americans now saw, usually for the first time, images of dead American soldiers who had paid the ultimate sacrifice for their country. Although the War Department would never release all these pictures, the imagery increasingly focused on the "solitary death" of American soldiers and grew harsher toward the end of the war. A concomitant shift was also visible in the war movies and newsreels of the last war years. To a degree unimaginable earlier in the war, they inched closer to a depiction of "the real war."[16]

The cumulative result of all this was that America fought a unique kind of propaganda war during World War II: it was a privatized war, shot through with appeals to the personal sacrifices or consumerist desires of the American people. The cultural politics of wartime radio propaganda provided a crucial link for the strengthening and relegitimation of the privatized culture of consumer capitalism.

This book analyzes how radio's propaganda effort was invested in this transition. Since radio was both one of the central hubs between the corporate-dominated public sphere and the private arena and one of the favorite entertainment media of the American people, it played a privileged role in this transformation. The epilogue concludes with an assessment of the legacy of the cultural politics of wartime propaganda. It argues that the reinforcement of this drive towards privatization and commercialization provided the ideological foundation for its rapid expansion into the postwar period.

PART ONE

Radio News, Propaganda, and Politics during World War II

CHAPTER I

Radio News, Propaganda, and Politics

From the New Deal to World War II

In the late 1930s, radio was no longer young. Over the previous ten years it had matured into the most popular entertainment medium in the country. The radio networks had expanded into vast organizations, touching every corner of the United States through their affiliations with local stations. Sponsored national radio programs, managed by advertising agencies for their commercial clients, dominated the daytime and nighttime schedules. And radio had forever altered the daily routines and rhythms of most Americans. Yet American broadcasting still lacked one dimension that would eventually define its importance and legacy as much as the entertainment programs: radio news and commentary.

A decade later, with the advantage of hindsight, observers were quick to point out the most important programming change from the late 1930s through the mid-1940s: the unprecedented growth of radio news programs. "The increased volume of news on the air is the greatest program change that has occurred in the last decade," wrote one analyst as he summarized recent developments in American radio. While news programs—news, commentary, and political talk shows—took up just over 5 percent of the program schedule in the late 1930s, their share had increased to almost 20 percent by the mid-1940s. The number of network news commentators had hovered at around half a dozen before World War II broke out in Europe; two years after the war's end, there were more than sixty national commentators on the air reporting the news and analyzing its significance. Locally, the numbers went into the hundreds.[1]

Obviously, these developments did not happen in a vacuum but rather reflected a significant and remarkable change in the way Americans got their news: by the early 1940s, radio became the number one news medium. Two public opinion polls of the period neatly captured the revolution in news dissemination. In 1939 and again in 1945, surveys conducted by public opinion institutes asked Americans to compare the respective importance of newspapers and radio as information media: "From which one source do you get most of your news of what is going on—the newspaper or the radio?" In 1939, over 60 percent of respondents mentioned the newspaper, and 25 percent mentioned radio; by 1945, the roles had been reversed: radio, 61 percent; newspapers, 35 percent.[2]

While radio news, especially foreign news coverage, was a novelty for Americans at the turn of the decade and during the war, this was decidedly not the case for radio propaganda. True, radio had not been around during World War I, yet it already had done duty during another calamity of equal proportions: the Great Depression. As William Leuchtenburg has argued, the Roosevelt administration justified the national mobilization of the New Deal through an "analogue of war." Especially in the early 1930s, newspaper columnists, Republican politicians, and most of the American people agreed that the country was indeed at war against an enemy as dangerous and devastating as any it had encountered in the past, and everybody pledged to do their part. Roosevelt had set the tone for his administration in his first inaugural speech when he announced that he would ask for "broad executive power to wage a war against the emergency, as great as the power that would be given to me if we were in fact invaded by a foreign foe." Republican Alfred Landon, governor of Kansas, promised the president his full cooperation: "I now enlist for the duration of the war." Hugh Johnson, the director of the National Recovery Administration (NRA), was equally quick to use the war analogy. He argued that the privations and sacrifices of the Great Depression had "anything that happened during the War backed off the board."[3] Nothing less than a war mobilization, as he argued in his first major radio address, could save the country.[4]

The symbolism and propaganda accompanying the NRA's policies provided the clearest expression of this analogy. Hugh Johnson was a general who had earned his stripes during World War I by helping to organize both the draft and government-industry cooperation through the War Industries Board.[5] The Blue Eagle—the official symbol of the NRA—was displayed in shop windows, on letterheads and invoices, and on clothing labels to indicate that companies were participating in NRA policies and fulfilling their patriotic duty. World War I soldiers had originally worn the emblem on bright badges during night attacks in order to avoid being hurt by friendly fire. Moreover, numerous cities organized military parades in 1933 to kick off NRA code drives. These efforts, together with the relentless propaganda in the press, on the radio, and in the movies, reminded many observers of the Liberty Loan drives of the Great War: "Not since the war-time Liberty Loan drives has the nation been so stirred to the support of its Government as it is to-day. The people are marching under the banner of the Blue Eagle, responding to the slogan 'we do our part.'" Another journalist came to the same conclusion: "Washington these days is like Washington in the summer of 1917. . . . The President is again the Commander-in-Chief."[6] Radio played a critical part in this peacetime mobilization.

This chapter discusses both government radio propaganda and radio news from the 1930s through the beginning of World War II. The main goal is to evaluate their respective influence on politics and to set the stage for a discussion of radio propaganda during World War II. Radio news was immensely influential in shaping public opinion because of its unique qualities as an information medium and because it was untainted by the legacies of earlier propaganda. Government-run radio propaganda, on the other hand, had already become suspect even by the turn of the decade. By the time the United States entered World War II, the strategies and narrative devices of the renewed propaganda effort seemed all too familiar. This did not bode well for government-run radio propaganda in the early 1940s.

Propaganda Legacies and Collective Memory

In the late 1930s, with war brewing in Europe and the renewed concern over the influence of propaganda in the United States, researchers made a timely discovery. In January 1937, Cedric Larson, a staff member of the Library of Congress, found the complete records of the Committee on Public Information (CPI) — the American propaganda agency during World War I — in the basement of an old War Department building. Larson teamed up with James Mock to study the materials, and in 1939 the two published the first comprehensive study of the propaganda crusade of the Great War.[7]

Larson and Mock's report confirmed Americans' fears about propaganda. First of all, they argued, the CPI had been tremendously successful in uniting the country behind the war in an unbelievably short span of time. The committee had almost immediately turned into "a gargantuan advertising agency," which undertook a breathtaking range of activities. The only adequate comparison that came to mind was the spectacular propaganda successes of the totalitarian dictatorships in the 1920s and 1930s. What disconcerted Larson and Mock just as much was how the rise of the nationalistic fervor during World War I had allowed the government to increase its censorship powers to a degree not seen in the United States since the late eighteenth century. As they put it, "America went under censorship during the [First] World War without realizing it."[8]

Foremost in the minds of many Americans in the late 1930s was one lesson learned from World War I: never again would they be drawn into war by propaganda, lured by a mixture of atrocity stories and high-sounding moral appeals. In part, this "propaganda consciousness" of Americans grew out of hearing all too many former propagandists confess to fabricating atrocity stories or boast of their success in whipping up the American public. In 1939, H. C. Peterson summed up the American public consensus on World War I propaganda: "The propaganda [both British and American] was not only responsible in a large degree for the American entrance into the war, but it was also responsible for the temper and irrationality of the peace treaty and the vindictiveness of the post-war years."[9]

Even after a year of war in Europe and the fall of France, as Harold Lavine and James Wechsler noted in their 1940 public opinion study, Americans' collective memory of World War I remained the strongest obstacle to Allied and domestic propagandists. They concluded, "Disbelief was the chief inheritance of America from the last war." Although the sentiments of Americans were solidly behind the Allied cause, Lavine and Wechsler concluded that this time propaganda would not sway the American public in either direction. If anything, it would produce the opposite effect: "If Allied propaganda intensified anti-war feeling in the United States, German propaganda intensified anti-Hitler feeling."[10]

An additional reason for Americans' propaganda consciousness was that the country had fought another war since World War I: the national crusade against the Great Depression. All media, including radio, had cooperated enthusiastically as they had done in the Great War and would do again during World War II. During the height of the NRA publicity from July through November 1933, for example, the National Broadcasting Company (NBC) alone donated close to seventeen hours of network time, and "countless more were organized by the local offices of the Recovery Administration." Two NBC stations in New York provided an additional six hours for NRA programming. During the same four months, NBC on two occasions even canceled commercial programs to make room for speeches by General Johnson. Between August 22 and September 23, the NRA scheduled twenty-two programs, although not all were picked up by the networks. The biggest single show was a mammoth two-hour broadcast on August 27, hosted by popular singer Kate Smith and backed by the participation of well-known radio, stage, and screen talent.[11]

By 1935, most observers agreed with E. Pendleton Herring's assessment of the New Deal publicity two years after its initiation: "No longer is official propaganda confined largely to war. . . . Never before has the Federal Government [during peacetime] undertaken on so vast a scale and with such deliberate intent the task of building a favorable public opinion toward its policies."[12] As might be expected, conservative journalists and politicians quickly soured on the New Deal propaganda and were particularly critical of the government's use of radio. One opponent of the administration termed it "the greatest political show ever put on in this country" and reserved his strongest criticism for radio, which in 1933 "was almost wholly pro–New Deal"; a good part of the press had at least resisted this government usurpation of the communication media. Part of this indictment of government propaganda included charges that a member of the Federal Radio Commission (FRC)—the forerunner of the Federal Communications Commission (FCC)—had used the government's leverage over the industry to intimidate broadcasters. Indeed, a FRC commissioner had sent a letter to all radio stations in August 1933, demanding that broadcasters refuse their facilities to advertisers and sponsors who did not collaborate with the NRA codes. Part of this letter read as follows: "It is hoped that radio stations, using valuable facilities loaned to them temporarily by the government, will not unwittingly be placed in an embarrassing position because of the greed or lack of patriotism on the part of a few unscrupulous advertisers."[13]

The NRA experience foreshadowed the relationship between FDR's administration and the news media. As the decade progressed, the majority of newspapers came out in opposition to the New Deal. In 1932, Roosevelt had been elected by 57 percent of the popular vote with the editorial support of only 41 percent of the dailies (and 45 percent of the weeklies). In 1936, when Americans reelected the president with 60 percent of the popular vote, his newspaper support had shrunk to 37 percent (and 40 percent of the weeklies). By 1940, this gap had grown even further: 55 percent of Americans voted for FDR, but only 25 percent of daily newspapers (and 33 percent of weeklies) supported him.[14] Over the same period, Roosevelt increased his number of network appearances. He delivered fifty-one speeches over the radio networks in 1932 and fifty speeches in 1933. In both 1936 and 1940, he gave seventy-two radio speeches. An even better indication of the administration's increased reliance on radio was the introduction of radio units in numerous government departments. As Jeanette Sayre has summarized this development, "The Roosevelt landslide of 1932 ushered in a new era in broadcasting by federal agencies. . . . They [the New Dealers] used all media in explaining the functioning of the agencies, but the press, soon hostile to the Roosevelt reforms, was less available to them than radio."[15]

The best-known examples of this government radio publicity were FDR's "fireside chats." Roosevelt took to the air twice during the first week after his inauguration on March 4, 1933, yet it was his first informal speech on March 12, on the banking crisis, that revealed his talent as a radio orator. About half of American families owned a radio in 1933, and it has been estimated that approximately 30 percent of the nation's radios were tuned in to the president's first fireside chat. "I want to talk for a few minutes with the people of the United States about banking," Roosevelt began in his soothing voice. He went on to explain the banking crisis in a way laymen could understand, and by announcing a bank holiday and restoring the trust of the American people in their financial system, he succeeded in averting the most serious crisis facing his young administration. The implications of this adroit use of radio were not lost on political commentators. The *New York Times* observed: "His use of this new instrument of political discussion is a plain hint to Congress of a recourse which the President may employ if it proves necessary to rally support for legislation for which he asks and which the lawmakers might be reluctant to give him."[16]

By the mid-1930s, the networks were broadcasting over a hundred special government programs on a noncommercial basis every year. By 1935, eight federal agencies produced regular weekly programs, with more agencies planning series for the coming year. In February 1936, *Variety* commented on the large increase in the number of government radio programs: "Government use of radio is mounting to the point where the broadcast industry earmarks [a] large chunk of its time for Federal programs." Most of this New Deal radio propaganda was controversial and became the target of harsh partisan criticism.[17]

The programs produced by the Office of Education of the Department of the Interior aroused the most controversy. From 1935 to 1940, this office produced twelve noncommercial network programs, which generally ran from half a year to a year. The goal of this Educational Radio Project, as contemporaries referred to it, was to put educational programs on network radio and to promote education by radio on local stations and in schools. In general, the broadcasts presented informational, scientific, or historical programs, but they also included clearly partisan series such as *Democracy in Action* (1939–40), which explored the "contributions of government to solutions of complex problems in American industry, health, social security, foreign trade, labor welfare, etc."[18]

At the height of its activities, the Office of Education maintained the biggest radio department of any government agency. By June 1936, the project employed 75 people; in the fiscal year 1939–40, the office had a quarter-million-dollar budget and between 170 and 200 employees on its payroll. Overwhelmingly it hired unemployed writers, actors, and technicians who had signed up with the Civil Conservation Corps or others who could not find work in commercial radio. The office had extensive contacts with educational groups and civic organizations, and it frequently benefited from the voluntary collaboration by big-name radio talent such as Orson Welles.[19]

Of course, Roosevelt and his administration did not have the air all to themselves. Both Governor Huey Long of Louisiana, and Father Charles Coughlin, who would emerge as two major detractors of the administration, had discovered radio as well and by the mid-1930s commanded huge audiences. Similarly, big business attacked the New Deal policies and staged a concerted campaign "to sell free enterprise" under the tutelage of the National Association of Manufacturers (NAM). The purpose of this ongoing campaign was not just to humanize business, but also to clearly target New Deal policies, focusing on the goal of "outselling the politicians."[20]

This pro-business public relations campaign grew by leaps and bounds beginning in the mid-1930s, which coincided with the second, more radical, phase of the New Deal. Since the campaign penetrated all media, it naturally also found its expression on the radio. Both General Motors and Ford started sponsoring symphony hours, which included "intermission talks" that promoted the American system of free enterprise. William J. Cameron became known for his attacks on New Deal policies, which he delivered during the *Ford Symphony Hour*. When the

NRA was declared unconstitutional in May 1935, for example, Cameron celebrated its termination in his talk: "Constructed of baseless fancies and colored by rainbow hues, a perfect welter of gorgeously incompetent plans faded and melted at the first touch of reality. . . . Every attempt to subjugate our citizens as vassals of the state has failed. A vast sense of relief possesses the whole people."[21]

The NAM produced a serial called *The American Family Robinson* and sent it to radio stations to play whenever it fit into their schedules. In 1936, a total of 222 stations carried the program at least once a week. In each show, the father of the family expounded on issues such as labor conditions or political and social trends. The cast of characters also included Professor Broadbelt, who was portrayed as the "prototype of the panacea peddler, organizer of Arcadia, Inc." This serial was part of the well-organized anti–New Deal and antiunion propaganda that the NAM pursued through every medium of communication. Its central message was that American businessmen were still the true leaders of the nation.[22]

A final example of this kind of radio publicity was the DuPont company's *Cavalcade of America,* though in this case the strategy was more specific. DuPont began sponsoring the series about the same time that Congress was uncovering the company's World War I profiteering schemes, which exposed DuPont as one of the main "merchants of death" of that war. The radio series highlighted the progress of science as well as outstanding examples of humanitarian assistance in American history in episodes like "The Seeing Eye," on the organization that trained dogs to lead the blind; "The Willingness to Share"; or a broadcast on Anti-Tuberculosis Christmas Seals. As one observer remarked, "Such programs . . . are likely to get the public out of the habit of thinking of DuPont as exclusively or primarily a manufacturer of munitions."[23]

This flurry of business publicity between the middle and late 1930s led *Fortune* magazine to argue in 1939 that businessmen had just discovered the power of public relations: "The year 1938 may go down in the annals of industry as the season in which the concept of public relations suddenly struck home to the hearts of a whole generation of businessmen." The reason for this development, the writer continued, was that "the New Deal . . . [had] spread the word public relations broadcast over the land."[24] The truth, of course, was that American business had pursued this route for quite some time. What was new was the degree to which FDR and his administration had succeeded in selling their policies to the American people, as well as the level at which the public relations battle was raging in the middle to late 1930s.[25]

Furthermore, with Roosevelt's reelection in 1936 and his unsuccessful "court-packing plan" a year later, fears of an authoritarian government and the extensive use of government propaganda, combined with the sheer hatred of FDR among many businessmen and commentators, revived comparisons of the Roosevelt administration with fascism and of FDR with Hitler. Gordon Carroll expressed this criticism in his article "Dr. Roosevelt's Propaganda Trust," published in the *American Mercury* in 1937. Roosevelt, Carroll argued, had "Hitlerized his constituents." Hundreds of government agencies had been created for no other purpose than to spread the New Deal policies and Weltanschauung: "Each of these bureaus, departments, boards, or administrations is utilized constantly by the *Führer* in putting over his propaganda message to the public—in an 'educational and informational' manner." Most important, as in European fascist regimes, American radio had become the "No. 1 instrument of State propaganda."[26]

While the partisanship of such vituperative attacks was easy to detect, these critics were right in pointing out that a new element had been added to the political landscape. The Roosevelt government not only was intervening in economic affairs on an unprecedented level but also had inserted its voice in the cultural affairs of the country. Through newsreels, documentary films, theater, murals, and radio, the state was reaching out to the American people. The 1930s was the decade of greatly expanded state propaganda and information not only in Europe but in the United States as well. In Europe, however, corporate states swallowed the arts and entertainment whole and turned them into obedient vehicles of their propaganda machinery. In the United States, this development stopped far short of such wholesale usurpation but introduced an important new element: by the 1930s, the state had become an important actor in the cultural politics of the country.[27]

Yet as the New Deal impulse weakened by the end of the decade, Congress garnered the necessary votes to end most of the New Deal radio propaganda in 1940. Hardest hit was the Radio Project in the Office of Education, the largest and most important New Deal radio unit.[28] For Republicans concerned about the Roosevelt administration's use of radio and other media, World War II could not have come at a worse time. They were just about to rid themselves of these political nuisances when the war gave government-run propaganda another lease on life.

Radio: A Different Kind of News Medium

Historians have little difficulty in pinpointing the moment when American radio made its debut as the preeminent medium for foreign news: the Munich Crisis in September 1938. Early that month, Hitler had raised the stakes in his gamble to dominate Europe by demanding self-determination for Germans living in a region of Czechoslovakia known as the Sudetenland. He left few doubts that he meant to repatriate these Germans by annexing the Sudetenland as part of an enlarged German Reich. High-level negotiations ensued, during which Britain's prime minister, Neville Chamberlain, journeyed to Germany three times in less than three weeks in a desperate attempt to save peace. Peace hung in the balance, and as Europe mobilized, America temporarily awoke from its isolationist slumber. Bent on minding their own business and fearful that a European war would once again entangle them, Americans became glued to their radios for daily and sometimes hourly updates and interpretations of the latest developments of the crisis.[29] Within a couple of days, American listeners were bombarded with news programs, special news bulletins, European roundups, and expert commentary on the crisis.

The coverage of the eighteen-day standoff in Europe turned into a news event extraordinaire in the United States that allowed Americans to listen to history in the making. The programs were something entirely new, with the suspense and drama of a Hollywood thriller—except that this was for real. The networks spared no expense in covering the event: transmission costs for foreign news reports escalated, and regularly scheduled commercial programs at home were interrupted and even canceled at will. Commentators and reporters in the European capitals and stateside held twenty-four-hour vigils and slept when they could, ever ready to bring the latest news to American audiences. Listeners soon expected multiple live, on-the-scene European reports, as well as news roundups, which took them from New York to Berlin and Paris, Prague and London—all within a few minutes. No doubt, radio news coverage came of age during the crisis.

One name that became inextricably linked with the coverage of the Munich crisis was that of H. V. Kaltenborn. Kaltenborn was fifty-eight years old in the fall of 1938 and, in his own words, had prepared for this moment all his life. He was fluent in several European languages, was widely read and well traveled, and had an intimate familiarity with European politics, geography, and culture. Moreover, he was not new to radio: his authoritative voice had been heard on an unsponsored news program on the Columbia Broadcasting System (CBS) for the past several years. Yet it was only through his indefatigable, around-the-clock reporting and well over one hundred largely extemporaneous commentaries during the Munich crisis that he became a household name in the United States and earned himself the unofficial title of "dean of news commentators." Kaltenborn's headquarters were in Studio Nine of the Columbia Broadcasting Company in New York, where he slept on a cot for the duration of the crisis. From there he surveyed the news, providing the New York linchpin for the European roundups and, most important, digesting and interpreting the complex European developments for American listeners.[30]

The immense interest these programs garnered in the United States was evident both in the huge listening audiences and in the thousands of letters that flooded the network studios, congratulating them on a job well done. Kaltenborn claimed that he received fifty thousand letters and telegrams during the three weeks of nonstop coverage. While the level of listener response spoke to the nation's overall interest in the crisis, individual letters also provided a glimpse into why Americans felt so keenly involved and interested in the radio news coverage.

One notion expressed in the correspondence to Kaltenborn was the excitement of being present as historical events unfolded across the Atlantic Ocean: "Columbia's achievement in giving, for the first time in history, an opportunity to its audience to be a witness of history in the making, deserves the highest praise, and your comments are the talk of the town of Hollywood." The writer went on to state that everyone in Hollywood—from writers and producers to actors and stagehands— was impressed by the drama conveyed by radio. Tied up in this allure was the sense of time traveling and vicarious experience, as well as a palpable apprehension as listeners waited for the next act of the drama: "I am now waiting to listen to Hitler's speech. I feel the keenest excitement and romance in being able to hear directly from Europe."[31]

Many people who wrote to Kaltenborn confessed—with some embarrassment—that this was their first "fan letter." Others asked for transcripts or posed specific questions concerning the crisis. A few even ventured into possible future scenarios, taking on the role of news commentators themselves. There was little doubt that, for many listeners, this had become an all-absorbing event, as one woman from New Jersey attested in her letter: "My radio stayed tuned in on Station WABC from the time I arose in the morning until the time I retired at night, for I did not wish to miss a single one of Columbia's timely news bulletins nor a single one of your very clear and interesting analyses." Another listener described her own trepidation and sense of involvement: "I lose sleep and let my house go to sit near our radio whenever you are due to speak."[32]

Americans from all across the continent expressed their gratitude to Kaltenborn and the CBS news team for their objective reporting and intelligible interpretations: "At such a time, when the layman is baffled by so many abtruse [sic] and conflicting reports, your far-sighted and unbiased explanations are a boon to those of us who are sincerely trying to understand." It is also clear that radio sizably increased the news audience in the United States and opened it up to segments of the population that had given up on other media, particularly newspapers: "Like so many housewives, I do not usually keep up with current events, but I have became [sic] so interested, through your help, that I find I am not only so much better informed, but also able to form my own opinions, and less confused by the newspaper reports." One last letter to Kaltenborn summarized many of the sentiments expressed in this "fan mail," including the benefits the radio industry and networks were reaping from this new programming, which was widely seen as radio's best public service to date:

Maybe when you will have an opportunity to get to your mail—which must be stacking up in piles from a continent of millions of listeners—[you will realize how] grateful—unspeakably grateful—[Americans are] to you and the Columbia Broadcasting Company. Your broadcasts here made history. Never will this generation experience anything so dramatic—so breathtaking—so all compelling in a lifetime. You have stayed at your post, weary and tense, and the nation has stayed with you, listening with bated breath, tense with anxiety. . . . Thinking people will salute you.[33]

In Europe, Hitler won the battle of nerves by staring down England and France. The democracies lost the confrontation by agreeing to the partitioning of helpless Czechoslovakia. In the United States, the crisis only heightened American determination to stay out of any possible European conflicts. In the meantime, U.S. observers had begun to write a new chapter in the annals of radio history. Praise for radio's news coverage came not only from listeners but also from within the field of journalism. *The Nation* congratulated radio, and especially Columbia, on the "superb job" of bringing frequent broadcasts directly from Europe and called the coverage "radio's greatest educational achievement."

James Rorty was equally and uncharacteristically effusive when he wrote later in the same magazine that "a new dimension has been added to politics and diplomacy. For the first time history has been made in the hearing of its pawns." He went on to commend radio on its "magnificent" performance and noted with surprise and satisfaction that "commercialism took a back seat during the crisis."[34]

Though it would take another year or two and the outbreak of war in Europe to entrench news programming firmly in radio's schedule and the audiences' daily routines, an important milestone had been passed in establishing radio as the emerging primary news medium in the country. The reasons for this transformation are captured in the letters from Kaltenborn's listeners: the immediacy of the reporting, the firsthand accounts, the extension of one's environment and vicarious traveling through radio, and, finally, the intelligible reporting and interpretation that radio provided.

Some of these qualities came naturally to radio; others were consciously developed and matured with the new dimension of radio reporting. As Paul W. White, chief of the CBS news division, pointed out in a book on the new craft, radio news staff very deliberately created a "new language" for journalism. No longer was it mandatory to pack the five W's (who, what, where, when, and why) and an H (how) into the lead sentence of the first paragraph, as was the practice in print journalism. Newspaper writing was unnecessarily stilted and unintelligible, argued White. He cited a number of studies which demonstrated that most press agency reports and subsequent newspaper articles were written at a level well above the reading ability of many Americans—especially since the education of many Americans had ended after the freshman year in high school. In contrast, radio used more accessible language almost immediately and instinctively: "It wasn't until radio really got going that news reached Americans in simple, direct English. The response was favorable and immediate. People were no longer baffled."[35]

This change was also corroborated in a study undertaken by the Office of Radio Research of Columbia University. In 1939, Paul Lazarsfeld, the director of the office, and his staff embarked on an in-depth analysis comparing the appeal of newspapers and the radio as news disseminators. The use of "plain English" was mentioned frequently as one explanation for radio's special attraction, as one respondent emphasized: "When you are reading, sometimes you don't know the words, then you skip them. When they talk to you, *they talk in plain English*." Added another fan of radio news: "I understand more easily when I am listening. *It is explained better*" [italics in the original].[36]

Yet Lazarsfeld and his researchers also made clear that radio news listeners were not necessarily converts from or apostates of the newspaper business. Many of these listeners were new to the news audience—period. Like the writer who confessed to Kaltenborn her confusion and bafflement when reading newspaper articles, many other Americans who had been out of the loop news-wise were now reached by radio. Lazarsfeld's research, for example, demonstrated that lower- and lower-middle-class Americans expressed a particularly strong preference for radio as a news source. Many of them had not read the political news covered by newspapers. Another broad audience that felt particularly attached to the new medium consisted of rural Americans, who no longer had to rely on local papers for coverage of national and international news. Very likely, two additional cultural attributes of radio appealed to Americans not given to solitary brooding over the written word. First of all, listening to the radio was a socialized activity, which one could enjoy with others. The other factor was the human voice, which made radio more interesting, real, and personal. Again and again this latter aspect reverberated through the responses of the Americans surveyed by Lazarsfeld: "It is more *interesting* when a person talks to you. . . . I like the voice. It is *nearer* to you. . . . A voice to me has always been more *real* than words to be read" [italics in the original].[37]

Lazarsfeld's study indicated that radio was significantly expanding the American news audience. Yet it would be a mistake to assume that only less educated, lower- and lower-middle-class Americans listened to radio. Rather, radio reached all segments of the American public and would soon be the preferred medium for Americans of every social and economic class. In short, almost all Americans would listen to radio news, but nowhere close to all Americans read the political news sections in the papers. Radio drew in millions who had previously passed on political news—because it was too onerous, too baffling, or simply too boring. Listening, in turn, was considered a "friendly activity," made more appealing by the warm, personal touch of the human voice. No doubt, radio news helped to democratize the news environment in the United States and introduced scores of Americans to the excitement of political news.[38]

The fact that many Americans viewed radio as a "friend" also had repercussions for their evaluation of radio news. In general, the American public trusted radio more than any other single source of information. In August 1939, the public opinion institute of Elmer Roper asked Americans which source they would trust most if they heard conflicting stories about the same event—radio, the newspapers, or an official spokesperson. Forty percent of those interviewed answered that they would trust radio, while 26 percent opted for newspapers, and only 13 percent said they would believe an official spokesperson. Certainly, the overall low respect for newspapers—partly because of their overwhelming opposition to FDR and their one-sided editorials in the 1930s—had something to do with this outcome. Radio's novelty and its largely unvarnished reputation, especially in the field of news coverage, probably were factors as well. But the most important reason was the medium itself: Americans simply trusted radio more.[39]

The degree to which this novel coverage of news throughout the latter half of September 1938 had impressed and unsettled many Americans became evident the following month. On Halloween night of the same year, Orson Welles directed and produced an adaptation of H. G. Wells's science-fiction fantasy *War of the Worlds*, which told of a Martian invasion of Earth. The broadcast played on Welles's regular program, *Mercury Theater on the Air*, which was unsponsored but garnered a regular audience of several million listeners. That night, with the Munich Crisis still fresh in listeners' minds, Welles would create a furor. About one million Americans—roughly 20 percent of the program's listening audience—were duped by the show, many of them frantically packing up their belongings and jamming the highways in a futile attempt to escape from the deadly invaders.[40]

Researchers later found that the characteristic that contributed most to the realism of Welles's program was its effective use of news bulletins. Welles had rewritten the play to give it the appearance of news and rapidly unfolding events, covered in similar fashion as the recent crisis in Europe. This similarity, combined with Americans' faith in radio, was the main reason for the panic. As one listener described the sentiments of many: "We have so much *faith in broadcasting*. In a crisis it has to reach all people. That's what radio is here for."[41]

Covering the International Crisis

Radio news programs of a simpler kind than the coverage of the 1938 European crisis had been part of radio for some time, yet they had usually been relegated to the niches of the radio schedule. By the late

1920s, news broadcasts had been added to program offerings, but they consisted largely of a selective reading of the newspapers over the air. Station owners and network executives liked to squeeze these broadcasts into their schedules, however, since they provided two appreciable advantages. They were inexpensive to produce, and they were considered educational programs, through which both networks and individual stations hoped to fulfill the FCC-enforced public service obligation.[42]

Yet beginning in the early 1930s, the radio networks laid the foundation for the establishment of larger, full-fledged news departments. Columbia made its most important early hires in this area in 1930, when both Edward Klauber and Paul White joined the network to establish a serious news department. Klauber had previously worked for the *New York Times* and as public relations director for a major corporation. He quickly rose in the ranks of Columbia and by late 1931 he held the position of executive vice president, from where he supervised the expansion of the CBS news team. White had made his career solely in journalism, initially in the newspaper business and since 1924 as a correspondent for United Press, one of the main American news associations. NBC set about the task of building a news department at about the same time as CBS. Its most important early addition was Abe Schechter, who joined the network in 1932. Like his counterparts at CBS, he had held a variety of jobs in the field of journalism and had worked for both newspapers and press associations.[43]

As radio was becoming serious about the news business, it quickly was able to upstage the newspapers in covering several key events in the early 1930s. In 1932, radio issued the first reports of the kidnapping of Charles and Anne Morrow Lindbergh's baby. The same year, CBS negotiated a special contract with United Press to receive the results of the presidential election and devoted all evening to this coverage. Radio again beat the newspapers to the story of the assassination attempt against FDR prior to his inauguration in early 1933. Because of these coups, the battle between radio and the newspapers, which had been brewing for a couple of years, finally broke out into the open.[44]

The key strategy of the newspapers in what became known as the "press-radio war" was to withhold from radio the fodder for news, that is, to forbid the press associations from serving the network and radio stations. In 1933, still holding the shorter end of the stick, the networks agreed to a short-lived peace treaty. According to the plan, a separate Press-Radio Bureau would be set up to supply broadcasters with news. Yet, and here was the crux, the individual items were not to exceed thirty words and were to be sufficient only for two five-minute newscasts, one in the morning at 9:30 or later and the other in the evening at 9:00 or later. The intent clearly was to avoid competition with the morning and late editions of the daily papers. The only exception to this rule applied to news of "transcendent importance"; such bulletins could be read over the air immediately. The truce and the agreement lasted only as long as it took some enterprising souls to establish competitive news services for the radio industry. The most successful among several upstart associations was the Transradio News Service, established in early 1934. By 1935, it had made such sizable inroads into the radio news business that both United Press and the International News Service abandoned their restricted service to radio and, late that same year, started to supply any broadcaster who was interested in their services. The Associated Press stuck to its boycott of radio news until 1940, when it also entered the fray.[45]

Other memorable events in the history of radio news during the mid-1930s pointed to the increasing importance of the medium. Two radio commentators, Boake Carter and Gabriel Heatter, built their reputations in 1935 when they covered the "trial of the century": the defendant, Bruno Richard Hauptmann, stood accused of the kidnapping and murder of the Lindbergh baby. He was found guilty and immediately sentenced to die in the electric chair. In September 1936, H. V. Kaltenborn and his brave French technician scored a coup in international radio coverage when they reported from the front lines of the Spanish civil war, with the roar of battle clearly audible in the background. Later that same year, Americans gathered in record numbers before their radio sets to hear an unprecedented event in English royal history: Edward VIII declared to the world that he was abdicating the throne because he was unable to carry the burdens and responsibilities of the duties as king of England "without the help and support of the woman I love." The king had fallen in love with a twice-divorced woman from Baltimore.[46]

The networks increased their forays into the field of foreign news reporting over the next few years, as European affairs became more and more tumultuous. Both NBC and CBS had had representatives in Europe since the early 1930s. Until the Munich Crisis, however, these individuals' first task was not to report but rather to transmit newsworthy events or to arrange for educational or cultural broadcasts: political speeches, concerts, talks by renowned novelists and artists, and occasional interviews. By early 1938, each network had two people on the

scene in Europe, one in England and the other on the Continent. For
NBC, Fred Bate was stationed in London, and Max Jordan covered the
Continent; their respective CBS counterparts were Edward R. Murrow
and William L. Shirer.

Bate, Jordan, and Shirer had worked for newspapers or press associations prior to their broadcasting careers. Jordan, a German-born nat-
uralized citizen, had worked for the Hearst papers in the 1920s before
joining NBC. Bate had lived in Europe since 1912 and had worked for
a number of Americans news organizations. Both Jordan and Bate had
been in Europe on assignments for NBC since the early 1930s and had
established elaborate networks and connections. Jordan, in particular,
had been very successful in signing contracts with the German, Austrian,
and Hungarian governments, which gave NBC privileged use of their
broadcasting facilities. These arrangements were further solidified because most European countries were only familiar with state-owned
broadcasting, and officials generally assumed that NBC was the official,
national broadcasting station of the United States. Murrow and Shirer,
in contrast, were new in their respective jobs. Murrow had joined CBS
in 1935 as director of talks and was sent to Europe in 1937 to take over
as European director of CBS. Shortly after his arrival he had signed up
Shirer, who had just lost his job with the floundering United News
Service, as his Continental liaison. Surprisingly, considering their late
start, Murrow and the CBS staff would soon outshine the NBC news
team, establishing themselves as the premier news network in the United
States by the early 1940s. In the field of broadcasting, this was the beginning of a journalistic legend: the "Murrow Boys" would dominate
the CBS newsrooms for the next several decades.[47]

In the late 1930s, however, NBC and especially Max Jordan remained
tough, and for the most part equal, competitors. In fact, the first major
success for CBS, a European roundup in early 1938, was born out of
defeat. The occasion was the Austrian Anschluss in March 1938, when
Hitler's troops marched into Vienna and united the two countries.
Shirer was in Vienna as the unannounced takeover occurred, yet he
could not get the story out because Nazi officials now in charge of the
broadcasting facilities denied him access to the microphone. Murrow
was on assignment in Warsaw. When the two connected, they agreed
that Shirer would fly to London to broadcast an uncensored eyewitness
account, and Murrow would fly to Vienna to continue monitoring the
situation. Both were able to reach their destinations through Berlin.
Shirer took the last seat on a flight to London, while Murrow hired a
plane all for himself. Yet "Ubiquitous Max"—as NBC's Jordan was

known in journalism circles—had scooped them: after rushing to Vienna, he talked his way past the Nazi officials who denied Shirer access to the broadcasting station, submitted his report to the censors, and relayed the first eyewitness account of the Austrian takeover to the United States.

In New York, CBS chief William Paley was furious that NBC had beaten them to the punch. He called Klauber in New York and ordered a half-hour roundup from Europe for the same evening. Until that point, Klauber and Murrow had done only two roundups, but these had required months of preparation because of the technical difficulties involved in such programs. Now they had exactly seven hours. Immediately, the CBS office in London started buzzing. Shirer reached Murrow in Vienna, and they agreed that Murrow would try to take care of the Berlin and Vienna end, and Shirer would arrange for connections from London, Rome, and Paris. The ensuing frantic work paid off: at 1:00 A.M. London time (8:00 P.M. in New York) , CBS canceled its regularly scheduled music program and brought its listeners the first ad hoc European roundup, which went off without a hitch. White and the CBS news staff were ecstatic about the program and asked for another one—the following night.[48]

As Shirer put it, that evening "radio had made a discovery. It found a new job to perform." Edward Bliss, Jr., concurs with this assessment in his history of broadcast journalism: "This was the first *news* roundup from overseas. It changed forever the way foreign news was reported." Bliss quotes another commentator, who pointed to the long-term impact of this discovery: "This was the start of a broadcast journalism tradition that eventually brought the Vietnam War into America's living room."[49]

With the Czech crisis, firsthand news coverage of international events became a permanent feature of American radio. Alongside it grew the demand for radio commentators who stood ready to digest and interpret the latest news for American listeners. Increasingly, too, these programs no longer had to broadcast on a sustaining basis because sponsors were eager to scoop them up as fast as they were put on the air. The annual percentages of sponsored network programs clearly chart this change. In 1938–39, the program category of "news, commentators, and talks" represented 7 percent of all sponsored network programs on the air. By 1940–41, it had increased to almost 13 percent. By the 1943–44 radio season, this type of programming accounted for nearly 18 percent of the commercial network shows.[50]

Americans came to rely on regular news periods on radio between

7:30 and 8:30 A.M., at noon, during the dinner hour, and for a last update between 10:30 and 11:30 P.M. Most Americans followed the war through radio: the Polish invasion, which marked the beginning of war in Europe, the "phony war" of 1939–40, the blitzkrieg in the West in the spring of 1940, the fall of France, the Battle of Britain, and so on. Radio news and commentaries became a steady, daily diet.

This new listening habit created two important advantages for the networks and the radio industry as a whole. First of all, advertisers and their clients were eager to sponsor these new programs, making them the number one growth field of the industry in the late 1930s and early 1940s. As in entertainment programs, companies hoped to profit from the popularity and, in the case of news commentators, respectability of the broadcaster. Kaltenborn, for example, quickly signed a lucrative contract with the Pure Oil Company in 1939. As the advertising agency made clear, Pure Oil expected some tangible benefits from this sponsorship. It hoped that "the names of Pure Oil and Kaltenborn [would become] linked in the public mind just as in the case of Lowell Thomas and the Sun Oil Company." The broad purpose was to have some of the broadcaster's aura rub off on the product and create a feeling in the listeners that "the Pure Oil Company is a fine company to do business with."[51] Straight network news would also receive sponsorship, yet the commercials usually just framed the broadcasts, which made the connection less direct and intimate.

Second, and equally important, radio news had a very practical, political dimension for broadcasters. It was considered public education and one of the major avenues for public service programming by the networks. In its continual tug-of-war with the FCC, broadcasting news was an important new arrow in the quiver of the private commercial radio industry. It was proof that American radio worked best when it was left alone—without strict supervision or possible new governmental restrictions. *Time* magazine summarized this sentiment well in 1941, particularly with an eye to the rise of the CBS news programs: "If any single job since radio began could unanswerably justify the business of broadcasting as now conducted, CBS' news coverage since 1938 might well be it."[52]

Yet radio news was only one component of this new growth sector in broadcasting. The other was radio commentary. Prior to 1938, there were few sponsored, national radio commentators, yet their numbers quickly swelled after the 1938–39 season. For networks, they proved both a blessing and a curse: a blessing because many became more popular than the news programs themselves; a curse because the line between objective reporting and interpretation blurred much more easily in these programs, and commentators' biases sometimes brought public criticism and reprimands—something radio tried to avoid by all means. Moreover, as radio reshuffled the journalistic landscape of the United States in the 1930s and early 1940s, radio commentators in particular gathered huge audiences, up to fifteen to twenty million in some cases, and the question of their influence on public opinion became increasingly relevant and pressing. Naturally, no single issue was more important than the debate between interventionists and isolationists in the years between 1938 and 1941, and radio indeed played a critical role in this confrontation.

The faith and trust that Americans put into radio news coverage turned out to be a decisive advantage in the battle. Rather quickly and with official government sanction and support, radio news and commentaries churned out a steady stream of interventionist messages. To be certain, radio was not alone in these efforts: by 1940 and 1941, Hollywood was producing decidedly pro-interventionist films such as *Confessions of a Nazi Spy, The Great Dictator,* and *Sergeant York.* Despite the fact that they drew the wrath of leading isolationists and had to answer charges of propagandistic manipulation before a congressional investigation committee in the fall of 1941, both media were instrumental in creating public support for FDR's increasingly audacious interventionist policies.[53]

But it was radio that covered the international crisis and war day in and day out, and its daily reports and commentaries decidedly weighed in on the side of interventionism. As David Holbrook Culbert has argued in his in-depth study of the six most important news commentators of the time, only one—Fulton Lewis, Jr.—staunchly defended the isolationist viewpoint. The others actively combated isolationism and, despite industry and network regulations, never abided by the calls for impartial reporting. As Culbert concluded, "Radio emerged as a major source of interventionism."[54]

The isolationist controversy also showed once again that FDR and his administration were not shy about using their leverage over radio in order to eliminate its fiercest opponents from the air. This became clear in the removal of Boake Carter as well as Father Charles Coughlin, who were outspoken opponents of FDR and staunch supporters of isolationism. Both of these broadcasters were past the height of their popularity, but they nevertheless commanded audiences of several million listeners and were thorns in the side of the Roosevelt administration. In the case of Carter, the administration applied pressure through an informal channel. It asked an influential Democratic supporter and former director of General Foods, Carter's sponsor, to relay the White House's concern over the programs to both the sponsor and its advertising agency. Based on this government intervention and the parallel boycott of General Foods by the Congress of Industrial Organizations (CIO) because of Carter's steady antilabor rhetoric, the agency overseeing the news commentaries coerced Carter to tone down his attacks in early 1938. When his ratings dropped over the next several months, General Foods canceled its sponsorship. Father Coughlin, the outspoken radio priest whose acidic antiadministration broadcasts attracted several million listeners weekly, would soon suffer a similar fate. In 1939, the National Association of Broadcasters (NAB) established a new code that prohibited stations from selling time for the discussion of controversial topics and forbade editorializing by newscasters. While the policy would be constantly circumvented over the next years, the industry used the statutes to demonstrate to the government that it could govern itself by banishing the troublesome preacher from the air. In terms of political matters and especially its internationalist agenda, according to Richard Steele, "radio's political content did not stray far from administration orthodoxy."[55]

One of the earliest and best-known examples of a confirmed internationalist working as a radio commentator was H. V. Kaltenborn. In the fall of 1938, his intimate knowledge of European affairs had brought him national fame; by early the next year, he had secured a sponsor for his own news program. A longtime supporter of aid to the Spanish government in its fight against the fascist Franco forces, Kaltenborn seized upon the issue in January 1939 in connection with a speech by FDR that hinted in the same direction. After the outbreak of war in Europe in September 1939, he was one of the first to suggest that America should change its neutrality laws in order to aid England and France yet remain neutral otherwise. Over the next two years, Kaltenborn emphatically supported every new initiative by the FDR administration that moved the United States closer to an interventionist stance. He endorsed the successive changes in the neutrality laws as well as the lend-lease bill, applauded the conscription law of 1940, and demanded increased defense production. In early 1941, despite the fact that American public opinion was coming around to his position, Kaltenborn's approval ratings dropped precipitously, especially after he attacked Charles

Lindbergh (a vigorous isolationist) on his program. His sponsor, the Pure Oil Company, which did most of its business in the Midwest, was becoming increasingly nervous. Its advertising agency informed Kaltenborn that "more unusually violent adverse letters have come into the Pure Oil Co. in connection with Lindbergh." Pure Oil instructed the commentator to keep his emphasis on the coverage of foreign news and to "exercise extreme caution in the handling of controversial subjects." The crisis would eventually subside, and with America's entry into the war, Kaltenborn was once again in the driver's seat.[56]

Another example of less than impartial news commentary during these years was the work of Raymond Gram Swing. By the time he began his radio career in 1936, Swing was in his late forties and had already worked for numerous papers and magazines as well as authored a book. By all accounts, he was not a commentator destined to great glory in radio because he was considered too scholarly, pedantic, and stuffy. Yet with the invasion of Poland even Swing found a sponsor, the General Cigar Company, and eventually a mass audience. His success surprised everybody in the business, including Swing himself, who had only one explanation: "The simple truth of my success is that the war has scared Americans to death." By 1940, Swing was carried five times a week by the Mutual network and had garnered an audience of roughly nine million listeners. This audience, as one historian put it, "was highbrow, high-domed, and high income." Swing was considered the choice of the foreign news aficionados—reserved, intellectual, and deeply analytical.[57]

Moreover, Swing was also the only American news commentator with an international audience. Once a week he spoke over American shortwave, summarizing U.S. politics for an estimated audience of thirty million. Most of his listeners lived in Great Britain, where his program, *Things American,* had a particularly loyal following. The reason for this was not only that Swing was very sympathetic to the English cause; at least as important was his unusually close relationship with the FDR administration. In fact, he was widely perceived as an "unofficial spokesman for the Department of State and the President." Secretary of State Cordell Hull was a personal friend, and Swing strongly endorsed FDR's foreign policies. In 1940, Swing was also the first radio commentator to join the Council for Democracy, an anti-isolationist organization and he later served as its chairman. Indeed, there is every indication that Swing's service to the Roosevelt administration was fully appreciated and encouraged. For one thing, he broadcast over shortwave, which was under the authority of the U.S. government. Moreover, in early 1941, the administration began sending Spanish and Portuguese translations of his broadcasts to Latin America.[58]

By mid-1940, after the German blitzkrieg in the West and the French surrender, the scales tipped decisively in favor of increasing American aid to Britain. Even commentators who had withheld their opinions up to that point—like Elmer Davis—now became more forthright in their editorials. Davis had joined the CBS network in the fall of 1939, and his five-minute commentary was a steady feature of the CBS news program until his appointment as director of the Office of War Information in 1942. Like the rest of the nation, Davis had hoped that the United States would stay out of the war. Yet with Hitler's successes in the spring of 1940, America for the first time had to contemplate the real possibility of a German victory. Davis spoke for himself and many other Americans when he described these events in his radio commentary in April 1940: "The unrecognized premise of a good deal of American isolationism was a conviction that the Allies were going to win anyway so we needn't worry about how the war would come out. That conviction, recently, has been shaken; and accordingly, a lot of people are worrying, for the first time." While Davis voiced his increasingly urgent pleas for aid to Britain most strongly in his magazine articles, his radio commentaries now left no doubt regarding his position: he was solidly in the camp of the interventionists.[59]

This biased war coverage on the air was not limited to commentators, however; it also intruded into the regular news programs, especially in the second half of 1940. The best examples of this trend are the news reports of Edward R. Murrow. When England stood alone to face the German onslaught in the fall of 1940, Murrow covered the Battle of Britain and particularly the nightly bombing raids on London. Certainly, his reports were news accounts, describing the falling of the bombs, their impact, and the destruction they wrought. Murrow developed his own inimitable style. In contrast to Swing's scholarly analyses or Kaltenborn's schoolmasterly lectures, Murrow's reports became known for their colorful, vivid imagery. Neither melancholy nor soapy, his reports were so rich in detail and description that listeners could almost smell the fumes from the fires burning in the streets of London and feel the heat emanating from the smoldering ruins. Without question, this was radio reporting at its best, but there was also no doubt about its impact, least of all in Murrow's mind. As he described his approach to a London newspaper in 1941, "The official news is perhaps less important than the more intimate stories of life, work and sacrifice in Europe today." He went on to explain that a night with London's fire fighters brought "the war much nearer to the wheat farmer in Kansas than any official communiqué."[60]

While the German censors were making meaningful reporting more difficult and banning the coverage of British bombing raids on German cities, Winston Churchill and his government made sure American reporters had as much freedom as possible without compromising safety. This proved to be a smart move on the part of the British authorities because Murrow's reports were full of drama and carried a clear message: Britain needs and deserves help. The following news report from London exemplifies this trend well:

It is now 4:15 in the morning in London. There will be piles of empty shell casings around London's anti-aircraft batteries when dawn breaks an hour from now. All night, for more than eight hours, the guns have been flashing. The blue autumn sky has been pockmarked with the small red bursts of exploding anti-aircraft shells.

Never in the long history of this old city by the Thames has there been such a night as this. But tonight the sound of gunfire has been more constant than the *bestial* grunt of bombs.[61]

As Murrow and his colleagues continued to cover what was now termed "a people's war" on the part of the British, their admiration and sympathy for the people of London and Great Britain only increased—and shone through their broadcasts ever more brightly. During the bombardment of London, the American reporters were as exposed to the bombs' deadly charges as were Londoners themselves, and they became brothers-in-arms. Murrow and fellow reporter Larry LeSueur, in particular, relished the opportunity to be in the midst of things, even if this meant risking their own lives. Indeed, they seemed to seek out danger as a badge of courage. Murrow did not use the air-raid shelters, and both he and LeSueur roamed through London in an uncovered Jeep during bombings. They broadcast live from London rooftops during air raids and rode in English bombers on missions over German cities. The offices of both CBS and NBC were in the most heavily hit part of London, yet the broadcasts continued even under increasingly chaotic circumstances, with bombed-out staff and reporters sleeping in the studio. It also created a camaraderie with the British, which Murrow casually reflected on in one broadcast in which he extolled the courage of the average Londoner:

Talking from a studio with a few bodies lying about on the floor, sleeping on mattresses, still produces a strange feeling but we'll probably get used to that.

Today I went to buy a hat—my favorite shop had gone, blown to bits. The windows of my shoe store were blown out. I decided to have a haircut; the windows of the barbershop were gone, but the Italian barber was still doing business. Someday, he said, we'll smile again, but the food, it doesn't taste so good since being bombed. I went to another shop to buy flashlight batteries. I bought three. The clerk said: "You needn't buy so many. We'll have enough for the whole winter." But I said: "What if you aren't here?" There were buildings down in that street, and he replied: "Of course, we'll be here. We've been here for a hundred and fifty years."[62]

Murrow kept his focus squarely on the common man and woman and how to reach them. He wanted to let them know that England was fighting a "people's war," not a war for its colonies, as the American isolationists charged. He wanted Americans to know that England was standing tall, united in its cause—indeed, that it stood as the final dike protecting Western liberties and European civilization. He wanted Americans to see Great Britain as their natural ally and hurry up a bit in extending a helping hand. Because of his reputation and impact, Murrow's role evolved into much more than that of a broadcaster. As his friend and fellow reporter Eric Sevareid put it, Murrow had far greater influence than the American ambassador to London: "He was an ambassador, in a double role, representing Britain in America as well as America in Britain." Like Swing, he was a diplomat without a portfolio, a spokesman for a cause.[63]

Yet Murrow was not the only one who came to fill an assignment and realized that he had found a vocation. Few of the American correspondents covering the Blitz over London could restrain their emotions and opinions. When Sevareid, who also covered London for CBS, had to leave the city sick and exhausted in the fall of 1940, he did not conceal his sympathies and emotions in his farewell broadcast:

London fights down her fears every night, takes her blows and gets up again every morning. You feel yourself an embattled member of this embattled corps. The attraction of courage is irresistible. Parting from London, you see clearly what she is and means. London may not be England, but she is Britain and she is the incubator of America and the West. Should she collapse, the explosion in history would never stop its echoing.[64]

The networks and the radio industry as a whole had expended a lot of energy and paper in 1939 trying to ensure impartial news coverage during the war. The industry-wide NAB code of 1939 stated that news broadcasts should not editorialize and that the interpretation of the news should be free of bias. Among the networks, CBS adopted the toughest code, which attempted to distinguish between newscasters, news analysts, and news commentators: the first one read the news, the second put it in perspective without offering personal opinions, and only the last group was allowed to voice biased, editorial opinions. Foreign news correspondents presumably fell into the second category. While the distinction between news analysts and commentators had always been fuzzy and blurry, by the fall of 1940 it was nonexistent as far as radio news from Europe was concerned.[65]

Conclusion

By the early 1940s radio broadcasting had, for better or worse, become a key medium that was deeply entrenched in the political culture. Prior to America's entry into World War II, it had already decisively influenced the politics of its time, yet it had also accrued some heavy liabilities. For Americans at the threshold of the war, all of this had become part of the way in which they thought about and experienced radio.

Radio news had a crucial impact on the formation of a national consensus in these critical years of U.S. history. Regular daily radio news and commentary were relatively novel phenomena in the lives of most Americans in the late 1930s, yet the medium matured rapidly. Radio was viewed as a friendly medium by its listeners, who considered it honest and trustworthy. On controversial issues, as one poll indicated, Americans were more likely to believe radio than any other source. Foreign news coverage in particular was often live and on-the-scene, making listeners feel as if they were witnessing history in the making. While it is difficult to gauge radio's impact through charts and numbers, there can be no doubt that its interventionist bent created an environment that facilitated American involvement on the side of the Allies and paved the way for the interventionist orientation of the postwar years. FDR indeed had some very powerful spokesmen for his foreign policies on the air.

The future of radio government propaganda, on the other hand, looked less rosy. For Americans living at the turn of the decade, the propaganda of World War I and the New Deal was very much part of their collective memory, and it informed their responses to a renewed battle for their hearts and minds over the next few years. FDR and his administration were no newcomers to government radio propaganda in

the early 1940s. In fact, the strategies for government-supervised propaganda through radio, as well as many of their narrative modes, had
been well rehearsed in the 1930s. Finally, FDR's opponents were on their
toes—ready to slash the new government propaganda as soon as it
proved politically feasible. All of this ensured that government-
sponsored radio propaganda programs during the early war years were
initiated in a tense, alert, and partisan political culture.

CHAPTER 2

Uneasy Persuasion

Government Radio Propaganda, 1941–1943

FDR and his administration were very much aware of the public's distaste for propaganda, as well as the suspicions of their political opponents. From 1939 to 1941, Roosevelt and his advisers were forced to walk a very fine line. They went out of their way to assure politicians, the media, and the public that the government was not going to censor information; nor was it going to initiate a large-scale propaganda bureaucracy as long as the United States was not a belligerent. FDR persistently rejected the early demands for a government propaganda agency, which high-ranking cabinet members such as Secretary of War Henry L. Stimson, Vice President Henry Wallace, and Secretary of the Navy Frank Knox were calling for. Roosevelt and his close advisers understood that a central propaganda agency established prior to America's entry into war would become the target of every political enemy of the administration.[1]

Yet during the same period, the government vastly increased its informational network, especially under the cover of the emerging defense effort. The two departments most actively involved in the radio defense effort were War and Treasury, both of which started their broadcast activities well before America's entry into the war. In late 1940 the War Department began collaborating with the networks on programs illustrating life in military training camps. As early as April 1941, it had established a Radio Division within its Bureau of Public Relations. This division was headed by Edward W. Kirby, formerly director of public relations of the National Association of Broadcasters, and started out with seven staff members, all with prior experience in broadcasting.[2]

Early in 1941 the Treasury Department began collaborating with the networks through both commercial and noncommercial radio programs to promote the sale of defense bonds and stamps. Its best-known non-commercial offering was *The Treasury Hour,* later called *The Treasury Star Parade.* The program was produced in New York, with transcriptions offered to all radio stations interested in playing them. The number of subscribing radio stations quickly rose from fewer than 300 in late 1941 to 830 stations in the country (out of a total of 920) by the summer of 1942; some radio stations even played the same show several times a week. Well-known writers such as Norman Rosten, Arch Oboler, Stephen Vincent Benét, Thomas Wolfe, Violet Atkins, and Neal Hopkins volunteered their time and service; scores of actors and actresses, including Bette Davis and Robert Montgomery, did the same.[3]

Yet these programs were just the tip of the iceberg. By late 1941 a basic infrastructure for information and publicity under government supervision was once again in place, justified by America's campaign of preparedness. The main links of this network were the Office of Government Reports (OGR), the Information Division of the Office of Emergency Management (OEM), and the Office of Facts and Figures (OFF). The OGR was created in mid-1939 to monitor American public opinion and to relay "the opinions, desires and complaints of the citizens" to the Executive Office. An important new agency created in connection with the inauguration of the Defense Program in June 1940 was the Division of Information of the OEM. Its task was to provide central information services to the Office of Civilian Defense, the Office of Price Administration, and other new defense agencies. Finally, the OFF was established as the first centralized agency to oversee all information and propaganda campaigns for the defense effort. From late 1941 to mid-1942, it coordinated most of the domestic propaganda campaigns. In June 1942 it was replaced by the Office of War Information, under the leadership of Elmer Davis.[4]

When Japanese bombs fell on Pearl Harbor in December 1941, thus, the U.S. government was not caught unprepared. A basic propaganda network was in place, though it had too many heads and too little coordination. Even more significantly, most Americans were ill prepared to answer one critical question: What was this war all about? With hindsight, many people consider World War II a "good war," probably the clearest case of a war that provided justifiable reasons to fight. Yet for many Americans in late 1941 and early 1942, these reasons were not obvious. When asked by a government survey as late as the spring of

1942 whether they had "a clear idea of what the war is all about," respondents were evenly divided. Half said they knew "what the war was about," but the other half said they did not.[5]

This, then, was the biggest challenge throughout 1942, and radio joined the propaganda campaign. The purpose was, as described by poet-turned-propagandist Archibald MacLeish, to explain to Americans what their country was fighting for and "to make the war their own." While all of radio—both commercial and noncommercial programming—joined the war effort right away, in this chapter and the next I will discuss noncommercial, government-sponsored broadcasts only. In contrast with commercial radio, these broadcasts were directly initiated and supervised by one of the propaganda agencies and were aired without commercial sponsorship, similar to network sustaining programs.*

Despite the collective memory of the Great War and the New Deal crusades, as well as considerable partisan political doubts, government radio propaganda gained a new lease on life, which extended from mid-1941 through early 1943. Yet it was based on an uneasy truce because the public had not forgotten past lessons and remained distrustful of government propaganda. And it was fraught with tensions because Republicans and conservative politicians remained skeptical about the Roosevelt administration's political intentions. Robert Taft spoke for his party when he commented on the renewed battle for the hearts and minds of Americans: "The New Dealers are determined to make the country over under the cover of war if they can."[6] And as the government radio propaganda got under way, many Americans had a nagging sense of déjà vu: all this seemed very familiar.

Government Radio Propaganda after Pearl Harbor: Fighting for What?

The first noncommercial government radio program after the attack on Pearl Harbor was broadcast on December 15, 1941. The show had been

---

*The Federal Communications Act of 1934 stipulated that radio networks had to provide free airtime for public service broadcasts in return for their free use of the airwaves. These programs were also known as "sustainers," because they usually ran during the less desirable hours of the networks' broadcasting schedules. Noncommercial government propaganda shows made up a large part of this public service programming during World War II.

scheduled since mid-November to celebrate the sesquicentennial of the Bill of Rights. William B. Lewis, the new director of the Radio Division of the OFF and former vice president of CBS, had asked his friend Norman Corwin to write a radio play. Corwin, one of the best radio writers in the late 1930s and 1940s, had worked for CBS for a number of years. He had just completed his series of weekly drama shows, *Twenty-six by Corwin,* and agreed to do the program. Even before America's entry into the war, this show was planned as a first-class radio event and was scheduled to play during prime time. Lewis sought to sign up Hollywood stars, and President Roosevelt was scheduled to conclude the performance with a short talk.[7]

The fact that *We Hold These Truths,* as Corwin's play was titled, was broadcast just eight days after the bombing of Pearl Harbor gave it new significance. It also assured the participation of a first-class cast: James Stewart, Lionel Barrymore, Bob Burns, Rudy Vallee, and Orson Welles were among the actors, while Leopold Stokowski led the New York Philharmonic Orchestra in the national anthem. The president gave a short talk as planned. Corwin wrote a measured yet emotional radio play, in which he mixed the recitation of the first ten amendments to the Constitution with dramatic historical interludes and somber reminders for his listeners of what the Bill of Rights represented:

And then they framed amendments to the Constitution. . . . The Congress of the thirteen states, instructed by the people of the thirteen states, threw up a bulwark, wrote a hope, and made a sign for posterity against the bigots, the fanatics, bullies, lynchers, race-haters, the cruel men, the spiteful men, the sneaking men, the pessimists, the men who give up fights that have been just begun.[8]

It was no coincidence that the play had been written for the moment—for a confused and bewildered American people still trying to figure out what this war was all about. Corwin had been a committed antifascist and internationalist long before the official declaration of war, and *We Hold These Truths* was his first opportunity to indicate the stakes involved in the war to a large national audience, an estimated sixty million Americans.[9] As he stressed in his play, the legacy of the Bill of Rights included having to fight for the liberties it secured:

> *Smith:* Why, the more these amendments make us free, the more they'll be hated by those who don't want freedom because it spoils their game. . . .
>
> *Friend:* You mean to say we're gonna have to fight all over again to keep our independence? Hope it don't get a habit.

Smith: I hope it does! It's a pretty good habit to get into, fightin' for your rights. There's always somebody waitin' for a chance to steal valuables—and if freedom ain't a valuable, I don't know what is.[10]

We Hold These Truths brought Corwin national recognition and made him an immediate candidate for the production of a larger propaganda series that the OFF had in mind in early 1942. Archibald MacLeish, who headed the propaganda agency at the time, and Lewis, who led the Radio Division, succeeded in signing Corwin up for the job and convinced him to start the series as soon as possible. The series—called *This Is War!*—premiered on Valentine's Day of 1942. For the next thirteen weeks, the half-hour program was heard every Saturday at 7:00 P.M., EST, broadcast by all four networks simultaneously over more than seven hundred stations. The scheduling as well as the national four-network hookup were unique for a government series and were not repeated throughout the war (except for FDR's fireside chats). The program was also shortwaved in seven foreign languages.[11]

As the first show, "America at War," indicated, the series was candid, direct, and hard-hitting: "What we say tonight has to do with blood and bone and with anger, and also with a big job in the making. Laughter can wait. Soft music can have an evening off. No one is invited to sit down and take it easy. Later, later. There's a war on."[12] The show was direct in addressing the American audience and in its incitement of hatred for the enemy. "What is the enemy? We know what we are, but what is the enemy?" the film star Robert Montgomery rhetorically asked his audience in this first episode. Then he answered his own question:

The enemy is Murder International, Murder Unlimited; quick murder on the spot or slow murder in the concentration camp, murder for listening to the short-wave radio, for marrying a Pole, for Propagation of the Faith, for speaking one's mind, for trading with a non-Aryan, for being an invalid too long. . . . The enemy is a liar also. A gigantic and deliberate and willful liar.

Corwin referred to popular images of enemy atrocities, not much different from German atrocity stories during World War I: "The enemy is laughter over the bloody stump, the cold smile of the officer watching while the hostage digs his own grave, the coarse joke over the girl just raped. The enemy is the torture gag, officially approved, given the nod by the High Command."[13]

Corwin wrote only six of the thirteen shows, yet he established the overall character of the series. Not all of the episodes were as harshly worded as the first one, and most tried to put the current conflict in perspective. Americans were reminded of heroic battles of the past, of the Revolutionary War and the Civil War. They were warned not to become stooges for the Nazis by passing on rumors, and they were candidly prepared for the sacrifices to come, including the possibility that many Americans would die in the fight. As poet Stephen Vincent Benét told his audience in the fourth show, entitled "Your Army":

Men are going to die—very good men are going to die. They are going to die in the jungles for the shape of a Virginia field and the cross-roads store back home—they're going to die in the cold, for the clear air of Montana and the smell of a New York street. . . .
    And—what are *we* going to do, sitting here at our radios? Squabble some more? Write letters to the papers? Curse out the Government? Spread the lies that divided a people? . . . There's bad news now, and there's going to be bad news for quite a while. The Army knows that. Our enemies aren't pushovers— they are skillful, savage and relentless. They have trained for years for this chance to enslave the world—and that's just what they mean to do.[14]

A confidential survey conducted by the Hooper polling firm for the OFF showed that *This Is War!* had garnered very respectable ratings. For the first seven episodes, they fluctuated between 19 and 24 percent, or an approximate average audience of twenty million listeners per program. Apparently, Americans, frightened by the war and reached in large numbers through the four-network hookup, were willing to give government propaganda another chance. Moreover, the report also suggested that many listeners had not been turned off by this propaganda, since the majority of those tuning in for the seventh broadcast had listened to at least one previous episode.[15]

Yet judging from some audience responses, which Corwin read on the last broadcast, "Yours Received and Content Noted," even after the attack on Pearl Harbor, many Americans remained skeptical of propaganda. "Must you reach into our living rooms and remind us of the facts of death?" asked one listener, Ethel Meriden. "I believe the purpose of your program is to arouse hate among the millions of your listeners," Mrs. M. Hansen wrote. "This is wrong." Others objected to the demand for sacrifices: "For years, before the war, I was up against it," wrote Henry J. Miller, referring to the hard times he had lived through during the Great Depression. "I was out of a job most of the time, but now I've got work and make a little money. . . . Why shouldn't people like me who've never had the good things of life be permitted to make up

for lost time?"[16] These critical listener responses and the continued reluctance many Americans felt toward propaganda suggest that the series
was at best a mixed success.

If the popular vote was undecided, the political response was clear:
the series did not play well with FDR's political opponents. One constant suspicion among Republican and conservative politicians was that
FDR and his New Dealers would twist government propaganda to promote their own political vision. As *This Is War!* demonstrated, their
fears were well justified. In the first episode, for example, Corwin clearly
revealed his own political bias. He emphasized that America had not
wanted this war, that it was minding its own business when it was
attacked, yet he simultaneously commended the New Deal policies of
the 1930s: "We were busy educating our people, giving them a decent
slant on things, trying to see that the hungry got fed and the jobless got
work, trying to remember the forgotten man, trying to deal out a better
deal around the table."[17]

In the second program of the series, entitled "The White House and
the War," writer William N. Robson stressed FDR's leadership qualities
and the similarities between FDR and the great presidents George
Washington and Abraham Lincoln. He reminded listeners of past struggles, such as Washington's close escape in the early stage of the Revolutionary War and Lincoln's despair in the first two years of the Civil
War. World War II was to test America's strength and steadfastness once
more. The program emphasized that there was another great president
in the White House, one hardened by his own debilitating illness and
miraculous recovery: "Again the great house and the man in it. The
anguish, the loneliness, the adversity, the responsibility; this time [it's]
the greatest struggle of mankind."[18] Clearly, propaganda like this made
Roosevelt's political opponents squirm in their seats.

An additional note of criticism came through an internal review of
the OFF, provided by a special survey of its Intelligence Bureau. As part
of a larger questionnaire, the bureau demonstrated that the better-
educated and more prosperous people in the cities primarily listened to
the series. This high-brow appeal, the researchers argued, kept the series
from fulfilling its primary purpose, which was to reach people who were
not yet aware of the consequences of the wartime crisis: "Listeners are
too high on the social and educational scale for the program to accomplish its purpose among the millions in the population who may be
needing its message most."[19]

Corwin scoffed at the notion that *This Is War!* had reached the "wrong" audience. As he saw it, there was a desperate need to explain this war to all the American people: "This is no time to make surveys, to take a clinical and academic point of view about radio and war. . . . There is a desperate necessity to explain this war to the people. They are confused. They are earnest. They want to fight, and they want to be sure what they are fighting for and what they are fighting against."[20]

Another writer, Arch Oboler, went even further, arguing that Americans would not start winning the war until they hated their enemies, and that radio drama had to work in this direction: "[Wartime drama] must do what we know will arouse the greatest response—through the intellect, yes, a little; but basically through the emotions, the emotions of self-pity, fear, hate, the desire for attainment, mass patriotism, translated into the will to action."[21]

Oboler collaborated with the Institute for Education by Radio to produce a thirteen-play series, which aired over NBC in the spring of 1942. His notion of "action motivated by hatred" was most clearly expressed in a piece appropriately entitled "Hate," in which a pastor in a small Norwegian town under German occupation inadvertently helps the German forces by trying to stay out of politics and by preaching to turn the other cheek. The pastor awakes to his foolishness only after he unknowingly aids the massacre of ten townspeople, including his own son. The play ends with him strangling a Nazi officer and joining the resistance.[22]

Corwin and Oboler were certainly right on one point: in the spring of 1942, many Americans felt confused about the war—and the officials in the OFF knew it as well. The monthly surveys of American public opinion undertaken by the Intelligence Bureau of the OFF from February through July 1942 chronicled an increasing dissatisfaction with the course of the war coupled with a resurgence of disunity and isolationist sentiments. As the March report succinctly summarized, "The superficial unity following Pearl Harbor is not only gone but the sentiment favoring acceptance and consideration of a peace offer from Germany, even by Hitler, is by no means insignificant."[23]

To be sure, only a minority of Americans were willing to ponder such a peace offer: 15 percent of those surveyed by the OFF said that they would consider a peace offer by Hitler, even though they conceded that this would mean a de facto victory for Nazi Germany; 30 percent said they would consider a peace offer by the German military after it had overthrown Hitler. These were worrisome sentiments, and, more important, they were on the rise. The seemingly unending string of Allied defeats in early 1942 and the growing realization that the war would last longer than expected were the main driving forces behind the growing uncertainty and skepticism.[24]

This increased skepticism was accompanied by the crescendo of critical commentary in the isolationist and antiadministration press. The most vocal newspapers represented only a small section of the national press, but they were located in important metropolitan areas: the *Chicago Daily Tribune,* the *New York Daily News,* and the Hearst newspapers. Although the editorial policies of these papers were driven either by genuine isolationist concerns or by fervent hatred for the FDR administration rather than pro-fascist sentiments, the effect was the same: they largely echoed Axis propaganda and fostered divisions among Americans and between the United States and its allies.[25]

From the beginning of the fighting in Europe, Great Britain had been at the top of the isolationists' list of enemies because it had involved the United States in World War I and, in their opinion, had done the same this time around. England, as the isolationists charged, liked to have others fight its wars:

> She [England] has systematically sacrificed her Allies to her safety and her own immediate objectives.
> She sacrificed Norway—
> She sacrificed Belgium in identically the same manner—
> England abandoned France at Dunkirk—
> In a word, England's plain policy seems to be to HAVE Allies, but not to BE an Ally.
> (*Hearst Newspapers,* January 28, 1942)

Equally persistent were the isolationists' attacks on Russia. Had not Russia abandoned the Allied coalition in 1917? What would prevent Stalin from once again switching sides? After all, he had collaborated in the German conquests from 1939 to 1941 by adhering to the nonaggression pact signed with Hitler and had pursued his own territorial conquest against the Baltics and Finland. What were his territorial goals in eastern Europe? Did the United States have to fight Russia next, after Germany and Japan were defeated? Even in the spring of 1942, when the Soviet Union was absorbing the brunt of the German offensive and the survival of the Russian army hung in the balance, isolationist papers fueled persistent American skepticism about Russia's reliability as an ally:

Matters seem to be progressing very favorably in Russia—for Russia. Of course, Russia is not a full partner of the United Nations. She is a semi-partner of the

Axis. She is making friendly treaties with Japan—protecting Japan on her Siberian frontier.

There is always in the Russian mental process the suggestion of the brutal selfishness and utter untrustworthiness of this wild animal which is her symbol. (*Hearst Newspapers,* March 30, 1942)

Roosevelt was attacked with similar venom as the English and Russian allies. When he asked for suggestions for naming the war Americans were fighting, the *New York Daily News* printed a whole string of derogatory letters in its "Voice of the People" column:

The President wants a name for the war. Why not call it by the name history will give it—Roosevelt's War? (April 9, 1942)

I favor "R.I.P. War"—standing for, among other things, Rogues in Power, Reds in Plush, Religion in Peril and Rights in Paun [*sic*]. (April 9, 1942)

Several suggestions for F.D.R. about naming the war: the Pyrrhic Victory, the Raw Deal, the Slaughter Pen, the Revenge of the Refugees. (April 11, 1942)

A final line of criticism pursued by isolationist papers was their attempt to commit the United States to a defensive war, which included a good amount of second-guessing and hindsight analysis. As the *Chicago Tribune* editorialized on January 12, 1942, with obvious reference to Pearl Harbor: "Had the plea of that committee [America First] against the neglect of our own national defenses been answered, the nation would have been spared much of the bitter news of recent days." The point was clear for the isolationists: America had overextended itself and now was paying the price. To this criticism, the *New York Daily News,* on February 25, 1942, added its own dire prediction: "The point is that if the arsenal of democracy is stripped of too many of its own defenses it will be laid open to invasion and conquest."

Shortly after the declaration of war, FDR and his advisers had decided not to impose the same draconian censorship as had been in effect during World War I, when the Espionage Act and Sedition Act had deemed any critical statement or opinion treacherous. These laws were still on the books in the early 1940s and were used in individual cases. In order to indicate this departure in policy, Roosevelt had appointed an experienced and well-liked journalist, Byron Price, as head of the Office of Censorship in December 1941. In general, the government professed to rely on the voluntary censorship of the newspaper editors and the heads of the radio news departments and on the basis of this "self-censorship," the sweeping abuses of World War I were avoided. But the administration curtailed and manipulated the flow of information in other ways.

The most egregious example was military censorship. Based on the twin wartime imperatives of protecting American lives and national security, journalists and news agencies frequently received belated and cursory reports about the progress of the war. Moreover, this often happened after they had heard more detailed reports from their English counterparts over the BBC. Domestically as well, Roosevelt struck out against his opponents in the press: in early 1942, for example, charging that the reports by the *Chicago Tribune* constituted seditious reporting, he authorized Attorney General Francis Biddle to initiate a grand jury investigation against the newspaper. The investigation evaporated only after the Justice Department was unable to amass convincing proof to warrant prosecution.[26]

It is also safe to say that the broad-scale censorship of a popular, conservative newspaper would have carried with it a considerable political toll, with administration critics claiming foul play and criticizing it as the pursuit of partisan politics under the cover of the wartime emergency. Therefore, Roosevelt had to counter the isolationist charges primarily in the public arena, although the content of the debate had shifted markedly. It focused less on whether or not the United States should fight and mainly questioned what kind of war America was to fight. In response to the demand for a defensive war, FDR addressed the nation in his second wartime fireside chat on February 23, 1942. He had asked listeners—about two-thirds of the American population—to have a map ready to help them follow his discussion. The president described the novel kind of warfare that required America to fight its enemies in faraway places and all around the globe. Emphasizing that his isolationist critics had been wrong before and were wrong again, he ridiculed what he called their "turtle policy":

Those Americans who believed that we could live under the illusion of isolationism wanted the American eagle to imitate the tactics of the ostrich. Now, many of those same people, afraid that we may be sticking out our necks, want our national bird to be turned into a turtle. But we prefer the eagle as it is— flying high and striking hard.

I know that I speak for the mass of the American people when I say that we reject the turtle policy and will continue increasingly the policy of carrying the war to the enemy in distant lands and distant waters—as far away as possible from our own home grounds.[27]

Government officials were encouraged by the popular appeal of FDR's speech, as well as by the congratulatory letters that poured in by the thousands. Listeners congratulated Roosevelt on his "calm, delib-

erate, and measured statements" and agreed that the speech was an effective response to the isolationist challenge. Indeed, these letters conveyed the degree to which Americans still admired their leader. FDR
had a cold the night he delivered his address, and many letter writers
combined congratulations on the speech with more personal notes, including admonitions that he needed to take care of his health. As one
letter illustrates, many listeners thought of Roosevelt as a friend or a
relative:

If I am addressing you too informally, it is only because you have brought
yourself so close to us, the people. You may believe me that as I listened to you
last night your every cough made me wince, and prompted me to admonish
you, as I would one of the family, to take good care of yourself, for the country's
sake, as well as your own.[28]

Yet FDR's advisers understood that it took more than the president's
personal popularity to overcome Americans' uncertainty about the war
and distrust of their allies. They needed to wage a concerted and sustained campaign for Americans' hearts and minds. As Archibald Mac-
Leish put it in a speech on March 19, 1942: "The principal battle ground
of this war is not the South Pacific. It is not the Middle East. It is not
England or Norway, or the Russian steppes. It is American opinion."[29]

Radio continued its participation in the government propaganda
campaigns. And at least in one respect radio—like no other medium—
was able to bring the war closer to Americans. A number of historians
have argued that in 1942 America was fighting a "sanitized" war. In this
early stage, as George Roeder has demonstrated, photographs were prohibited from portraying the savagery and cruelty of the war. Thomas
Doherty pointed out that movie directors likewise were instructed to
keep "the awful devastations of combat from the homefront screen—
sometimes by outright fabrication, usually by expedient omission."[30]
What made dramatized radio documentaries more real was that they got
away with more graphic descriptions of the horror of the war because
they did not *show* casualties of war. One of the dramatic approaches used
by radio writers during World War II was the "you-technique," which
made listeners feel as if they were partaking in the action. This narrative
strategy was employed in the *This Is War!* programs as well as in *The
Man behind the Gun,* a series that presented life in the military from
various angles—from training camps, submarines, aircraft carriers, and
so forth.

Like a number of other shows, *The Man behind the Gun* attempted to place listeners in the middle of the action by directly involving them. Rather than describing a situation, such as "The radio man listens on his earphones, waiting for a report from the scouting force," the narrative focused on the listener: "You're sitting there, with the earphones digging into your skull, waiting and listening . . . listening for the sound of a circuit key being opened somewhere in the thousands of miles of sky all around you . . . waiting for the sound of static . . . the sound of the scouting force calling you."[31]

The writer of the show, Ranald MacDougall, argued that the "you-technique" provided an endless number of variations, which drew the listeners in by personalizing and dramatizing the plot. This technique was ideal for broadcasting, since it played on listeners' imaginations and pulled them out of their armchairs and into the cockpit of a fighter plane, onto the deck of a destroyer, or into a ditch on the front line. The "you" used in radio was a powerful technique, especially since it was a human voice that addressed each listener as an individual.

As one program of the series *The Treasury Star Parade* demonstrated, this and similar techniques were ideal for "personalizing" the war. In the "Ballad of Bataan," Norman Rosten eulogized the American and Allied soldiers fighting on Bataan and Corregidor. In early May 1942, Corregidor finally fell to the Japanese, yet the Allied soldiers had held the peninsula for weeks against an overwhelming force. It was this kind of endurance, sacrifice, and determination, as Rosten emphasized, that was needed on the home front as well:

> You, listening at home, safe in your chairs,
> surrounded by safety, who do not feel
> the bullet strike, or the sun's whip on your back,
> how can you know these weeks of battle?
> How can you feel the bayonet turn in the wound,
> or gangrene eating the bone away?
> What image describes the grenade exploding
> in a foxhole, or the loneliness of the evening?
> How do we tell the anguish of thirst?
> How is the leaking blood weighed and described?

Rosten told those still expecting to strike a deal with the enemy or hoping for humanity and decency in dealing with the Nazis and Japanese to wake up to the cold-blooded reality of this war:

> Those who had the strength, men and nurses,
> tried to swim the three-mile bay to Corregidor;

tried to fight the shark-infested waters
under the roaming eye of planes.
O, you flying assassins in your armored sky,
look away this time, do not see them!
[Planes diving]
Did anyone say mercy?
Does the new order deal in sentiment? . . .
Does one ask for mercy from murderers?
[Machine guns strafing in and out]
There's the kind of mercy:
the pureblooded Aryan kind![32]

Despite the confusing ploy of blaming Aryans for supposed Asian brutality, radio dramas like these had the potential of achieving one of the key goals of radio propaganda. They drew listeners out of their secure environment and into the war, making them feel, for a few minutes at least, the anxiety, the sheer fright, and the pain of soldiers in combat.[33]

Enemies and Allies

As should be clear by now, the question of why the United States should fight often became a question of what and whom it should fight against. As Frank Capra so brilliantly demonstrated in his film propaganda series *Why We Fight,* one question could not be discussed without the other. In Capra's propaganda films, totalitarian ideology and Allied ideals were depicted as completely irreconcilable opposites: they showed the striking differences between democracy and dictatorship, freedom and slavery, tolerance and bigotry, light and dark.[34]

In the spring of 1942, radio writers turned increasingly to describing "the nature of the enemy" so that Americans could understand what the stakes were. Most of this radio propaganda was directed against Nazi Germany for a simple reason: Roosevelt and his military advisers had decided on an Atlantic First strategy, yet in early 1942 Americans' anger and hatred was overwhelmingly directed toward the Japanese. Early in April 1942, the Intelligence Bureau of the OFF included the following question in its regular survey: "Granting that it is important for us to fight the Axis every place we can, which do you think is more important for the United States to do right now—put most of our effort into fighting Japan or into fighting Germany?" Sixty-two percent of respondents chose Japan, 21 percent chose Germany, and 17 percent had no opinion—three to one in favor of fighting Japan first.[35]

John Dower has argued that the attack on Pearl Harbor was only one of the reasons that made it easier for Americans to hate the Japanese enemy; the other was racism. The most demeaning and spiteful expression of this hatred was reflected in the frequent portrayal of the Japanese as "subhuman creatures," unworthy of being compared to other human beings.[36] Radio propaganda was no exception. In one program of *The Treasury Star Parade* entitled "A Lesson in Japanese," Neal Hopkins taught his listeners about the Japanese:

Listen! Have you ever watched a well-trained monkey at the zoo! Have you seen how carefully he imitates his trainer? . . . The monkey goes through so many human movements so well that he actually seems to *be* human! But under his fur, he's still a savage little beast!

Now consider the imitative little Japanese . . . who for seventy-five years has built himself into something so closely resembling a civilized human being that he actually believes he is just that.

In the same play Hopkins referred to yet another popular image—the Japanese as an agile reptile, thoroughly at home in the jungles of the southern Pacific. Describing the strongly inflected sound of the letter *s* in the Japanese language, he commented:

You know, snakes have the same characteristic—hissing! What a sharp similarity. . . . The Japanese—some of them painted green—some of them covered with green mosquito netting—wiggling their way across the ground on the plains of Luzon—through the jungles of Java—the hills of Burma—Listen!

[A soft hissing, building under]
Do you hear them? . . . Do you hear the little green snakes?[37]

Portrayals like these both reflected and reinforced the deep-seated hatred of the Japanese. In contrast, even in the middle of the war, Americans found good things to say about Germans. When asked to describe the Germans in July 1942, most respondents chose terms such as "warlike" and "cruel," but they also called the Germans "hard working." The three descriptions most frequently selected for the Japanese enemy were "treacherous," "sly," and "cruel."[38]

It was in this context that the U.S. government launched one of its most successful and long-running radio propaganda series, with the goal of focusing attention on the German enemy first. *You Can't Do Business with Hitler,* written by Douglass Miller and based on a book with the same title, was begun by the Office of Emergency Management in April 1942. (The OEM merged into the OWI in June 1942.) For fifteen years prior to the war, Miller, who announced the broadcasts, had been commercial attaché to the American embassy in Berlin. His book, published in mid-1941, was a popular exposé of Nazi war aims and the Germans' methods of fighting the war; it also described the possible repercussions of a Nazi victory for American business. Miller painted a gloomy picture. He emphasized that Nazi Germany used business as a weapon in its strategy for global supremacy and that a defeat of the Allies would slowly but surely strangle American business and free enterprise. An adamant interventionist who saw no common ground between Nazi Germany and the United States, Miller strongly advocated a declaration of war against Germany as early as mid-1941. As he stated, "The current situation leaves us two alternative settlements for a future world—a German settlement or an American settlement."[39]

The premise of an irreconcilable conflict was also the starting point of every program of the series. Each episode opened with Hitler addressing his obedient followers:

> *Voice* [On filter—vehement—hysterical]:
> Meine deutschen Volksgenossen—Männer und Frauen. In diesen Schicksalsstunden sind wir von unbeugsamen Siegeswillen gefüllt [*sic*]. Der Reichsadler fliegt vom Nordkap bis zum [*sic*] Griechenland und unsere siegesreichen Truppen verfolgen. . . .
>
> *Miller* [Low, emphatic]:
> You Can't Do Business with Hitler!
>
> [*Music:* Build to abrupt peak and cut sharp]
>
> *Announcer:* We are now at war. There are but two alternatives: total victory or total defeat. There can be no such thing as a military stalemate that would result in the survival of Hitlerism.[40]

From its inception, the series enjoyed a "runaway radio popularity" according to *Variety.* Within weeks, 720 radio stations from all over the country requested transcriptions of the program. "With no advance publicity," as the *Variety* reporter emphasized, "the transcription has smashed all records in the radio industry and is being air-waved by as many as ten competing stations in the same areas where rival stations refuse to carry the same programs except when the President speaks to the country." Originally, the OEM had planned only thirteen programs—as in the case of *This Is War!*—but *You Can't Do Business with*

Hitler was repeatedly extended and ran until March 1943, for a total of fifty-six episodes.[41]

The program covered every aspect of Hitler's Germany and Nazi conquest, as even a partial list of broadcast titles will attest: "The Anti-Christ," "Swastikas over the Equator," "Work or Die," "Women versus Hitlerism," "Trial by Terror," "No God for Poland," "Health by Decree," "Education in the New Order." The first thirteen programs emphasized Nazi Germany's way of mixing business with military strategy and conquest. A set of broadcasts also took aim at both isolationists and fascist sympathizers in the United States, recalling the propaganda strategy Goebbels employed so adroitly in France in 1940: to divide and attack the enemy from within. The later shows increasingly focused on the everyday social changes brought about by Hitlerism—changes that awaited Americans if they were to lose the war.

One of the most frequently repeated themes of the series was the destruction of the family and the mistreatment of women under Nazi rule. As the broadcasts stressed, Hitler's regime had systematically destroyed the family as a social unit because he needed soldiers who were absolutely obedient to his commands. The most despicable outcome of this policy, as was reiterated in a variety of themes in shows such as "Women versus Hitlerism," "The German Mother," "Origin of the Nazi Species," or "The Nazi Estate of Matrimony," was that both German women and women from occupied countries were forced to have children out of wedlock to replenish Hitler's armies.

The dramatized programs by Miller and the other writers frequently provided brief history lessons of actual changes that had occurred in Nazi Germany. In fact, every program was spiced with references and quotations from published books: "Unbelievable? Want proof? See a book entitled *Nazi Germany: Its Women and Family Life* written by the brilliant sociologist, Clifford Kirkpatrick." Like Capra's *Why We Fight* and Corwin's *This Is War!, You Can't Do Business with Hitler* was "doc-udrama," propaganda that relied heavily on documented dramatizations of the enemy's way of life, including propaganda the Axis powers themselves used for domestic consumption.

Yet *You Can't Do Business with Hitler* was more didactic and emotionally restrained than much other government propaganda. This was probably because Miller and his colleagues faced a particularly tricky situation with respect to the German enemy—again a legacy of World War I. Many Americans remembered the exaggerated propaganda campaigns against the "Huns" during World War I. Now that the Nazis were perpetrating unbelievable atrocities all over Europe, American propagandists had to restrain their material, or at least provide evidence that they were not making outlandish claims. If they wanted to cry wolf again, American propagandists had to make sure they had documentation on which to base their charges.

You Can't Do Business with Hitler owed much of its success to the application of these didactic and familiar dramatic techniques. Nazi policies were personalized through these dramatized plots, arousing disbelief, hatred, and, at times, pity for the victims—who included Germans. Finally, the ultimate threat was always the hint of what would happen to America if it were occupied by the Nazis.

As indicated, the series enlightened a large number of Americans about the changes that had occurred in Germany since the Nazi takeover. As it emphasized, Germany had undergone a social and political revolution since 1933. The subjugation of women, the disintegration of the family and parental authority, the purging of all faiths, the indoctrination of a Nazi youth, and a complete disregard for common decency and humanity were the mainstays of the New Germany. As the shows emphasized, Hitler and the Gestapo reigned with an iron fist over both Germans and the conquered countries, which fared even worse.

What was surprising about the series was its exaggerated portrayal of a gulf between the Nazis and the rest of the German people. Judging from these programs, Germans suffered almost as much under Nazi rule as did people in the occupied countries. According to a number of these broadcasts, Germans also were subjugated to ruthless policies against their will. In an episode entitled "Work or Die," the audience was told how the average German worker had been enslaved in a systematic eight-year-long campaign. Similarly, two episodes, "Beast of Burden" and "The Sell-Out," focused on how German businessmen had become beasts of burden, "groomed by the Gestapo to serve, feed and obey the New Order in Germany." According to the broadcasts, private business was disappearing in Germany and was being replaced by "Hermann Goering, Inc."[42]

As during World War I, the U.S. government tried to pursue a propaganda policy that distinguished between the leaders of the enemy country and the people themselves and repeatedly called on the people to overthrow their governments. The policy ultimately failed and disintegrated, especially in the last two years of the war, just as it had done in the previous war. Once a significant number of American soldiers were dying at the hands of Germans, Americans awoke to the fact that most enemy people were in fact supporting their militaristic leadership.

In the case of the Japanese, as mentioned earlier, this transition was easier for Americans to make. From the outset of the United States' participation in the war, consistently fewer Americans were willing to distinguish between the Japanese people and their government than in the German case. While public sentiment gradually hardened toward the Axis enemies, Americans' attitudes toward Germans remained conflicted up until D-Day. Even in the spring of 1944, 65 percent of Americans interviewed in an OWI survey thought that the German people would like to get rid of their Nazi leaders but doubted that they would succeed. In contrast, only 13 percent thought that the Japanese people disliked their leadership.[43]

It was sound propaganda policy, therefore, to keep the focus on Nazi Germany. In June 1942, the OWI expanded on the idea used in the *You Can't Do Business with Hitler* series to produce a show covering all Axis powers. *This Is Your Enemy,* which ran until September 1943, was a more polished production, yet it substantively duplicated much of *You Can't Do Business with Hitler,* which kept running concurrently. Particularly, the new series retained an emphasis on Nazi Germany: out of sixty-eight episodes, only seven dealt with Japan and two with Italy; the rest focused on the Nazi threat.[44]

The listener responses to *This Is Your Enemy* preserved by the OWI reflect a favorable reception. The letter writers compared it to *You Can't Do Business with Hitler* and called both series "highly informative," "grim and realistic," and "fact-filled drama." One letter from a listener in Buffalo, New York, captured the tenor of the responses: "I listen to your program every Sunday and although it is harsh and cruel I think it does the American people good to know whom we are up against."[45]

By September 1942, the FDR administration achieved one of its goals. According to the surveys undertaken by the Intelligence Bureau of the OWI, a majority of Americans now agreed that Germany had to be subdued first: "Last spring they wanted to hit hardest at Japan. . . . Americans are now convinced that we should turn most of our strength on Germany." Clearly, government radio propaganda alone could not be credited for this turnaround. The escalated U-boat war in the Atlantic hand in hand with government propaganda in all media brought about this shift. Yet series like *You Can't Do Business with Hitler* and *This Is Your Enemy* played over radio stations in every corner of the United States in 1942 and educated Americans—sometimes for the first time—

about the enormous changes that had taken place in Germany, as well as the monumental task ahead of them.[46]

On the other hand, no amount of government propaganda could brush off the residue of latently positive and conciliatory sentiments Americans seemed to harbor toward Germans, especially in comparison with their Asian enemy. Similarly, noncommercial government radio propaganda also found its limits when it came to selling America's allies to the people. As mentioned earlier, both Axis propaganda and the isolationist newspapers in the United States hammered away at two of the most important allies of the United States, England and Russia. Elmer Davis, director of the OWI, had eloquently described the warped logic behind the isolationist attacks in one of his regular radio talks over CBS in February 1942: "Some people want the United States to win so long as England loses. Some people want the United States to win so long as Russia loses. And some people want the United States to win so long as Roosevelt loses."[47]

In the case of Russia, government propaganda generally pursued the route of least resistance, that is, emphasizing the terrible and widely acknowledged sacrifices the Russian people were making in the face of battle. Radio programs stressed the terrific fighting spirit and heroism of individual Red Army soldiers. Yet the U.S. government also tried to portray a different and changed Russia, a "New Russia" that emerged out of battling the Nazis. In "A Letter from a Red Army Man," broadcast in late March 1942 as part of *The Treasury Star Parade,* Boris Grabatov stressed this "New Russia." He portrayed Russians as not all that different from Americans. They loved to celebrate and sing, they loved their families and their way of life, and yet they knew that they had to do their part in defeating "the Hitler beast." Like Americans, they were fighting for their families, their country, and the future of humankind: "This is our battle to the death. Across many lands and many oceans, I clasp your hand, my American friend."[48]

Selling the Russians to the American people was one of the most difficult tasks ever assigned to a government propaganda agency, as revealed by the storm of protest that greeted the premiere of the controversial movie *Mission to Moscow* in early 1943. Under pressure from the OWI, the movie presented a whitewashed version of the Soviet Union that was not much different from the United States except, as film critic James Agee wryly noted, "that in Russia everybody affects a Weber and Fields accent and women run locomotives."[49] Americans' skepticism toward Russia remained strong despite this concerted propaganda campaign. Americans readily acknowledged the sacrifices being made by the Russian people. In fact, throughout 1942, they consistently thought that the Soviet Union—of all the United States' allies—was trying hardest to win the war. On the other hand, Americans distrusted the Soviet Union the most when it came to postwar planning. In November 1942, 51 percent of respondents to a government poll believed that Russia would cooperate with the United States after the war (up from only 38 percent in February 1942), whereas 75 percent trusted in English postwar cooperation, and 80 percent believed China would be a dependable ally after the war.[50]

The problem facing the OWI with regard to Great Britain was the opposite of the Russian quandary. An overwhelming majority—roughly 85 percent—was willing to trust England as a postwar ally, but during 1942, Americans questioned its commitment to winning the war. If Americans thought Russia was trying the hardest to win the war, England was thought to be doing the least. Coupled with this skepticism was a persistent belief by a strong minority (one-third of Americans) in 1942 that the British were trying to get Americans to do the fighting for them.[51]

Lewis and other officials in the OWI were concerned about this strong, vocal minority and decided to do something about it. Again Lewis sent word to Corwin and asked if he would be willing to produce a series in collaboration with CBS to enhance Americans' appreciation for the British contribution to the war. Corwin again eagerly accepted and headed to England to produce a series of broadcasts based on his firsthand observations. As he reminisced later, he shared the OWI officials' sense of urgency: "I expected and understood (though I did not condone) a certain measure of American antipathy toward the British. But the scope and the utter senselessness of most anti-British sentiment puzzled me." *An American in England,* as the new series was titled, was produced in London, shortwaved to the United States, and broadcast over the national CBS network. To add to its appeal, Edward Murrow was signed up to narrate the programs.[52]

Corwin portrayed the British as Americans had already come to know them through Murrow's news reports and other descriptions: resilient and unbending, holding out with a mixture of understated humor and a stiff upper lip. Moreover, he tried to convey the fears and deprivations the English experienced in their everyday lives, from ducking bombs to queuing for rationed food. But this ambitious transatlantic project ran into a number of problems, some of them technical, others having to do with programming. Ironically, *An American in England* had more listeners in England, where it was broadcast over the BBC, than in the United States, where it ran opposite Bob Hope, who then had the highest-rated show on American radio.[53]

The Impact of Government Radio Propaganda

Corwin's series from England points to one of the weaknesses of a number of the noncommercial government radio series. Because they were broadcast as sustaining programs, most of them were assigned "leftover" air times—time slots that sponsors did not want to occupy. These frequently were hours on weekend afternoons or, as with *An American in England,* slots that networks had given up on because of competition from a show on another network. Another noncommercial government series hampered by its status as sustainer was *The Man behind the Gun.* Despite its initial popularity, the program was moved three times within its first twenty-six weeks and twice thereafter. As its writer, Ranald MacDougall, argued, the networks often seemed to be fulfilling their duty without caring about the results: "Seemingly, the networks are content merely to list their [noncommercial] programs in impressive booklets, without particularly caring that these programs are not being listened to by the public they are meant to serve."[54]

There is no doubt that the networks pursued a dual agenda by collaborating with a number of government agencies in airing noncommercial government radio propaganda. Network executives followed their hearts in aiding America's war effort, but they also wanted to prove their worth to the government and especially the FCC. As MacDougall implied, to make sure that the government was not overlooking their contribution, they regularly summarized their voluntary network collaboration in thick booklets, which they sent to the OWI and the FCC.[55]

Most of the government radio propaganda series ran as regular sustaining programs. The series that gathered the largest audiences, *This is War!,* was an exception, since it was broadcast over all networks simultaneously during prime time—a privilege that was usually reserved only for FDR's fireside chats. The other show that beat the odds based on its own appeal was *The Army Hour,* which aired on Sunday afternoons over NBC and ran throughout the war, attracting several million listeners every week. Series such as *The Treasury Star Parade, You Can't Do Business with Hitler,* and *This Is Your Enemy* also became standard fare by playing regularly over most of the country's radio stations, often being repeated several times per week. Yet their status as noncommercial, public service programs did relegate them to the niches of the radio schedule. Thus, whereas the networks eagerly collaborated with the government propaganda agencies and tried to remain in good standing with the FCC, they certainly did not risk disrupting their regular, profitable prime-time schedules.

The second factor that limited the effectiveness of this radio propaganda certainly had to do with America's legacies—from both World War I and the New Deal. As some letters and opinion polls amply certified, Americans did not swallow government propaganda hook, line, and sinker. This fact was further illuminated by propaganda studies undertaken during World War II, such as the frequently cited study by Carl Hovland and others that analyzed the effect of the propaganda film *The Battle of Britain*. The film, the fourth in Capra's *Why We Fight* series, was intended to convey three key messages: teach Americans about the righteousness of their cause; highlight the integrity and fighting ability of Great Britain; and increase the fighting morale of American soldiers. Hovland and his team of researchers concluded that the film succeeded most fully in meeting the first goal. Comparing the research group with a control group, the authors found an increased level of historical understanding of the causes of the war and a slightly heightened sense that Britain, and especially the Royal Air Force, had performed a heroic deed in fending off the German attack. Yet this newfound knowledge did not change the soldiers' opinions on two crucial issues. The overall attitude toward Britain had improved only slightly, with a large minority still distrusting Britain's will to fight. The willingness of the soldiers to fight and die for the cause, finally, remained low.[56]

Other studies concurred with these findings. The reception of propaganda as well as other media messages was a complex and personalized process, as social scientists found out during World War II. People constantly read and absorbed images and messages selectively, through several filters. They ignored mediated messages that did not fit with their preconceived notions, distorted media images, or adjusted new facts to merge with their overall worldview. This wave of communication studies during World War II led to a complete revision of the dominant paradigm in media research. Before the war, most researchers had firmly upheld the "magic bullet theory" (also referred to as the "hypodermic needle theory"), which argued that media messages directly and instantaneously produced a predictable change in personal opinion and behavior among the recipients. The fear and suspicion of propaganda prior to and at the beginning of World War II were based on popularized versions of this model. The new, emerging paradigm, in contrast, emphasized the limited influence of propaganda and the media and was appropriately termed the "limited effects model."[57] As these forerunners of recent reception theory confirmed, the government was definitely dealing with audiences that constantly negotiated, reread, or actively resisted their messages. In general, the media research conducted during World War II, as well as common sense, reminds us to be cautious about taking the effects of propaganda for granted—unless we want to fall back on the simplistic notions of the "magic bullet theory."

Conclusion

The year 1942 marked the high tide of noncommercial government radio propaganda. During these months there was a fragile, war-driven consensus among network executives, government officials, and the politicians in Congress that Americans needed to be told or reminded what this war was all about. The overall impact was mixed and limited. Series such as *You Can't Do Business with Hitler* continued to find audiences, not least of all because Americans were poorly informed and curious about the changes that had occurred in Germany over the past ten years. These programs taught Americans valuable lessons about the nature of the enemy and helped the FDR administration in pushing through its Atlantic First strategy. On the other hand, as the pro-Allied propaganda demonstrated, no amount of propaganda could break Americans' resilient skepticism. Even though most Americans acknowledged that Russia was bearing the brunt of the fight in Europe in 1942, and gave them credit for it, at least half of the population continued to distrust the Soviet Union. Along the same lines, while most Americans trusted Great Britain and thought it would prove a loyal postwar ally, a large minority criticized its war effort in 1942 and doubted its determination to fight and win the war.

Noncommercial government radio propaganda continued throughout the war. CBS followed up Corwin's *An American in England* with two similar programs: one entitled *An American in Russia* and the other a series on Latin America produced by Orson Welles. Corwin continued to write war drama, including a number of outstanding pieces like *Untitled* (1944), a eulogy for an American soldier who died in action, or *On a Note of Triumph* (1945), a thoughtful, provocative radio drama played over CBS on V-E Day.[58] NBC also continued its collaboration with *The Army Hour* and other government programs. But some of the urgency that had spurred the propaganda shows in early 1942 had clearly dissipated a year later.

Beginning in 1943, there was a rising wave of criticism directed against government radio propaganda and the role of the OWI as a whole by politicians no longer willing to suspend their opposition to government propaganda initiated by the Roosevelt administration. With an eventual Allied victory in sight, Republicans and conservative Democrats had seen enough government propaganda, which to them confirmed their worst fears, that is, that the Domestic Branch of the OWI had become FDR's public relations agency or at least was propagating overall policies in line with those of the New Deal. Not surprisingly, they went after the Domestic Branch at the first chance that presented itself: the appropriations hearings for the OWI beginning in 1943. In the summer of 1943, Congress cut the budget of the Domestic Branch—which included the Radio Division—to one-third of its former appropriation. Moreover, it prohibited the branch from publishing pamphlets or producing radio propaganda series.[59]

Before considering in greater depth the political backlash against government radio propaganda during World War II, one further layer needs to be added to this discussion of noncommercial radio propaganda. This is the government's involvement in domestic foreign-language programming. Aside from radio news and commentary, no segment of radio broadcasting was influenced more by the war. More important, through the OWI and the FCC the government severely censored the stations and programs directed at sizable ethnic audiences. The urge to control and change these programs further fueled the political objections to government-sponsored radio propaganda.

CHAPTER 3

Closing Ranks

Propaganda, Politics, and Domestic
Foreign-Language Radio

Amid fears of sabotage and fifth columnists in the hectic months after the attack on Pearl Harbor, *Variety* opened the radio section of its May 20, 1942, edition with the sensational headline "FOREIGN STATIONS 'CONFESS.'" The article told of an "amazing recital" of abuses by domestic foreign-language radio stations over the past months and years, which had finally come to light at the annual conference of the National Association of Broadcasters in Cleveland the week before. The story that especially aroused the tempers of the conference participants was the revelation by the manager of the New York City radio station WBNY, who had overheard one of his Italian announcers dedicate a musical number to the captain of a steamship, mentioning both the name of the ship and its departure time from New York harbor that same night. This was a flagrant violation of the Code of Wartime Practices, which among other things banned news concerning landings and departures of ships because thousands of American sailors were endangered by German and Italian submarines lurking off the Atlantic Coast.

Variety echoed the opinions of a number of conference participants when it accused "cheap-minded, cynical Axis-lovers" like this Italian announcer of openly mocking the government's good nature by taking advantage of American free speech and civil liberties. At a time when Americans were practicing blackouts in fear of imminent enemy attacks on both coasts and German saboteurs were arrested along the East Coast after being dropped off by German U-boats, nobody was inclined to take this revelation lightly. In fact, *Variety* followed up on the story in its next week's edition in an article entitled "Is There a Radio Underground?" It reported that the managers of radio stations had asserted that there were only a "few bad apples" among the foreign-language broadcasters, which did little to dissipate *Variety*'s suspicion "that 'only a few' of them have been really helpful"—helpful to America's enemies and saboteurs.[1]

This well-publicized episode echoed the very grave concern over fifth columnists that the American government and the American public shared in the early months of 1942. For worried and confused Americans, it was a stark reminder that the United States might still suffer the same fate as France had in 1940. The dominant view of France's quick defeat in the spring of 1940 was that it was made possible by the concerted efforts of a fifth column, which had divided and weakened the country from within.[2]

Nevertheless, unlike in World War I, the Roosevelt administration decided not to curtail foreign-language media indiscriminately but rather to use them as propaganda vehicles to reach large ethnic audiences. During World War I, the Espionage Act and the Sedition Act had enabled the postmaster general to ban any newspaper that dared to challenge or criticize the policies of the United States government. Moreover, against the backdrop of the virulent one-hundred-percent-American movement, every foreign-language newspaper had to print English translations alongside the original text. In the years after 1919, observers agreed that the most frequent and flagrant abuses of power by the Committee on Public Information had been perpetrated against foreign-language media, needlessly alienating large segments of the American ethnic population.[3]

During World War II, the U.S. government, intent on demonstrating to friends and foes alike that democracy and tolerance presented a strong, viable alternative to fascism and racial totalitarianism, launched a powerful campaign to turn the nation's pluralism and ethnic diversity into a strength. Contrary to Nazi and fascist propaganda, this campaign would prove to the world that democracy had not made the United States soft and flabby, and that the country's racial and ethnic mixture had not sapped it of the will to fight and win wars. Aside from the indiscriminate and racist exclusion of Japanese Americans, the Roosevelt administration pursued a concerted campaign to boost the integration and patriotism of other ethnic Americans. Foreign-language radio was assigned a crucial role in this government effort.

The agency charged with overseeing the unity campaign was the Foreign Language Division of the Office of Facts and Figures, which after

June 1942 merged into the Office of War Information like all other propaganda units. Established in late 1941, the division monitored the domestic foreign-language media and disseminated pro-democratic, Americanizing material. It oversaw approximately sixteen hundred newspapers and nearly two hundred radio stations working in up to thirty foreign languages, both of which catered to between twenty and thirty million Americans. The division operated with a maximum of seventeen staff members. These included eight officials, each of whom was individually responsible for one major language group.[4]

The second part of the strategy—aside from disseminating pro-Allied propaganda—consisted of the covert expansion of a surveillance network to monitor German- and Italian-language groups especially closely. The agency in charge—established within the Justice Department in early 1940—was the Special Defense Unit. Its task was to oversee and analyze domestic and foreign-language press and radio to detect antidemocratic, particularly pro-Nazi or pro-fascist, propaganda. The second main agency within this surveillance campaign was the Neutrality Law Unit, created about the same time, which pursued neutrality laws violations, industrial sabotage, and treason. These two units provided the core of the American "propaganda prophylaxis" from 1940 to 1942.[5] They collaborated closely with the Foreign Language Division of the OFF/OWI throughout 1942.

As the episode of the Italian broadcaster illustrates, during World War II it was the radio stations, with their ability to cross national borders and to signal enemy navy vessels and submarines, that caused the main headache for the officials in the Foreign Language Division. Domestic German- and Italian-language programs within the United States became the main concern of various government agencies. In the early 1940s, German Americans and Italian Americans were still the biggest foreign-language groups in the country. At the time of the 1940 census, there were close to five million first- and second-generation German Americans living in the United States; Italian Americans numbered close to four million. A total of 200 newspapers and twenty foreign-language stations catered to German Americans; 130 papers and sixty-five radio stations provided news and entertainment in the Italian language.[6]

During the early months of 1942, an informal coalition emerged that took an intense interest in foreign-language programs, especially those in German and Italian. The group consisted of various German and Italian refugee organizations, the Foreign Language Division of the

OFF, and the FCC. In the months to come, the Foreign Language Division, especially the head of its radio section, Lee Falk, spearheaded a two-part, concerted policy toward domestic foreign-language programs. It initiated morale- and unity-building foreign-language programs and also removed from the air broadcasters who were considered pro-fascist.

By early 1943, both parts of this policy would come under increasing partisan fire. One line of attack criticized the agency's attempts to rein in foreign-language radio and its use of heavy-handed censorship. The other, less obvious, charge was that the OWI had collaborated with foreign atheists and communists, that is, refugees, who spread their insidious messages throughout the United States—with the official approval of the federal government, no less. These attacks discredited the work of the Foreign Language Division and further threatened the precarious status of the Domestic Branch of the OWI. In the broader political context, they became part of the ongoing political power play between the Roosevelt administration and its opponents, which despite the wartime emergency continued at a high-pitched level.

Control and Censorship of Foreign-Language Radio

Until the early 1940s, foreign-language broadcasting went generally unnoticed by the English-speaking public at large and rarely received coverage in trade magazines or newspapers. Without the war, it very well might have remained that way. After the German attack on Poland in September 1939, however, U.S. government agencies started to take notice. As early as February 1940, the FCC and the Federal Bureau of Investigation (FBI) discussed ways to neutralize the possibly subversive effects of foreign-language broadcasts.[7]

This situation was exacerbated by Italy's entry into the war on June 11, 1940. In response to mounting governmental pressure, the NAB called a special meeting for July 1940, inviting the managers of radio stations broadcasting domestic foreign-language programs to discuss ways to safeguard their continuation. The licensees of these stations insisted that they could supervise these programs themselves, without government intervention. They proposed an internal monitoring system like the one already adopted by individual radio stations such as WOV in New York City. According to this proposal, all scripts would be scrutinized before programming, monitored while being read over the air, and kept in a file for later reference. Furthermore, an executive committee was appointed to discuss ways to elicit community support in fostering Americanism among ethnic groups through radio programs.[8]

When the FCC undertook a survey of stations broadcasting foreign-language programs toward the end of 1940, it found that, despite these precautions, popular suspicions of a fifth column working inside the United States had already taken their toll on the industry. Although 199 domestic stations (out of a total of about 850) still carried foreign-language programs in one or more languages, 57 had already dropped theirs. Thus, even before America's entry into the war, there was a marked decline in foreign-language broadcasts. In all, 1,721 weekly programs were still broadcast in thirty-one foreign languages, for a total of 1,330 broadcasting hours per week. Most numerous among these were small local stations operating on 250 watts. More important, however, were the close to 50 stations with greater power that broadcast ten or more hours of foreign-language programs per week. Foremost among these were programs in Italian, Polish, Spanish, Yiddish, and German.[9]

A study conducted in 1941 by Rudolf Arnheim and Martha Collins Bayne of the Office of Radio Research at Columbia University on foreign-language programs confirmed that broadcasters continued to cater to the tastes of their traditional ethnic audiences. During the week of February 13 through February 19, 1941, these researchers set up fifty-nine listening posts throughout the United States to monitor a total of eight hundred hours of foreign-language programs, more than half of the total broadcast during one week.[10]

Their findings showed that foreign-language broadcasts presented a very different kind of programming than that transmitted by the networks. Regular sponsored programs such as dramatizations, talks, or newscasts took up less than one-third of the airtime. The remaining two-thirds were devoted to participation programs, which largely consisted of listeners' musical requests to fill time between commercial spots and public service announcements. German-language broadcasters relied especially on music programs, which accounted for an average of 91 percent of the broadcast hours. Italian-language shows averaged 61 percent music programs, which was still markedly above the network average of about 51 percent. As might be expected, the music played during these broadcasts was almost exclusively ethnic and was sung in the native language of the listening audience. As Arnheim and Collins Bayne stated, it consisted of old songs, which typically "reflect very little of what goes on at present [but rather] suggest a dreaming back to that

Germany or Poland or other homeland that listeners left many years ago."[11]

Of immense concern to the FCC, as well as other government agencies, were the news reports broadcast during German- and Italian-language programs. Arnheim and Collins Bayne's findings confirmed part of the lingering suspicion against these broadcasters: "Though a certain pro-Axis bias is apparent here and there, it is clear that it is a settled policy of stations to tone it [the pro-Axis bias] down."[12]

The American public was clearly lining up behind the Allies after the fall of France, and it agreed with FDR when he condemned Italy's entry into the war on the Axis side as "a stab in the back" of France. Consequently, at home Americans grew resentful of the numerous German- and Italian-language media, which had often reveled in the rise of their former homelands in the 1930s and frequently continued their support of the fascist regimes during 1940 and 1941.

To be sure, such overt support dwindled after the outbreak of the war. But contemporary observers routinely estimated that between 10 and 15 percent of German Americans and Italian Americans were strong supporters of the fascist regimes in Europe at the turn of the decade. For example, when the Nazi propaganda film *Campaign in Poland* opened in Yorkville in mid-1940, the German Americans of that New York City neighborhood flocked to the theater, filling the five hundred seats in the house; another crowd stood in the back throughout the show. All through 1940, the German-language program on radio station WBNX in the Bronx featured German military music as its main item of entertainment. In restaurants in Italian-American neighborhoods, as one reporter noted, one could still overhear patrons closing discussions of world events with the phrase "Roberto vincera." "Roberto" was an acronym based on the names of the Axis powers, Rome, Berlin and Tokyo, and the phrase translated as "Roberto will win."[13]

Two other groups that continued to closely watch the German- and Italian-language programs were political refugees from these countries. Together with labor unions and left-wing and Jewish organizations, these refugees were termed "premature antifascist" in the 1930s. Now their criticisms fell on more receptive ears. In October 1940, in an article in the *New York Times,* Gaetano Salvemini, probably the most prominent antifascist Italian émigré residing in the United States, launched his first major attack. He charged that the Italian-language programs broadcast in New York played an integral part in perpetuating support for the fascist ideology among Italian Americans and listed the names of nine broadcasters, all of whom worked through the New York radio stations WOV and WHOM, as the primary felons.[14]

On the German side, charges by the antifascist refugees were no less acrimonious. On December 12, 1941, an article by Kurt Hellmer in the *Aufbau,* a weekly German-Jewish newspaper published by German refugees in New York, charged the German-language broadcaster George Brunner, of WBNX, with subversive activities. According to Hellmer, Brunner, among other things, played a popular German beer hall song, "Ach Du Lieber Augustin" ("O, You Poor Augustin"), after the announcement of the declaration of war by the United States. The lyrics of this song poke fun at Augustin, who fouls up everything he touches and in the end is left with nothing. To the German listener, this sequencing could easily have been mocking America's potential as a war ally: the United States, like Augustin, had taken on much more than it could chew and in the end would be left with nothing. As Hellmer claimed, these songs could indeed have been used as a secret code, "incomprehensible for American observers, who were not familiar with the words and contents of the song."[15]

This accusation was supported by Jack Iwo, a columnist for the *Neue Volkszeitung,* a Social Democratic German refugee paper published in New York, who concluded that there was little difference between Brunner's news hour and German shortwave. In one show, for example, Brunner had dwelt on the fact that the United States was inhabited by only one-sixteenth of the world's population, yet it controlled five-sixteenths of the world's copper and zinc production. Claims like these were taken straight from German propaganda, Iwo argued, which accused "plutocratic England and the United States" of protecting their world dominance, denying Germany its own Lebensraum in the East.[16]

Soon after the bombs had fallen on Pearl Harbor, the FCC and the Foreign Language Division geared up for a full-fledged investigation of all major stations on the East Coast that broadcast foreign-language programs. The stations that soon found themselves under investigation were WBNX, WHOM, and WOV of New York City, WPEN of Philadelphia, WCOP of Boston, and eventually WGES of Chicago. These were, in terms of both broadcast hours and audiences reached, the biggest foreign-language stations in the United States, although none broadcast in foreign languages exclusively. On March 20, 1942, Alan Cranston, chief of the Foreign Language Division of the OWI, sent an initial list of nine broadcasters to William B. Lewis, head of the OWI's Radio Division, with the recommendation that "the individuals mentioned should be barred from the air immediately."[17]

It was not a coincidence that all these broadcasters worked on New York City stations. The OWI's explicit policy was to tackle the biggest and most concentrated foreign-language market first. Moreover, these stations were closest to the offices of both the OWI and the FCC and had already been indicted by several New York refugee papers.[18]

The first station to come under intensive pressure was WBNX of New York City. During the week of December 11 through 18, 1941, the FCC systematically monitored the German-language programs sent over WBNX. Like the articles published by German refugees in *Aufbau* and *Neue Volkszeitung,* the FCC investigators noted the suspicious sequencing of reports and music in these programs. Similar to the refugee papers, the investigators concluded that "in accordance with the general situation, the broadcasts are strongly camouflaged, still they must be considered definitely pro-Hitler."[19]

The first casualties of these government investigations were Herbert Oettgen and George Brunner, two German-language broadcasters working for WBNX. Oettgen was dismissed from WBNX not because of remarks he made on the air but because he was the owner of Radio Rundfunk Records Company, which distributed offensive Nazi recordings such as the "Horstwessel Song" or "Wir Fahren Gegen England" ("We Drive towards England"). Prior to the war, Oettgen had also played such recordings on his musical program broadcast over WBNX. The trigger to his dismissal was Dorothy Thompson's column in the *Washington Evening Star* of February 28, 1942, in which she accused him of advertising and selling Nazi marching songs, playing them on the air, and boasting of his friendship with known Bund leaders. When Walter Winchell repeated the same charges on his radio broadcast on March 8, Oettgen was taken off the air.[20]

George Brunner's case was less clear-cut than Oettgen's. Brunner had been with WBNX as a German-language announcer since February 1933. Since 1936 he had conducted the *German-American Housewife Hour,* a commercial participation program that played three times a day for half an hour each. The broadcast was announced by Brunner and, since May 1940, his Jewish assistant, Ruth Parsey. According to another of his colleagues, who was known for his anti-Nazi broadcasts over WBNX, Brunner was "not known to be a Nazi but rather an old-line German army officer who hope[d] Germany [would] win the war." He argued that Brunner was above all a shrewd businessman who played what his audiences liked.[21]

Until shortly before his removal from WBNX on June 19, 1942, the most damaging evidence that could be marshaled against Brunner was that brought forth by the German refugee papers and the FCC report in the weeks immediately after the attack on Pearl Harbor. Apparently, this was not enough to remove him from the air. In the following months there were no further complaints against Brunner, although his programs were still considered suspect.

What finally tipped the balance against Brunner were charges by Rudy R. Strauss, a German refugee living in New York, who in June 1942 accused Brunner of using a secret code in his broadcasts. Strauss claimed that he had listened to thirty to thirty-five consecutive broadcasts by Brunner, ending on June 12, 1942; he thought he had "detected a pattern of mistakes and corrections," hinting that Brunner might have devised a code to contact German submarines off the coast of the United States. When Strauss reported his suspicion to Lee Falk of the Foreign Language Division, Falk lost no time but immediately suggested that the FCC record several of the broadcasts and hand them over to the Army Signal Corps for investigation. Without waiting for any confirmation of his suspicion, he asked the FBI to remove Brunner from the air. When the FBI answered that such a move was "one entirely foreign to the scope of [the] Bureau," Falk finally decided to tell the station manager of WNBX about his actions and convinced him to take Brunner off the air immediately.[22]

This episode came to a head against the background of the revelations published in *Variety,* mentioned earlier. In June and July 1942, the aftershocks of the revelation of a potential "foreign-language radio underworld" still rippled through the broadcasting industry. At a convention of the NAB held in Cleveland in late May, managers of stations broadcasting foreign-language programs had created an internal watchdog agency, the Foreign Language Radio War Committee, under the chairmanship of Arthur Simon of WPEN of Philadelphia. On its first day, the committee drafted a special wartime radio code for foreign-language broadcasters in which the members promised to scrutinize and monitor their foreign-language programs and agreed to a checkup of all broadcasters in the field through questionnaires and fingerprinting. Finally, in July Simon sent a circular to all station managers suggesting that they "contact Lee Falk, Chief of Radio, Foreign Language Division, OWI, before engaging anyone in connection with the preparation of foreign language programs."[23]

These events had certainly firmed up the position of the Foreign Language Division among foreign-language radio broadcasters. What the episode surrounding Brunner's removal showed as well was that neither the OWI, the FCC, nor the FBI had any jurisdiction over the removal of radio personnel. In fact, in August 1942, Elmer Davis, head of the OWI, and James Fly, head of the FCC, met with Byron Price, chief of the Office for Censorship, to confirm their respective jurisdictions: the OWI could propose and initiate programs and try to persuade the stations to play them; the FCC controlled the licensing of stations and could be asked to monitor alleged subversive programs; only the Office of Censorship, finally, was granted the right to censor broadcasts, to take punitive action against stations, or to remove personnel. As will become clear, this division held true on paper only: Brunner was not the last foreign-language broadcaster removed from the air by the Foreign Language Division in concert with the FCC.[24]

The Campaign for Ethnic Unity

While the investigations of foreign-language stations continued throughout 1942, so, too, did the efforts by the Foreign Language Division to initiate and produce foreign-language programs. The blueprint for this government involvement in domestic foreign-language radio was spelled out in a memorandum from Alan Cranston, chief of the Foreign Language Division and future California senator, to William Lewis. Referring to a new study on foreign-language programs undertaken by the FCC in the early part of 1942, Cranston pointed to the "rapidly diminishing" number of broadcasts in foreign languages. According to Cranston, this "serious situation" had developed because of a number of related reasons: criticisms by American listeners, withdrawal of advertisers' sponsorship, as well as suspect foreign-language broadcasters. He considered it a serious mistake to let the situation deteriorate any further and suggested that his "section of the Office of Facts and Figures take immediate steps to furnish inspiring and informative programs about America at war to stations with foreign language audiences." For this task, Cranston proposed that the Foreign Language Division enlist the help of advertisers and ethnic organizations and actively participate in the production and distribution of programs. As he concluded, "It is of utmost importance that foreign language programs be maintained as a channel through which the sympathy and participation of the foreign groups in this country can be enlisted in the war effort."[25]

The first series sponsored by the Foreign Language Division pre-

miered in March 1942 over WOV (Italian) and WBNX and WWRL
(German). *Uncle Sam Speaks,* which ran through July 1943, was a weekly
program written by Marion Dix. Announced as an informational program, the series portrayed situations in which a patronizing, avuncular
figure named Uncle Sam responded to fictitious letters and inquiries
read to him by his two "nieces," Pat and Maggie. The main purpose of
the program was to entice listeners into volunteering their services for
war-related work, to advertise jobs in the defense industry, and, more
generally, to invite ethnic listeners to support the war effort and partake
more fully in American society. The leitmotif of the programs supported
this notion of cooperation and unity: "Uncle Sam has advice on everything and finds work for each of you."[26]

Along these general lines, Uncle Sam helped a Czech refugee eager
to express his gratitude to America for allowing him into the country
by directing him toward the Voluntary Farmers Corps. A war veteran
too old to enlist was told that his services were still needed by organizations like the New York State Guards. Writing with a similar concern,
a disabled worker was referred to the United States Employment Service, which had established a service office for disabled workers. Finally,
Uncle Sam was able to console anxious letter writers like the little girl
who was concerned about the future of her Italian parents. If they had
done nothing wrong and would close shoulders with their American
neighbors in support of the war effort, Uncle Sam told her, there was
nothing to be afraid of.[27]

In March and April 1942, respectively, the Foreign Language Division also started distributing *This Is War!* and *You Can't Do Business
with Hitler* after transcribing them in foreign languages. In all, between
late April 1942 and mid-January 1943, the division transcribed thirty
programs (out of a total of fifty-six) of the *You Can't Do Business with
Hitler* series to stations broadcasting in foreign languages.

It is impossible to determine how many listeners were influenced by
these propaganda programs. But the following enraged response by a
German American who heard *You Can't Do Business with Hitler* over
WGES in Chicago indicates that these programs certainly rankled some
listeners:

> In every German American home one will hear "do you listen to that filthy
> propaganda 'You can't do business with Hitler'?" Well and the answer always
> is Pfui Teufel [yuck]; any good and decent German American will not listen
> and as soon as that phrase is announced they will turn off the German hour
> program!

The listeners will boycott such storekeepers who advertise with such broadcasts. And your Jewish outfit will not benefit by that. What German American people expect is good music and not filthy propaganda, otherwise we do not need a German Hour! Why can't you ether [?] in a clean and decent way of broadcasting? Must everything be as filthy as the Hollywood Films they are showing all over? Everybody knows that it is nothing else but war propaganda and filth and the people are fed up on that kind of mudsliding [sic] and you do likewise!
Disgusted,
American born German![28]

Anti-Semitic listeners like this German American were certainly not pleased with the events yet to come. The Foreign Language Division not only continued to initiate foreign-language programs but also soon received help from a number of refugee organizations that produced similar broadcasts. The first two organizations to get involved were the Mazzini Society, which included Italian refugees and Italian American antifascist groups, and the German-American Congress for Democracy, which brought together German refugees and German American labor unions with a Social Democratic orientation. In September 1942, the German refugees associated with the *Aufbau* started producing their own show, the *German-American Loyalty Hour.* All these programs followed the same pattern: they explored the pitfalls and horrors of the fascist regimes in Europe and, to a lesser degree, emphasized ways that German Americans and Italian Americans could support the American war effort.

The program most in line with the *You Can't Do Business with Hitler* series was *We Did It Before—We Can Do It Again,* produced by the German-American Congress for Democracy. On the recommendation of the Foreign Language Division, it went on the air over WBNX late in June 1942 following the removal of Oettgen and Brunner. Originally, the shows, which ran weekly until October 1943, were well-conceived, well-dramatized portrayals of the horrors of Nazi rule over Europe and the heroic struggle of underground organizations holding out in the face of overwhelming power. Each show opened with the same catchy tune:

We did it before
and we can do it again,
yes we will do it again.
We knock them over
and then we get

the guy in back of them;
we did it before,
we can do it again![29]

Unfortunately, by early 1943 the broadcasts lacked both in originality and in performance, and they deteriorated into overdramatized proclamations, devoid of any clear conception. By mid-1943, Joseph Lang, station manager of WHOM in New York, reported to Falk of the Foreign Language Division about the "very poor quality" of the broadcasts, which did neither the station nor the country any good. Lang informed Falk that the last "program consisted entirely of German folk songs, but the program ended with 'We Did It Before and We'll Do It Again'"; he asked whether the shows were still backed by the OWI. Falk informed Lang that his agency no longer checked the program's scripts and emphasized that the German-American Congress worked independently.[30]

This incident illustrates the attitude of the Foreign Language Division toward the refugee broadcasts. Because the broadcasts were never officially part of the OWI's work, Lee Falk and the Foreign Language Division could easily distance themselves from them if they started to backfire; yet if the broadcasts turned out to be a success, they could just as easily embrace them as their own.

The latter situation arose in the case of the other German refugee broadcast series, *We Fight Back: The German-American Loyalty Hour,* written and produced by the German refugees connected with the *Aufbau*. In these half-hour shows, the producers presented a well-dosed mixture of inspirational talks by prominent German Americans, news from Germany, and cultural programs. They were especially successful in signing up prominent refugees such as Kurt Weill, Thomas Mann, and Franz Liszt to participate in the programs. In November 1942, Falk thus wrote his chief, Alan Cranston: "Our 'We Fight Back' show with Thomas Mann made the New York Times this week. It was quite a show, with Mann and List [*sic*] of the Metropolitan."[31]

We Fight Back was the most ambitious German-language program produced during these years. It was also short-lived, with only twenty weekly shows broadcast over WHOM in New York between late September 1942 and early January 1943. The most distinctive feature, aside from serial dramas by well-known German writers, was their incorporation of Berlin-style cabaret and parody pieces.[32]

By October 1942, Falk was able to send Cranston an impressive list of achievements. In the "Monthly Report on Foreign Language Radio," from October 5, Falk noted that the regular weekly releases of his section included the following: *Uncle Sam Speaks* (Italian, 55 stations; German, 21 stations); *You Can't Do Business with Hitler* (Italian, 45 stations; Polish, 55 stations; German, 18 stations); a weekly newsletter, containing a short list of items to be included in news reports (Polish, 31 stations; Italian, 29 stations; German, 6 stations); two Mazzini women's programs (Italian, 17 stations); the weekly program by the German-American Congress for Democracy (German, 8 stations); and, finally, the *We Fight Back* series (German, 8 stations). Moreover, most of these shows were produced or transcribed by big stations broadcasting foreign-language programs and thus cost the OWI little or no money.[33]

What is apparent from this short review of German- and Italian-language programs initiated or coordinated by the Foreign Language Division of the OWI is how markedly they differed from the programs produced by foreign-language broadcasters prior to the war. Before the war, 90 percent of the German-language broadcasts consisted of old-time music programs, as demonstrated by a study undertaken by the Office of Radio Research. Now listeners were treated to classical music and cutting-edge, Berlin-style cabaret. While it is difficult to find direct responses to these wartime radio broadcasts in the German-American media, it is easy to imagine that this new programming did not play well with the established audiences.

The common response on the part of ethnic audiences was not resistance but evasion. Researchers at the time had already observed this reaction in connection with the coverage of controversial topics in radio news reports. This response also carried over into the German-language newspapers. For example, the two biggest daily German-language newspapers, the *New York Staats-Zeitung und Herold* and the *Chicago Abendpost,* never discussed the government-sponsored radio programs in 1942 and 1943. The *Staats-Zeitung* at least announced these broadcasts in its daily radio schedule, although it never listed the *We Fight Back* series. The *Abendpost* listed none of the series.[34]

This reluctance of the traditional German-language audiences could become even more overt, as indicated by a related incident at the *National Weeklies,* a German-language chain published in Winona, Minnesota, by Emil Leicht. The newspaper appeared in eight different local editions in various parts of the Midwest. Early in July 1942, Cranston sent Gerhart Seger, a German refugee and vice chairman of the Social Democratic German-American Congress for Democracy, to Winona to take over editorial control of the chain. In a five-week tug-of-war, Seger tried a variety of approaches to commit the papers to a more forceful antifascist editorial line, from cajoling Leicht to "wielding the big stick of second mail privilege." In the end, however, Leicht rejected any changes in his publication. As Seger reported back to Cranston, Leicht had told him that rather than accepting the government's line, he would close down, save his subscriber list, and open up again after the war was over. Seger and Cranston grudgingly resigned themselves to the fact that there was no more they could do.[35]

This episode points to the uphill battle facing the Foreign Language Division in large parts of the country. Some segments of the ethnic audiences, not unlike the American public at large, probably harbored anti-Semitic feelings and resented the role that Jewish refugees played in the government campaigns. Some were probably still rooting for their former countries to emerge victorious from this war. But the largest number of these ethnic listeners probably tuned out because they simply did not care for the progressive political ideas advanced by Seger and others or for the urban, elite culture that replaced their traditional and familiar foreign-language broadcasts.

This episode also highlights the government's different approach toward foreign-language newspapers as opposed to similar programs. Clearly, it was much easier to get rid of a broadcaster than to close down a newspaper. This is not to say that the latter did not happen. In fact, the first paper that was temporarily shut down was a German-language newspaper in Philadelphia. However, closing a newspaper always caused a big splash and served as a fretful reminder of the well-publicized abuses the Creel Committee during World War I. The removal of broadcasters, on the other hand, usually went unnoticed by anyone outside the field of foreign-language broadcasting.

And it is indeed clear that the foreign-language stations got this message as well. By the end of 1942, Falk and the Foreign Language Division had removed one or more German- and Italian-language broadcasters from every major foreign-language station on the East Coast, as well as a few in the Midwest and on the West Coast. Moreover, the division had been instrumental in replacing these broadcasters with anti-Axis spokesmen, often German and Italian refugees. On WTEL in Philadelphia, for example, prominent refugee politicians took over the *German Hour*. These personnel changes went the furthest at the Italian-language station WOV in New York City, which by the end of the year had replaced five of its Italian-language broadcasters with refugees.[36]

Political Backlash: The Demise
of Government-Controlled Radio Propaganda

Another key difference that made radio stations broadcasting in foreign languages so much more susceptible than foreign-language newspapers to the wishes of the Foreign Language Division was the radio licensing system supervised by the FCC and the fact that the FCC closely collaborated with Falk's office. According to the Federal Communications Act of 1934, every station in the country had to periodically apply to the FCC for the renewal of its license. By the early 1940s, such renewal was required every two years. As the radio stations broadcasting in foreign languages came up for renewal in 1942 and 1943, then, it was legally within the prerogative of the FCC to delay issuing new licenses. Instead it could issue a temporary one- or three-month license, and could do so repeatedly.[37]

It was thus hardly a coincidence that all major stations broadcasting in foreign languages (including WOV, WHOM, and WBNX of New York City; WGES of Chicago; WPEN of Philadelphia; and WCOP of Boston) were put on temporary license at some point during 1942 or 1943. In fact, as was revealed in a major congressional investigation of the FCC in 1943, which charged it with amassing powers far beyond the authority outlined in the Communications Act, this policy was part of a cleverly planned tactic on the part of the FCC and the OWI.[38]

The clear evidence that the FCC had overstepped its authority in cahoots with Lee Falk of the Foreign Language Division was presented in a recorded interview of Sidney Spear, attorney for the FCC, in the context of a broader congressional investigation of the FCC. Spear described how the FCC had held the threat of license cancellation over foreign-language stations for a certain period, during which Falk convinced the station managers to drop targeted broadcasters. Those who knew of this method called it the "squeeze play":

We worked it this way. If Lee [Falk] found a fellow he thought was doing some funny business, he told me about it. Then we waited until the station applied for a renewal of license. Say the station was WBNX and the broadcaster in question was Leopold Hurdski [fictitious name]. . . . Well, when WBNX applied for a renewal, we would tip off Lee and he would drop in on Mr. Alcorn, the station's manager. He would say, "Mr. Alcorn, I believe you ought to fire Leopold Hurdski."

Then he would give Mr. Alcorn some time to think this over. After a couple of weeks, Mr. Alcorn would begin to notice he was having some trouble getting his license renewed. After a couple of more weeks of this same thing, he would put two and two together and get four. Then he would fire Leopold Hurdski and very shortly after that his license would be renewed by the Commission.[39]

A case in point was WGES of Chicago, which had been put on temporary license in August 1942. In September, Arnold Hartley, the station's manager, wrote Lee Falk asking if the Office of Censorship was suspicious of WGES. Hartley told Falk that the station had been asked to send a list of all German- and Italian-language broadcasts, along with transcripts of these programs and translations in English. He was clearly surprised at this distrust because WGES was already participating fully in the campaign of the Foreign Language Division. Aside from initiating its own anti-Axis programs, it had broadcast *You Can't Do Business with Hitler* in German and Polish, *Uncle Sam Speaks* in German and Italian, the Mazzini programs in Italian, and foreign-language news and public service announcements in both German and Italian. At the meeting of the Foreign Language Radio War Committee in Washington, D.C., in late October, however, Hartley was told in no uncertain terms that he had to remove two Italian-language broadcasters if he wanted his license renewed. He did so immediately after his return to Chicago, and by November 1, 1942, WGES received its two-year license. Two days later, Hartley notified Falk of the removals and pledged his full support of the OWI foreign-language radio effort.[40]

Stations such as WGES in Chicago or WOV in New York City could count themselves among the lucky ones of the foreign-language stations because they received their renewed licenses after a "waiting period" of only four months. Less lucky were stations such as WBNX or WHOM, both in New York City, which were put on temporary licenses in August and December 1942, respectively. The full licenses were not renewed until September 1943, after the investigation of the FCC revealed how it and the Foreign Language Division had manhandled these stations.

The FCC revelations were welcome fodder for long-standing foes of government agencies like the FCC and the OWI. As Eugene L. Garey, the general counsel of the congressional investigating committee, emphasized during the hearings, this unlawful cooperation between these agencies did not bode well for the future. Clearly, America could not tolerate these "Gestapo" measures. Nor should Americans be forced to listen to a bunch of communist, atheist, or foreign refugees, as he warned: "The voices of these aliens go into our homes, and the unwary are led to believe that they speak with authority and official approval.

They even censor our Christmas and Easter religious programs, and tell us what music we may hear."[41]

This was only one of the charges leveled against the OWI and the FCC. The others vacillated between attacks on OWI officials and broad accusations against the two agencies: that Lee Falk was a Gestapo-minded crackpot; that the OWI had unlawfully deprived American citizens (foreign-language broadcasters) of their livelihoods, had ruined their careers, and had damaged private enterprise; and that the OWI and the FCC had collaborated to dismiss foreign-language broadcasters by holding the threat of license suspension over the heads of station managers—which had indeed been the case.[42]

The effect of the hearings on the Foreign Language Division and the OWI was profound. Cranston, who followed the proceedings while touring California, encouraged Falk "to get out some kind of a strong rebuttal" for the agency by stressing its achievements and the courage it demonstrated in taking on these responsibilities. As Cranston wrote, "C'mon, dammit, cut loose on the bastards."[43] Yet the hearings had done their damage. While the FCC and its personnel would eventually escape almost unscathed, the hearings were instrumental in demoting the Foreign Language Division and the Domestic Branch of the OWI as a whole. [44]

The hearings also tapped into another ongoing controversy underlying all government propaganda in the early 1940s. They gave further ammunition to opponents of the OWI, who wanted to get rid of domestic government propaganda for partisan political reasons. FDR's enemies had rejected a central government propaganda agency before the war, and they did not like the creation of the OWI after America's entry into the war. The reason was quite simple: even though the nation had to unite behind its commander in chief, Republicans and conservative Democrats distrusted FDR's political motivations. They saw Roosevelt as a crafty, calculating manipulator and were wary of giving him and his New Dealers a free hand over domestic government propaganda.[45]

Parallel to the FCC investigation and the OWI appropriations hearing, which would cut much of the funding of the propaganda agency, another related conflict played itself out within the OWI. This controversy revolved around the overall role of the agency and the kind of information and propaganda campaigns it should disseminate. It pitted two groups against each other: the "idealists," who advocated educational and high-minded political appeals, and the "pragmatists," who were drawn from private industry and favored a largely commercial, privatized propaganda approach. The first group consisted of New Dealers and intellectuals who had been handpicked by the poet Archibald MacLeish when he was charged with leading the OFF in 1942. The other consisted of "dollar-a-year men," business and advertising executives, who were led by former CBS vice president William B. Lewis and whose numbers had steadily increased throughout 1942. The idealists included established writers such as Malcolm Cowley and Pulitzer Prize–winning historian Henry Pringle, as well as future notables such as Arthur Schlesinger Jr. and McGeorge Bundy. They accused the pragmatists, such as James Allen, a former motion-picture executive, and Price Gilbert, erstwhile vice president of Coca-Cola, of executing emotional, sugarcoated propaganda campaigns—in short, a "Madison Avenue" approach to war.[46]

Unfortunately for the MacLeish group, both the American political landscape and the dynamics within the OWI favored their opponents. Inside the agency, the head of the Domestic Branch, Gardner Cowles Jr., a former midwestern newspaper publisher, steadily sided with the "dollar-a-year men." By early 1943, most units within the Domestic Branch were headed by them. In addition, after the Republican resurgence in the 1942 election, Washington politics turned a few notches more conservative. The election also brought to Washington a fresh batch of politicians who, as Sydney Weinberg has aptly put it, "equated 'information' with 'propaganda.'" They quickly took aim at several pamphlets written by the "intellectuals" within the OWI, which they claimed perpetuated a liberal New Deal philosophy or glorified the Roosevelt presidency. These changes finally led to the resignation of the by now demoralized New Dealers in April 1943 amid charges that the slick promotional style of advertising had come to dominate the agency, making political information campaigns impossible.[47]

William Rose Benét, a friend of one of the writers who resigned, captured their collective frustration and disappointment in a poem published in the *Saturday Review* one month after the incident:

> Oh boy, but there's an ocean
> Of joy in promotion,
> Answering the question
> "What's in it for me?"
> [...]
> Aren't you on to the surprising
> Way they fall for advertising? . . .
> Try this delicious health-building War!

Buy *all* you need—then buy some more!
Never mind what we're fighting for!
Customers, customers, come and buy!
A short girdle does not bind the thigh.
We're the Salesmen of the OWI.[48]

By the fall of 1943, two years before the end of the war, the Foreign Language Division—like the OWI as a whole—had been demoted to a servicing agency, writing news releases but prohibited from producing its own radio propaganda. By mid-1943, the "Madison Avenue" style of propaganda would indeed dominate the work of the OWI.

Conclusion

War is said to be the "fuel of the melting pot," and World War II was no exception. Even though they were spared the infinitely worse treatment endured by Japanese Americans, for several years Italian Americans and German Americans lived under the shadow of their "enemy alien" status. This not only led to job discrimination, as several historians have documented, but also increased the pressure to adopt American ways.[49]

In terms of the government propaganda effort, this trend was exacerbated because the Foreign Language Division of the OWI coerced ethnic broadcasters to sign on to a prescribed vision of ethnicity that often had little to do with the national identity listeners remembered and cherished. Even apart from the work of the Foreign Language Division, stations cut back on foreign-language programs because of the suspicions surrounding ethnic radio. Whereas almost 200 stations had broadcast foreign-language programs in 1940, only 150 did so by September 1942. This number shrunk to approximately 130 in the fall of 1943, and it would continue to fall in the later war years.[50]

As Lizabeth Cohen has argued in her study on ethnic working-class communities in Chicago, domestic foreign-language broadcasting was one of the many strands that reinforced ethnic bonds and held these communities together. In the 1930s, with the domination of commercial network radio, this strand, like so many other institutions that had ensured the vitality of ethnic communities, became increasingly frayed across America. During World War II, at least in the case of German and Italian Americans, these ethnic ties were further undermined as the pressure increased to adopt both an updated version of ethnic identity and an Americanized outlook.[51]

The other striking feature of this propaganda effort is the degree to which government agencies lost track of their mission to use foreign-language radio in a positive, constructive manner. The only mitigating factor, as Lee Falk recalls, was that "this was not normal, work-a-day Washington or U.S.A.":

After the catastrophe of Pearl Harbor, the first two years of the war was a time of gigantic effort by the entire country to build our war machine which would eventually win the war. . . . Japan was sweeping through Asia. The Nazis were sweeping through Europe, all the way to Moscow. German submarines *were* sinking our ships just off the coast. At this time, we and our allies were losing the war to the Axis powers.

We in the wartime agencies like the OWI and the FCC and others were fighting this war on the home-front, against possible enemies in our country. In this emergency, some extreme measures were needed and some mistakes would be made.[52]

Yet these mistakes would cost the Foreign Language Division and the OWI dearly. First, they alienated part of the industry by manhandling broadcasters and managers in a style reminiscent of the Creel Committee of World War I. Second, the actions of the Foreign Language Division further exposed the government to political attacks like the FCC hearings. The investigation helped Republicans and conservative Democrats to curtail the authority of both the FCC and the OWI, which they viewed as "New Deal agencies" in the service of the Roosevelt administration. As a result, noncommercial government radio propaganda largely ceded after mid-1943. Clearly, this development took place within a much larger context, specifically the shifting tides of politics and the war. As the threat of enemy attacks on the United States and the fear of losing the war slowly receded, party politics regained utmost priority in the domestic arena. Domestic government propaganda was one of the casualties.

A Texas farm couple relaxing by their radio set. Radio was the primary mass-communication medium during World War II. By the early 1940s, roughly 90 percent of American families owned at least one radio set and, on average, listened to it for three to four hours a day. (Photo courtesy of Library of Congress.)

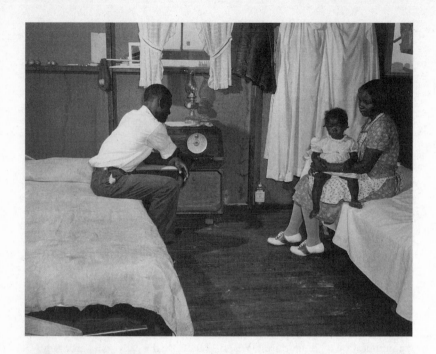

During the war, radio became even more central to the lives of most Americans. In a postwar survey, two-thirds of Americans praised radio for having done the best job of serving the public among all the media. The prominent position of the radio set is reflected in the pictures of (*above*) a family in a New Jersey Farm Security Administration camp and (*below*) an Illinois mother and son. (Photos courtesy of Library of Congress.)

H. V. Kaltenborn in a publicity picture in the early 1940s, after his switch to NBC. Kaltenborn became a household name for Americans in the late 1930s because of his nonstop radio news commentary during the Munich crisis. (Photo courtesy of National Archives.)

By the early 1940s, CBS emerged as the premier news network, led by Paul W. White, chief of its news division, and Edward R. Murrow, chief of its European staff. *Above:* CBS New York newsroom; Paul White is in the background (left in the left-hand window). *Below:* Edward R. Murrow at his desk in London during coverage of the D-Day invasion. (Photos courtesy of Library of American Broadcasting.)

Listening to news programs quickly emerged as an essential part of Americans' radio diet, especially for those who had little other access to the news. *Above:* For the nurse in a remote area in New Mexico, the radio was the primary contact with the outside world; papers were rarely delivered to her town. (Courtesy of Library of Congress.) *Below:* This was even truer for troops in the field, like this group of GIs listening to the latest news over the radio in their pup tents in northern France. (Courtesy of National Archives.)

Elmer Davis (*above left*), a popular radio news commentator, became the head of the Office of War Information (OWI), America's propaganda agency during World War II. Even though Davis advocated a "strategy of truth," he was unable to control public opinion. For example, while his office preferred to treat Japanese and German enemies similarly, the Japanese were quickly caricatured as animal-like (*below left*), whereas the Germans were always treated as humans (*above*), despite their brutal warfare. Radio programming and radio propaganda reflected this overall trend as well. (Photos courtesy of National Archives.)

The Radio Division of the OWI sponsored numerous radio propaganda series after America's entry into the war. Two of the most popular and long-running series were *This Is War!* and *You Can't do Business with Hitler*. *Above:* The artistic genius behind *This Is War!* was Norman Corwin (standing in the back with his hand raised). (Courtesy of Library of American Broadcasting.) *Below:* Rehearsal for the government propaganda show *You Can't Do Business with Hitler*. (Courtesy of FDR Library.)

As during the Great Depression, FDR's fireside chats were national events during World War II. Roosevelt deliberately used the programs sparingly, and his administration and the media publicized them generously. *Above:* FDR delivering a fireside chat in June 1944, after the fall of Rome. *Below:* In February 1942, the president delivered an address on the progress of the war and asked his listeners to have a world map handy so they could follow his discussions. (Photos courtesy of FDR Library.)

More than half of the American people regularly tuned in to FDR's fireside chats, and listeners wrote thousands of letters to the White House in response to the programs. According to this cartoonist, Hitler was aware of FDR's adroit use of the radio and here orders Reichsmarshall Hermann Göring to turn off his set as FDR's speech is announced. (Courtesy of Library of Congress.)

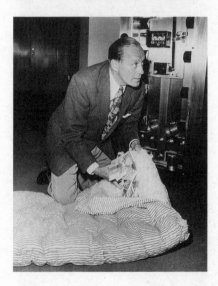

America's radio propaganda was eventually controlled by the "dollar-a-year men," radio and advertising professionals who staffed the Radio Division of the OWI. This propaganda effort ingeniously used the existing radio schedule and the drawing power of the radio stars to disseminate war messages—and more. *Above left:* The head of the Radio Division was William B. Lewis, a former vice president at CBS. (Courtesy of National Archives.) *Above right:* The stars of one of America's favorite radio comedy shows, Jim and Marian Jordan as Fibber McGee and Molly. (Courtesy of Library of American Broadcasting.) *Below:* Another favorite comedian, Jack Benny, who here plays off one of his show's most famous plotlines: Benny's stinginess and love for money, which he hides either under his mattress or in his vault. (Courtesy of Library of American Broadcasting.)

Most of radio's stars regularly participated in USO shows for the troops during the war. *Above:* Jack Benny in a USO show in New Guinea in July 1944. *Below:* The unrivaled GI comedian was Bob Hope. He attracted the largest crowds of any of the radio stars, as during this USO show in New Georgia. His shows became famous for regularly incorporating soldiers and their concerns into their routines. (Photos courtesy of National Archives.)

Irna Phillips was one of the most prominent soap opera writers during the late 1930s and early 1940s. Her shows, like all radio entertainment, incorporated propaganda and war messages as well as helped listeners navigate the many changes of home-front America. (Courtesy of Library of American Broadcasting.)

The low opinion which many Americans had about soap operas in the 1940s is eloquently captured in this cartoon. According to the cartoonist, of all the possible punishments for Adolph Hitler, nothing could be more torturous than having to listen to soap operas all day long and be left hanging in suspense while waiting for the following episodes. (Courtesy of Library of Congress.)

PART TWO

Selling the War to the American People: Radio Entertainment and Advertising

CHAPTER 4

The Rewards of Wartime Radio Advertising

By the end of World War II, radio had even more thoroughly won the hearts of the American people. It had delivered up-to-the-minute news from the war fronts; it had provided information, entertainment, and distraction throughout the nerve-racking years of the war; and it had been a steady, reliable companion. No other medium had endeared itself as much to the American people through the wartime experience, as indicated by the results of an extensive national survey conducted in November 1945. The National Opinion Research Center at the University of Denver, commissioned by the National Association of Broadcasters, interviewed almost three thousand men and women in this nationwide investigation of the public's attitude toward radio.[1]

Radio's high standing was indicated in one of the survey's first questions, in which respondents were asked to compare five institutions with which they had regular contact: schools, newspapers, radio, local government, and churches. Radio ranked by far the highest, with 82 percent of respondents judging radio's service as excellent or good, followed closely by churches. Newspapers and schools had a two-thirds approval rate, and local governments less than half. In a complementary question, the interviewees were asked which they would give up, if forced to choose: listening to the radio or going to the movies. Eighty-four percent responded that they would give up going to the movies; only 11 percent were willing to do without a radio. A final comparative question asked directly about the media's war service: "Taking everything into consideration, which one of these do you think did the best job of serving the public during the war—magazines, newspapers, moving pictures or radio broadcasting?" Sixty-seven percent of the respondents put radio at the top of the list, with newspapers ranked highest by 17 percent, movies by 4 percent, and magazines by 3 percent of the respondents. Clearly, Americans loved radio.[2]

This chapter focuses on radio advertising and its part in planning and executing radio's war effort. The central argument is that it was the corporate sponsors and advertisers who gained the most from commercial radio propaganda. Incorporated within Americans' favorite medium and presented by some of the most popular entertainers, this propaganda merged patriotic duty and public service with popular entertainment and the selling of American businesses. This cultural politics of propaganda enhanced the role and status of sponsors and advertising, paving the way for their renewed dominance in the postwar era.

To understand the power and potential of wartime radio advertising, it is not enough to study just the ads themselves. One needs to understand the multiple layers of communication involved in broadcasting—the radio advertising discourse. Moreover, it is important to view radio's participation in terms of the advertisers' overall contribution to the war effort through the War Advertising Council, which provided the larger context for radio advertising.

Depression, War, and Advertising

As America's entry into World War II seemed more and more inevitable in the fall of 1941, American advertising was on the defensive and was rather unsure of itself. Its two biggest concerns were the continued attempts by Roosevelt administration officials to curtail advertising and, with entry into the war imminent, the knowledge that a wartime economy would severely curtail the production of consumer goods and leave advertisers high and dry, with little to sell to American consumers.

In his history of wartime advertising, Frank Fox has emphasized that the high tide of government interventionism and activism against advertising was actually waning in the early 1940s. The climax of this development had been the passage in 1938 of the Wheeler-Lea Act, which had established a set of new advertising regulations and charged the Federal Trade Commission (FTC) to monitor advertising. The new law did not markedly change commercials, however, despite some interventions by the FTC.

Advertisers, like business as a whole, were still smarting from their inability to pull the nation out of the prolonged depression of the 1930s. During the Great Depression they had watched the growth of an increasingly hostile political culture, including the emergence of a state-sponsored economic liberalism, vast gains by the labor movement, the growth of a consumer movement, and increasingly brash public condemnations of the American economic system. Advertisers and business did not take this criticism lying down but instead staged a concerted campaign "to sell free enterprise" under the tutelage of the National Association of Manufacturers. Industry leaders remained suspicious of government activism in the early 1940s, as numerous editorials in the advertising trade press in 1941 attested. John Benson, president of the American Association of Advertising Agencies (AAAA), expressed this sentiment during the war: "Business has had the jitters ever since the New Deal. . . . The depression brought on a loss of confidence in business. It was in the doghouse for a decade or more. . . . Always on the defensive, we have been afraid of every tin horn bureaucrat in Washington."[3]

Two of the most unpopular government officials in advertising circles were Assistant Attorney General Thurman Arnold and Leon Henderson, director of the new Office of Price Administration (OPA). Both men were perceived as New Dealers eager to pull the rug from underneath advertisers' feet. In Arnold's case, advertising executives were most concerned about his antitrust legislation and feared that he would include advertising under monopolistic practices, making it liable under the Sherman Act. Advertisers feared Henderson because he had questioned the necessity of advertising in a defense or wartime economy and because, as director of the OPA, he had a crucial influence on the implementation of government economic policies and the allocation of resources and supplies.[4]

When Henderson softened his stance on advertising in the fall and winter of 1941, it repeatedly made headlines in the advertising trade press. The most important occasion was Henderson's address to the special joint meeting of representatives of the Association of National Advertisers (ANA) and the AAAA in Hot Springs, Virginia, in November 1941. Henderson restated what he called his "customary consumer skepticism" toward advertising but also emphasized that he was not "a charter member of [a cell] of conspirators whose main purpose in life is to alter, reform or perhaps even destroy advertising as we know it." Instead, he expressed his belief that "advertising performs a useful economic function" and "must survive as a thriving economic force."[5]

The advertisers' meeting at Hot Springs was a watershed event not only because of Henderson's heartening words but also because it helped advertisers develop a consensus concerning what advertising might achieve during a wartime crisis. This meeting of the minds boiled down to this: with little to sell or to advertise, advertising should sell itself, as well as American business and free enterprise. As James W. Young, senior consultant of the J. Walter Thompson Company, reassured his colleagues, advertisers did not have to fold up their tents during a wartime crisis:

Let us ask ourselves whether we, as an industry, do not have a great contribution to make in this effort to regain for business the leadership of our economy. We have within our hands the greatest aggregate means of mass education and persuasion the world has ever seen—namely, the channels of advertising communication. We have the masters of the technique of using these channels. Why do we not use it?[6]

To be sure, advertisers were used to this kind of pep talk, and calls for a "united front" among advertisers had been advanced repeatedly over the last few years. Therefore, Young's fighting plan did not automatically spur them into action. The representatives of the two trade associations did agree, however, to begin making plans to establish the Advertising Council, an umbrella organization for advertisers to fend off criticism of the industry and to deal with the challenges of a likely wartime crisis. As it turned out, the timing of the meeting was impeccable. A little more than two weeks later, in early December 1941, America was at war, and, after meetings with government officials, advertising executives began operations of the council.[7]

The War Advertising Council (WAC), as it was to be called during the war, brought together advertisers from all media. Its board of directors was composed of an equal number of representatives from each of three groups: commercial clients (companies with large advertising budgets), advertising agencies, and the advertising media. Chester J. La Roche, formerly an advertising executive with Young and Rubicam, served as the WAC's first chairman. Miller McClintock from Harvard University was hired as executive director to run the organization's day-to-day operations (later, Theodore S. Repplier of the War Manpower Board held this position). The WAC proved its effectiveness in the very first campaign in which it collaborated with the government in February 1942. This was the Treasury Department's payroll deduction plan, which asked all working Americans to have 10 percent of their monthly pay automatically deducted from their payroll and applied toward buying war bonds. Through extensive advertising of the payroll deduction plan, twenty-four million workers had enrolled by the end of 1942, funneling $365 million into the Treasury each month.[8]

The collaboration between the WAC and the government was further increased in June 1942 with the establishment of the Office of War Information, which became the central clearinghouse for government information and propaganda campaigns. All government agencies channeled their requests for media coverage through the OWI, which coordinated the campaigns and established a list of priorities, and the OWI submitted the campaign request to the WAC. If the WAC decided that advertisers could handle the campaign, it appointed a manager, generally an ad executive of a major agency, to run the government's appeal to the public like a regular advertising campaign. The advertising director submitted the basic copy platforms and sample advertisements to the OWI for factual information and clarification. Then the advertising plan was distributed to all advertisers and advertising agencies, asking them to devote all or part of their regular advertising to the recommended propaganda copy theme.[9]

All media campaigns were run free of charge to the government. Sometimes advertisers donated time and space, and in other cases industry associations funded the campaigns. The American Iron and Steel Institute, for example, underwrote the scrap salvage drive to the extent of $2 million. Similarly, the Glycerin Producers funded the fat salvage campaign, and the American Meat Institute paid for advertising on point rationing and black markets. Most of this advertising did not cost companies and advertisers very much because in May 1942 the Treasury Department changed its tax codes. The new tax code instituted an excess profits tax of 80 percent but also allowed companies to write off up to 80 percent of their advertising costs by including them in their overall expenses. The only condition was that the advertising help the war effort. As a memorandum by the Bureau of Internal Revenue put it:

Under section 23 of the Code, an individual may make a gift to the Government and deduct that gift from his income. . . . If advertisements featuring the sale of War Bonds, conservation, nutrition or other government objectives are clearly signed by a corporation, . . . the advertisement will be considered as an institutional or good-will advertisement of the manufacturer and hence, deductible, provided, of course, that the expenditure is reasonable and not made in an attempt to avoid proper taxation.[10]

How the Treasury was to weed out advertising "made in an attempt to avoid proper taxation" remained unclear. What was clear was that this new tax law provided the single most important boost to wartime advertising. Even if companies had nothing to sell, how could they pass up a chance to use practically free advertising paid for by the American taxpayer for institutional and goodwill copy? America's entry into the war had forced government and business to work in ever-closer collaboration. Advertising, as an extension of the free enterprise system, was part of this confluence.

Nothing better expresses the sea change that had taken place in 1942 than the meeting of the Association of National Advertisers in November 1942, one year after the conference in Hot Springs. In his keynote address, Paul B. West, president of the ANA, marveled over the "new fair-mindedness" that radiated from Washington. Like other advertisers, he viewed this newfound cooperation and trust between government and the business community as a crucial turning point. "I can say now, without fear of contradiction," West said, referring to the former government-advertising antipathy, "that our real progress began when we ceased drawing issues and fighting with our national 'enemies' . . . and discovered them as our natural *friends*." Likening this new unity to "the knights of old," West concluded: "We have learned as they did that strength comes from joining in a circle with all facing *outward*."[11] Advertising representatives were further encouraged by a survey conducted for the ANA in late 1942, in which one thousand Americans were interviewed about their views on advertising and business. The report reflected a growing confidence among Americans that industry and business were up to the task of providing economic leadership.[12]

In this changed climate, company heads and advertisers were increasingly willing to follow the rallying cries of visionary executives, who called on American business to see the war as an opportunity to shake off the ghost of the Great Depression. Emil Schram, president of the New York Stock Exchange, had suggested early in 1942 that the war provided a promising opportunity for American business. As he had argued in *Printer's Ink:* "In a certain sense American business is now being submitted to an acid test. If American business . . . proves once and for all its capabilities, it will occupy an unassailable position when the difficult period of post-war readjustment sets in." In an article entitled, "Opportunity!," Walter Weir of the Lord and Thomas Agency echoed the same sentiment for advertisers:

Here we sit with the greatest force for moving mass psychology that the world has ever seen. . . . We can demonstrate the power of advertising as it has never been demonstrated before. We can justify its existence as it has never been justified before. . . . And if we make advertising fight today, we'll never again have to defend its place in our economy.[13]

The selling of American business and free enterprise, or "the ad behind the ad," as Fox has called it, was indeed one of the most consistent themes in American wartime advertising.[14] It is also true that both business and advertising proved themselves during the war years and were in an "unassailable" position in the postwar period. Finally, because of the work of the War Advertising Council and its contribution to mastering the challenges of the wartime crisis, the advertising industry was more coordinated and unified than it had ever been.

Radio Advertising during Wartime

Radio was the big winner of the wartime advertising boom. Even in 1942, when the volume of advertising for most media decreased—by 5 percent for newspapers and 6 percent for magazines—radio was able to add advertising dollars and increase revenue by 9 percent. To be sure, except for newspapers, whose revenues stagnated because of paper shortages, overall advertising expenditures grew rapidly, fueled by the changed tax code of 1942. But radio outdid all the others: its advertising volume increased dramatically during the war years, almost doubling between 1941 and 1945.[15]

The only serious limitations for radio were the freeze on establishing new radio stations and on the manufacture of new radio sets because of the shortage of raw materials. Other than that, radio had room or, more accurately, time to expand. Radio had always had its unappealing time slots, times when listeners were otherwise occupied. Thus, networks had always found it difficult to sell some Saturday and Sunday time slots, except for the evening schedule. Even more unattractive were the late evening and nighttime hours, from 11:00 P.M. to 6:00 or 7:00 A.M. These and other assorted weekday times had usually been filled by network sustaining programs.

Because an increasing number of Americans started working evening and night shifts during the war, advertisers discovered a new market: all-night radio. It was estimated that about 20 percent of Americans worked the often new nighttime shifts, either from 4:00 P.M. to midnight or from midnight to 8:00 A.M., during the war years. Before the war, only about a dozen stations, spread across the country, stayed on the air all night. These stations did, however, almost blanket the country because they had powerful signals (operating at fifty thousand watts) and ran into little or no interference from neighboring stations. In 1942, the number of stations broadcasting at night expanded quickly. In New York City, where only WNEW had been on the air all night before the war (since 1935), three stations joined the night market in 1942. Advertisers especially appreciated this nighttime programming because listeners—particularly when they tuned in their radios at home—listened more attentively, with fewer disruptions than during regular broadcast hours. Also, as mentioned earlier, because of reduced interference, radio stations still reached distant states: New York stations sometimes received listener mail from as far away as Seattle.[16]

Not only were previously nonsponsored time slots filled with commercial programs, but the prime-time schedule also became more competitive. Networks had generally observed a "first come, first served" rule for evening spots that became vacant. NBC, for one, changed this policy in September 1943, announcing that it would also take into account the quality of the proposed sponsored show. With advertisers queuing up for evening radio like never before, NBC could afford to be choosy about its new clients.[17] What made these time slots even more appealing was the fact that they became "radio franchises" for the advertiser. Once a client had bought a particular time from a network, that time slot belonged to this company until it decided to vacate it. With plenty of advertising dollars available during wartime, these franchises became even more sought after, especially by those who anticipated a postwar spending boom.[18] All these developments increased the desirability of radio as an advertising medium.

By 1943, Chester La Roche, chairman of the WAC, was encouraging advertisers to include a wartime message in every ad. Radio advertisers, like their colleagues in other media, needed little prodding, as this Pepsodent ad on the Bob Hope show indicated:

Every hour of work that is lost through illness pushes victory just a little farther away. We all have to stay well to work well. It's more than ever necessary that we all take care of ourselves. Start now to practice common-sense precautions. Avoid wet feet, drafts, . . . and watch your throat, because that's where illness often starts. Gargle with Pepsodent Antiseptic regularly. It starts acting instantly to kill germs, even way back in your throat. . . . Get a bottle of Pepsodent Antiseptic tonight.[19]

Connecting a product to patriotism and the national call to duty or making it relevant in light of the wartime crisis was one of the most obvious and most commonly employed tactics of all advertisers. With the right twist, any product could enhance America's fighting power and help win the war.

All you homemakers know that this year the business of getting three well-balanced meals every day is going to take a lot of ingenuity. One food that can be a real help to you is VELVEETA. . . .

These days when you get a loaf or package of Velveeta, remember the fine nutrients hidden in that rich yet mild cheddar cheese flavor. There's milk protein. Food energy. Milk minerals. Vitamin A. And vitamin C, that's sometimes called riboflavin.

Plan to use this wonderful Velveeta nutrition *wisely*. Let smooth, golden Velveeta sauce turn leftovers into a nutritious and exciting main dish. . . . And use Velveeta to pack working power into the lunch box sandwiches.[20]

As in the case of Velveeta, Americans discovered that food they had eaten for years had "hidden" energy sources they had never suspected. Velveeta packed "working power" into lunch boxes. In their commercials, the Bakers of America announced a "new, enriched white bread" that, according to the ad, was the result of two years of cooperative work between the United States government and the baking industry. They invited Americans to celebrate with them "one of the greatest forward steps ever taken in the nation's interest" and "a great day for the national nutrition program."[21]

Another favorite genre of wartime advertising was the "service commercial," which explained to Americans how to make their possessions last longer. Johnson's Wax, the sponsor of *Fibber McGee and Molly,* used its commercial to emphasize the life-prolonging qualities of Glocoat, one of its products.[22] Oil companies such as Shell used the opportunity to advise Americans on how to care for their most prized possessions— their cars and their tires:

Your car and your tires are a national asset now! See that you keep them in good condition. To help you get longer wear from tires and car—Shell now offers you *Ground Crew Service,* patterned after rigid Army Air Corps routine. . . . It's absolutely FREE at all Shell dealers displaying Ground Crew Wings.

When you see your Shell dealer, ask him about the new 5,000 miles Ground Crew Log Book. It maps out an economical plan for servicing your car during the next 5,000 miles. Your dealer gives you a FREE check-up and tells you exactly what work needs to be done to *lengthen* your car's service and to get *extra* mileage from your tires. He records every step in the Ground Crew Log Book— just as Army Air Corps mechanics record the work they do on Uncle Sam's fighting planes.[23]

Survey after survey showed that Americans appreciated the informative aspects of such advertisements, despite their obvious hyperbole. Consumers most frequently noticed ads that told them how to conserve their possessions, explained rationing and other government policies, or simply provided recipes for stretching their rationing points. When asked about their overall appraisal of radio advertising, listeners indicated that this was the aspect of commercials they appreciated the most. Nearly one half of the participants in a nationwide survey responded favorably to this kind of advertising because it provided practical information. As one woman from Miami, Florida, put it, adding her own hyperbole: "I might fuss about ads on the radio but truthfully I would be lost without them."[24]

The wartime crisis provided all advertisers with an unparalleled opportunity to serve the public and simultaneously sell their product or brand name. For consumers facing a dizzying array of new point rationing books for various food groups, for example, service commercials did indeed provide much needed guidance; they also could use the ration point system as a selling point:

Delicious, crisp, crunchy peanuts! When you want peanuts like that, you ask for Planters Peanuts. Now, for a peanut butter that has all the rich peanut flavor that Planters means, ask for Planters Peanut Butter! You won't be disappointed either—this peanut butter is delicious, and makes a grand spread now that butter's 16 points a pound. . . .

Planters Peanut Butter is rich in energy-giving fats and oils and is a good source of B vitamins. What's more, this peanut butter is fully as rich in protein as beefsteak![25]

Another common development in radio advertisements was that war slogans became more patriotic: "Victory Is Our Business" (General Motors), "Camel—First in the Service" (Camel cigarettes), "Victory Will Come with the Rubber *You* Save" (General Tires), or "Care for Your Car for Your Country" (Pennsylvania Oil).[26]

Wartime advertising provided new opportunities for advertisers, to be sure, but it also created additional risks: besides the usual skepticism about advertising, listeners resented patriotic sales copy for pure and overt commercial reasons. Offensive ads could be heard on American radio stations throughout the war, in part because some advertisers subscribed to blunt and even shocking advertising tactics. Listeners who tuned in to a New York radio news program sponsored by a cemetery firm in 1942 were reminded, between battle reports and casualty figures, to be prepared for the worst: "You never know when to expect bad news, so be prepared. Buy a [cemetery] lot." Similarly, Pall Mall kept playing the plug "On land, in the air, and on the sea to victory," sung by a quartet, with the sound of airplanes and artillery zooming and whistling in the background. The company continued the ad on all but one network, which banned it, even though similar sound effects were generally censored in entertainment programs. Another favorite in the early months after the attack on Pearl Harbor was the blending of news bulletin reporting with advertisements: "Here is a late important news bulletin: use Smith Bros. cough drops."[27]

Equally controversial were commercials known as "brag ads," which boasted of the significant contribution of one particular product to American victory. Clearly, this was a subtle distinction, as most advertisers who had hardware to sell tried to show its usefulness for the war effort. Even manufacturers of American fighting planes could cross this line. When American pilots stationed in Europe read an ad for an American plane titled "Who's Afraid of the Big Focke-Wulfe?" (the name of a German fighter plane), a whole squadron signed the page and sent it back to the sponsor. Another complaint came from a soldier in training camp: "When I read the ads I don't see why I'm here in camp. We don't need men in this war—our machines are so perfect they'll do the job themselves."[28]

As brag ads became more common, other advertisers took advantage of the growing resentment against them by poking fun at them. As a manufacturer of lipstick emphasized in his commercial: "It won't build morale, it won't preserve our way of life, all [this] lipstick will do is make you look prettier. If it's victory you want, better buy a bond."[29] Few techniques aroused as much resentment, even among advertisers themselves, as the "singing commercial," yet these ads persisted despite continued attacks and despite the fact that some radio stations banned them from their programming.[30]

Listeners also continued to complain about loud and too frequent ads. Like the listener who wrote to *Radio Life,* many people had no choice but to turn their radios down during commercial breaks, and once out of their chairs, they sometimes turned them off: "If commercials were given in a tone lower than the rest of the program, none would need to turn the radio down to avoid disturbing neighbors, something which apartment house dwellers must think of. When compelled to turn the commercial down, we turn it off for the 'duration.'" Other listeners turned their sets off when commercials ran too long: "When advertising comes, sometimes I turn it off. . . . I turn it off if I can . . . it depends. If it's a short talk I'll leave it running; I might as well. I just don't listen until it's over. But if he keeps talking and talking . . . then I just turn it off."[31]

One of the most embarrassing moments for radio advertising as a whole was the publication of examples of offensive radio ads in *Reader's Digest* in August 1942. The article, entitled "Radio's Plug-Uglies," focused on advertisements for hygiene and medical products, which had always been a sore spot for broadcasters. One offender the article mentioned was a Lifebuoy commercial: "There's nothing so dismal as a foghorn [sound effect] unless it's Beee-Oh [sound effect again]. Lifebuoy— from head to toe it stops B.O. [body odor]." More frequently, radio commercials skillfully got around mentioning an offensive smell by simply describing a situation. For example, in 1942 an announcer read a supposed letter from a listener instead of the commercial: "My son, aged ten, wouldn't kiss me good-night. I told his father about it, and the next night he brought home a tube of Colgate's toothpaste. I use it twice a day, and my son no longer refuses to kiss me."

The final example mentioned in this article were two ads which went into more anatomical detail: "If you don't feel good, try Carter's Little Liver Pills. They wake up the flow of our most vital digestive juices. . . . Doctors say your kidneys contain 15 miles of tubes. Doan's Pills will help flush out poisonous wastes."[32]

Although these kinds of advertisements were not new, apparently a number of listeners finally had enough of them and founded the Plug Shrinkers Club in New York City. At the end of the article, the writer included a ready-to-mail application to the club, which read as follows:

Dear Fellow Plug Shrinkers: I am with you, heart, soul and offended ears. Enroll me as an Outraged Member.

Please tell (sponsor or product name) that his radio commercials are (check appropriate epithet) in bad taste . . . hokum . . . tiresome . . . repetitious . . . repulsive . . . long-winded . . . too intimate . . . too anatomical . . . silly . . . syrupy . . . poor sales policy. . . .

I understand that this entitles me to enroll as a Militant Member, in token whereof Plug Shrinkers will refrain from sending me one life-sized scientific drawing, reproduced in natural colors, of the contents of the Human Stomach after a hearty meal.[33]

What made advertisers and radio executives nervous about articles like this one was the fact that *Reader's Digest* had at least seven million readers in 1942. This sort of publicity reflected very poorly on radio broadcasting as a whole and could scare away advertisers and listeners. This article also highlights the fact that radio advertising had its share of controversy during the wartime, and that not all advertising had a war angle to it; indeed, common estimates are that well over half of all advertising was unrelated to wartime concerns.[34]

The discussion of radio service ads only begins to identify the potential and advantage of wartime radio advertising for sponsors. Even more important was the fact that *their* radio stars ran many of the propaganda campaigns. In the process, radio entertainment, commercial sponsorship, and patriotic service became intimately fused in these programs.

The Wartime Radio Advertising Discourse

If one wants to understand the potential of radio advertising during the war, it is not enough to look just at the commercials themselves. Broadcasting provided a multilayered communication environment and created a unique advertising discourse that was both complex and endearing.[35] Radio provided the most powerful and persuasive medium for advertising before and during the war years because it combined four layers of communication: (1) the unique character of the medium, which included both its friendly appeal and the supreme control advertisers had over it; (2) the popularity of radio entertainment stars; (3) the fusion of advertising and entertainment in radio broadcasting; and (4) the exclusiveness of radio sponsorship. During the war, public service through timely informational or propaganda programs added an additional ingredient to this discourse.

As a number of historians noted as early as the 1930s, radio was a novelty among the media. It relied on the auditory rather than the visual sense, and it brought a wide variety of programs directly into the home with a simple flick of the switch, often gathering families around this "modern substitute for the hearth-side." In addition, listeners sat by their radio sets in a relaxed mood, in a comfortable chair and a familiar environment. Radio became a part of many Americans' daily schedules.[36]

As far as advertising was concerned, radio added a whole new dimension. Before radio came along, advertising, for the most part, had to rely on commercials inserted into magazines and newspapers. These usually remained isolated from the preceding and following pages and interrupted the flow of a story or article just as long as it took the reader to turn the page. The same disconnection between commercials and their surroundings also applied to outdoor advertising (billboards unrelated to the environment they stood in) and direct mail advertising (individual letters with nothing to absorb the immediate snub of rejection). Radio was different. One reason for this difference was that listeners approached the medium with a distinct mind-set. As Hadley Cantril and Gordon Allport emphasized in a study of radio conducted in 1935, this made an immense difference for radio advertising: "In the case of radio, the individual actually *plans* to be seated in a certain chair at a certain time in order to hear a sponsored program. . . . This voluntary attention and friendly disposition on the part of the potential customer is of incalculable advantage to the advertiser."[37]

Radio programming presented the most appealing answer to the question haunting businessmen and advertisers alike: How could business endear itself to consumers? The answer was simple: by providing daily commercial entertainment which Americans grew to love. They quickly noticed that radio provided the most intimate form of communication. As Roland Marchand put it, "Radio surpassed all others in its capacity to deny its own status as *mass* medium." In this respect, radio exhibited a veritable Jekyll-and-Hyde personality: it intimated a personal touch and thereby "humanized the image of business," yet it prospered so quickly only because it reached unprecedented millions of listeners simultaneously across the country.[38]

But this intimate quality, though absolutely vital, was only the beginning of the advantages radio advertisers enjoyed over other advertising media. Advertisers not only had the opportunity to pitch their product to a friendly audience but also could decide which show to put on the air and retain some control over the program content. According to media critic Charles Siepmann, "The newspaper owner does not delegate to his advertising clients power and discretion to select and sponsor the news columns, editorials, features, and comic strips that are printed. Radio networks and stations do this."[39]

Americans liked, at times even adored, the radio actors and stars. In turn, through the commercial sponsorship and ownership of radio programs, specific products became closely associated with radio programs or personalities: Johnson Wax with *Fibber McGee and Molly*, Pepsodent with Bob Hope, and Jell-O (and, after 1944, Lucky Strike cigarettes) with Jack Benny. This proprietary relationship of radio sponsors and stars was firmly anchored in radio contracts. When Benny signed his new three-year contract with the American Tobacco Company (Lucky Strike) in October 1944, it included a section on advertisements: "Commercials—client has entire control over commercials, Benny appears or not as the client wishes."[40]

Moreover, sponsors clearly understood that their products and the popularity of radio personalities were intricately tied to radio shows, which was why George W. Hill, president of the American Tobacco Company, agreed to pay even for Benny's personal public relations expenses:

Exploitation of Jack Benny—entire responsibility to be assumed by Benny— public relations man employed by Benny, selected by Benny. Understood that the client has the right to object to any exploitation which in the client's opinion is detrimental to the client or his product. . . .

The client [is] entirely willing to make an allowance at the rate of $200,000 a year for three years for this purpose to Benny including the cost of his employment of public relations counsel.[41]

Hill had long been well known—even notorious—for his plain speech when it came to the commercial purpose of his radio sponsorship. When he entered radio in the late 1920s, he admonished a band auditioning for his show that he was aiming at the heart of mainstream America: "I want dance music that people will like to dance by, and I don't want their attention diverted by French horn gymnastics." When Benny, shortly after signing on with American Tobacco, assured Hill that he had a personal interest in seeing Lucky Strike doing well, Hill thanked him and was pleased to note that they saw eye to eye: "Boy, I am a salesman enough to know that it's the year's record that counts. . . . But I don't have to wait this time for the year's record; three shows are enough to convince me that you are going to sell the goods."[42]

In addition to the explicitly commercial relationship between sponsors and entertainers, most of the radio stars' public relations work during the war years was done in the name of winning the war. It was a service that performers pursued very sincerely. Yet as everybody in show business knew, fulfilling this "patriotic duty" also created a commercial advantage: it raised the visibility and popularity of performers, increased the ratings of their shows, and ensured secure profits for the future. What is striking when it comes to radio entertainment is that many Americans—who were generally savvy at detecting propaganda techniques, including advertising ploys—often found it difficult to apply this same skepticism to their favorite radio stars.

A case in point was a marathon war bond drive undertaken by Kate Smith over CBS on September 21, 1943. Smith was well known to most Americans not only for her rendition of "God Bless America" but also through her daily talks over CBS. In this war bond drive, Smith spoke for a minute or two at repeated intervals over eighteen hours of continuous broadcasting. She succeeded in selling $39 million in bonds in the course of that one day, the largest amount raised by a single person in radio's war effort. Robert K. Merton and researchers from the Bureau of Applied Social Research interviewed one hundred listeners (seventy-five who had pledged, twenty-five who had not) to identify the reasons for Smith's spectacular success.[43] Of particular note, according to Merton and his colleagues, were the intensity with which Smith's fans followed the war bond drive and the loyalty expressed in their responses.

We never left her that day. We stood by her side. I didn't go out all day, except to go shopping. Even then, I was anxious to get back and listen. Of course, my sister was holding down the post in the meantime and could tell me what had happened.

I was glad at the end of the day when her job was over and I didn't have to listen to her any more.[44]

Even for listeners who were not devoted fans, certain features of this bond drive enhanced their sense of participation. One was the length of the program, which elicited concern among listeners who wondered whether Smith could endure eighteen hours of nonstop broadcasting. In addition, Smith managed to establish a "conversation" over the air: listeners could call her between announcements, and Smith responded to those calls over the air and modified subsequent comments as a result.

Merton and his colleagues also found that Smith's reputation for sincerity, integrity, and altruism, coupled with the "sacrifice" involved in this long bond drive, dominated the impressions of her audience. Even in an extended poll of one thousand listeners, four out of five were convinced that Smith was interested *only* in the promotion of bonds. Merton considered this emphasis on Smith's sincerity all the more striking "when one considers the disenchantment of our informants with the world of advertising, commercials and propaganda."[45]

It is also striking when one compares the popular response with the way Smith's bond drive played in radio circles. Apparently, a number of CBS radio personalities and OWI Radio Bureau officials criticized the drive "as a purely personal publicity stunt." In fact, CBS advised Smith that she would not be asked to participate in the war bond drive in 1944. As the writer of an OWI memo on this issue added, "I intimated that the OWI would not be unhappy about this news."[46]

An additional area that is absolutely crucial for an understanding of radio advertising is the fusion of entertainment and advertising so typical of radio broadcasting. The most basic format for this concept was institutional advertising, which was common practice in the 1930s and 1940s. In July 1943, for example, Clipper Craft Clothes decided to sponsor a news broadcast by the well-known commentator Dorothy Thompson. The company executives hoped that this sponsorship would help them solve a peculiar problem: how to maintain a market for a good product whose price was low. By putting a "quality" news broadcast on the air, Clipper Craft Clothes hoped to reach an audience that bought quality clothes and to convince them to buy the company's low-priced products.[47] During the war, institutional advertising was even more appealing than before, especially to companies with few or no consumer products to sell, yet with a tax code that encouraged spending on advertising. General Motors took over the recently created NBC Symphony Orchestra under Arturo Toscanini, United States Rubber sponsored the New York Philharmonic on CBS, and Allis Chalmers financed a program by the Boston Symphony. In the commercial breaks, an announcer told listeners about the contributions of the respective company to American victory.[48]

More complex and intricate, however, were shows in which entertainment merged with the commercial itself, usually during the middle commercial. Each show included three commercials, one each at the beginning, middle, and end. Advertisers knew that the beginnings and endings were the periods most often missed by listeners. Only in the middle did advertisers have a near-captive audience, especially if they integrated the commercial into the entertainment itself.

"Integrated commercials" were not new, having been used in comedy programs since the early 1930s. Comedians Ed Wynn and Jack Benny are generally credited with regularly integrating commercials, in which they often poked fun at their sponsor and its products.[49] In the 1940s, Benny's writers still frequently integrated the middle commercial into the show. In one program in March 1942, for example, Dennis, the show's singer, insisted that he had seen a dinosaur in the Los Angeles Zoo. This led the discussion straight into the commercial for Jell-O:

Jack: Dennis, that's impossible . . . you couldn't have seen a dinosaur.

Phil: Of course not, she's in New York with Eddie Cantor.

Jack: That's Dinah Shore. . . . The name is Dinah Shore.

Mary: May I read my poem now?

Jack: Not now Mary, I'm leading up to something. . . . All right, Don. . . . *Dinah Shore.*

Wilson: Oh Jack, this one is utterly fantastic.

Jack: Don . . . I don't want to go through this every week. . . . *Dinah Shore.*

Wilson: But, Jack, people are beginning to talk. . . . Everybody says, there is that goofy Wilson.

Jack: I don't want to hear another word about it. . . . Now go ahead. . . . *Dinah Shore.*

Wilson: Oh, all right. . . . Ladies and Gentlemen . . . The next time you have dinner, be sure to serve Jell-O for dessert, whether you *dine at sea* or *Dinah Shore.*

Jack: Wonderful.

Wilson: You will find that Jell-O with its new locked in flavor is America's favorite gelatin dessert. [. . .]I'm sorry, Dinah.

Jack: Well, personally Don, I thought it was very, very clever.[50]

This ad also gives an indication of how common this kind of commercial was on the show. With Benny repeating the setup line three times, listeners knew that an integrated commercial was about to follow. The repetition also built up suspense and attention to assure that no listener would miss the pun.

This fusion of entertainment and commercial was so familiar to listeners, in fact, that comedians could even poke fun at the technique of integrated commercials itself. In an episode of *Fibber McGee and Molly* that centered on McGee's inability to control his temper, the entertainment led directly into dialogue with Wilcox, the announcer and "ad man" on the show:

Wilcox: Like a woman I know, who was always in a foul temper. Nerves were ragged. . . . Her name was Mimi Perkins and everybody called her screaming Mimi. And you know what cured her?

Fibber: What did, Junior, asked little Fibber innocently, as if he hadn't heard the answer every week for ten years?

Wilcox: Johnson's Wax. . . . Changed her whole life. . . . [Continues with usual commercial][51]

Middle commercials provided a difficult challenge to advertisers. If done poorly, they stuck out even more because they interrupted the program, which was, after all, what the listener had tuned in to hear. When they were integrated or presented with humor, on the other hand, listeners especially appreciated the effort. When asked, most listeners praised particular shows that they thought had tried to make commercials more enjoyable:

I think if more commercials were done in the type Bing Crosby does it, you'd get more enjoyment out of them, because they're cleverly done. . . . they're very humorous.[52]

Fibber McGee and Molly. He works it in with the story. [He doesn't] just stop the program and put in a commercial. It goes with the story. (Office boy, Brooklyn, N.Y.)

March of Time. They bring it in so naturally without slapping you in the face. (Vice president of construction company, Clayton, MO.)[53]

The integrated middle commercial in a sponsored radio show was, for the advertiser, the most ideally located commercial. It was placed within a pleasant advertising environment, which the listener had chosen. Moreover, it blurred the line between ad and entertainment—the ad became part of the entertainment. In fact, in wartime radio advertising the middle commercial frequently was not an ad, as in the following example from *The Pepsodent Show* starring Bob Hope. The typical dialogue between Hope and Frances Langford merges into the middle commercial, read by the show's announcer, Keating:

Langford: Bob, when I see all these boys . . . it just makes me want to do something for our country. . . .

Hope: Well! Frances . . . the boys are all for that, I'm sure.

Langford: No, Bob. I'd like to help. . . . I think everyone has to pitch in.

Keating: That's right, Frances . . . this isn't only a job for the soldiers, marines and sailors. They're learning to fight—that's their job. Our job is to provide them with the stuff that will knock the stuffings out of the Axis. And we can do that by joining the "10% Club." [Continues to explain idea of putting 10 percent of one's income into war bonds][54]

As in this commercial, during the war years the "ad" was just as frequently a war message through which broadcasts participated in radio's overall war effort. In fact, during these years listeners never knew quite what to expect: a commercial plug or a patriotic service or propaganda message. This conflation is important because the two contents meant something quite different. Whereas the commercial ad served the self-interest of the advertiser, the war message was a public service that advertisers broadcast for the American people.

One last example from *Fibber McGee and Molly* illustrates the ingenious ways in which the various layers of radio's advertising discourse could overlap in wartime broadcasting. In this episode, Fibber's craving for a good dinner has overcome his sense of civic duty: he went to the black market and got himself a nice steak. In his usual manner, he bragged about his achievement to his neighbors, among them Wilcox. Their dialogue continued right through the middle commercial:

> *Fibber:* Look—here's all you gotta do. Go down the alley next to the Snooker poolroom on 14th street, see, and whistle twice like a snipe. . . . when the guy opens the door—his name is Eddy, friend of mine—just tell him . . . [interrupted]
>
> *Wilcox:* What is this . . . *black market meat?*
>
> *Molly:* If it was any blacker it would make midnight look like high noon.
>
> *Fibber:* Well, gee whizz, if a guy is hungry for meat—
>
> *Wilcox:* I'm not so hungry for meat I want to patronize a rat in an alley to get a steak. What's the matter with you, Fibber? I always thought you were a pretty decent guy.
>
> *Molly:* Pour it on, Mr. Wilcox . . . pour it on.
>
> *Fibber:* Well, my gosh, what's a little thing like—
>
> *Wilcox:* It isn't a little thing, pal! This is the dirtiest racket that's come out of the war. These crooks are buying up meat, and selling it illegally, without any sanitation or inspection, and throwing the whole business of supply and demand out of kilter.
>
> When I buy things I want to know where they came from and who's back of them and what the quality is. That's why I'm proud to be selling Johnson's self-polishing Glocoat, with a tradition of fifty years of conscientious quality behind it . . . [Continues ad][55]

This is a perfect illustration of the powerful potential of radio advertising during the war years. The content of advertisements was interchangeable: at times it was a commercial ad, other times a service message, often both at once. The entertainment always merged with commercial sponsorship in radio, even if it just provided a friendly environment for the ad. In this cultural process, the multiple aspects literally merged, blurring the lines between entertainment, advertising, war propaganda, and public service. Finally, underlying all of this was the overwhelmingly favorable attitude Americans had toward radio. Only if one considers the various layers of this discourse does one understand the potential of wartime radio advertising.

One more aspect of commercial radio is crucial for an understanding of radio wartime advertising: namely, not everybody could sponsor a network radio program. According to network policies, generally only companies and businesses that sold consumer or durable goods had a "legitimate" right to sponsor a radio program. Networks considered everything else controversial broadcasting, and for such broadcasts they provided airtime free of charge to the two opposing sides on a sustaining basis only. Yet sustainers often aired irregularly, at unpopular hours, generally during times that had not found sponsors. This policy assured that sponsored network radio was firmly in the hands of American business during World War II, even when many companies had little or nothing to sell to the American public.

This fact was sharply brought to light in an FCC hearing on the transfer of the Blue Network in September 1943. The FCC commissioners questioned Mark Woods, president of the Blue Network, about the kind of advertising his network would accept. They specifically asked whether he would accept a program like the *Ford Sunday Evening Hour,* which had been on the air on NBC since the mid-1930s and which was known for the notoriously pro-business, anti–New Deal commentaries by W. J. Cameron, who spoke at the intermission of the musical program. Woods argued that the network would accept the program because he thought Cameron was presenting his own view and not necessarily that of the Ford Company. As the commissioners questioned Woods further, it became obvious that the networks denied other groups the same chance:

> *Chairman (of FCC):* All right. Now suppose the A. F. of L. wants their trade mark to be remembered [during the war], wants to build up and preserve good will, which they have acquired over the decades of its union work, so it wants to come on with a general program to build up good will for the A. F. of L. Would you sell them time?

> *Woods:* No sir, we would not sell them time for that purpose. . . . We will not sell them time because they have a particular philosophy to preach. We do not sell time for the discussion of that type of controversial issue. . . .

> *Commissioner Durr:* Where do you make the distinction between that and [Ford's or] General Motors' situation?

> *Woods:* We make the distinction in that we are in the national advertising business and selling time specifically for the purpose of advertising products. We do not sell time to groups for any other purpose whatsoever.
>
> *Commissioner Durr:* Well, General Motors today has no product to sell.
>
> *Woods:* No, but they do have a great stake in maintaining their name before the public, so that after the war is over they may be considered to have done an outstanding job in the war effort and are deserving of public support.[56]

Woods made clear that he was speaking not just for the Blue Network but for the whole trade; his network simply followed established broadcasting policy. To be sure, the networks did provide time on the air for organizations such as labor unions, cooperative associations, or the Little Businessmen's Association. But they did so on a sustaining basis, which, as the commissioners charged, provided only a "back-door entrance" and little more than a "hand-out." Such organizations were, in fact, shut out from commercial network broadcasting. During the war years, this network policy was even more obviously a political one because many advertisers had nothing to sell either—except for their trademarks, goodwill, and the free enterprise system.

The hold of big business on network radio is apparent when one considers the large percentages of network revenue that came from big advertisers. In 1943, NBC accrued nearly 60 percent of its revenue from ten companies, the Blue Network (after 1945 known as ABC) more than 60 percent, Mutual 52 percent, and CBS slightly less than half. Even at a local level, radio was "top-heavy": unlike newspapers, which on average received 70 percent of their revenue from local advertisers, radio stations relied on regional and national advertisers for 70 percent of their budget; only 30 percent came from local businesses.[57]

The power structure of commercial network broadcasting had significant repercussions for radio wartime advertising. For one thing, the relatively small number of big radio advertisers simplified the execution of the radio war effort. More important, radio's excellent performance and widespread popularity during wartime reflected well on those who had provided the programs and footed the bill. These businesses' wartime service through radio did not go unnoticed.

Finally, it is important to consider radio audiences and the way that listeners responded to wartime radio advertising. This is the most difficult aspect of historical media research because, unlike in contemporary media studies, historians are unable to question living audiences and have to work with the materials that have been preserved. Fortuitously, the 1940s were a period of relatively prolific audience research, which provides some answers to this question.

To start with, as one might suspect, Americans did not turn on their radio sets to hear radio advertisements. But in a nationwide survey on overall attitudes toward radio advertising, conducted in November 1945, most respondents indicated either that they "didn't mind" commercials or that they "put up with them." The question "Which one of the four statements comes closest to what you yourself think about advertising on the radio?" yielded the following responses:[58]

"I'm *in favor* of advertising on the radio because it tells me
    about the things I want to buy."   23%
"I *don't particularly mind* advertising on the radio. It doesn't
    interfere too much with my enjoyment of the program."   41%
"I don't like advertising on the radio but *I'll put up with it*."   26%
"I think all advertising should be *taken off* the radio."   7%
No opinion   3%

These percentages fluctuated somewhat, depending on how the questions were posed. When asked, for example, what—if anything—they liked about advertising, 43 percent of respondents said they appreciated ads because of the practical information they provided. On the other hand, one-third of those surveyed expressed strong annoyance about commercials and would have preferred radio without advertising. When asked, however, if they would be willing to pay five dollars a year for radio programs without advertising, only 20 percent of respondents were willing to do so.[59]

Taken together, these answers provide a general overview of the attitudes of listeners. Only 20 percent of respondents disliked advertising so much that they were willing to pay for it. On the other hand, only about 20 percent unequivocally supported advertising. The vast majority of respondents had mixed feelings about advertising, answering either that they were "putting up with it" or that they "didn't particularly mind it." The tenor of most answers suggested that respondents considered commercial radio a reasonable, or at least bearable, compromise:

Someone has to pay so that we can get the good programs. We wouldn't get the programs we get if it weren't paid for by sponsors, you can rest assured of that. (Machinist, Worcester, Mass.)

I like the programs enough so I'll stand the advertising. (Owner of electrical shop, Helena, Mont.)

The commercials are a nuisance. They interrupt the programs and they talk too much. But I guess we have to stand it as we get the service for nothing. (Retired police sergeant, Belleville, N.J.)[60]

The war did not radically alter the way most Americans felt about radio advertising. The responses sound quite familiar: Americans lived with their compromise before, during, and after the war. In general, they appreciated the effort to integrate commercials, as long as it made them more enjoyable. On the other hand, if the ads were too loud, long, or annoying, a flick of the switch could change that.

And yet there are some indications that radio's wartime service improved listeners' impression of radio advertising. As survey after survey showed, the greatest mistake of advertising was to be either dull, offensive, or unrelated to the circumstances of the listener. Advertisers had ample opportunity to make their ads relevant during the war years, as the lives of Americans underwent dramatic changes and as they encountered new demands: different diets and shopping habits, the salvage and campaign drives, the complexities of the economic stabilization program, and others. Advertisers provided useful hints on how to conserve and ration; as one popular slogan put it, "Use it up, wear it out, make it do or do without."[61]

Most listeners had "favorite" service ads, or at least ads that were memorable because they contained valuable information. The wife of a farmer from Sheridan, Arkansas, liked the Magic Miller Flour commercial because it told her not only how good the flour was but also, and more important, "how you can use the sacks [it came in]." Another listener recalled and appreciated a commercial that told her not to put bananas in the refrigerator. A woman from Tacoma, Washington, summarized her impression of the increased number of service ads: "Radio has improved. I get quite a bit of information from the advertisements."[62]

Wartime radio advertising did not radically alter Americans' attitudes toward commercials. It certainly did not hurt advertisers' reputations; it is more likely that it bolstered advertisers' standing with the American public because the ads were informative and of practical value. As businessmen and advertisers frequently repeated after the war, they had discovered a powerful new motto. Before the war their motto was "What helps business, helps you"; during the war it became "What helps the nation, helps business."[63]

Conclusion

When the members of the American Association of Advertising Agencies met for their annual meeting in December 1945, they did so in a celebratory mood. The general feeling was that advertising had proved itself during the war and had turned an important corner. James W. Young, chairman of the War Advertising Council eloquently expressed this impression in the keynote address. He first recalled the uncertainty and insecurity that surrounded advertising before the war: "Four years ago last month advertising, as a tool of business and as a social asset, was literally on trial for its life." But he invited his colleagues to marvel about the sea change that had occurred in a few short years: government administrators, who had attacked and criticized advertising before the war, "have learned to use advertising and to depend on it." The New Deal challenge had been defeated. Outside of government, the picture was much the same: "Never has advertising received so much favorable publicity as it has in the last two years. . . . Never have the clipping files shown so many favorable editorials about it." Finally, advertisers themselves had gained new confidence in their craft. All of this, Young charged, had been the "by-product" of a simple yet important lesson advertisers had learned during the war years: "The best advertising is public service advertising."[64]

This resurgence of advertising had come about gradually, increasing year by year. As early as July 1943, advertisers had remarked with visible pride how their standing both in Washington and with the American public was on the rise. On March 8, 1944, they reveled in a historic meeting between leading American businessmen and high-ranking government officials, including several generals of the armed forces. The meeting had been initiated by the WAC as an official occasion on which the achievements of American business and advertising were lauded by all sides. And in the fall of 1945, after the war had ended, government officials—including President Harry Truman—approached the WAC and asked it to continue its work into the postwar period. As Paul B. West, president of the Association of National Advertisers, argued in 1945, something new had been added to advertising: "Those who have dedicated their advertising to the national interest in time of war are learning that advertising can both serve and sell; that there is no conflict between good citizenship and good business."[65]

Advertisers liked to call this their "wartime discovery," but in fact there was not much new about this revelation. Advertisers had always used goodwill or public service commercials as part of their advertising strategy. What was new was the sheer scale and the relative unity of purpose, which brought leading advertisers together under the guidance of the WAC. Another unique feature of this "discovery" was the new-found intimacy between government and business during World War II, which elevated advertising into a "quasi-official position": advertising continued to speak for American business, but during the war it *simul-taneously* functioned as the main mediator between the U.S. government and the American people.

In fulfilling this function, advertising had propagated more than just public service advertising, as is apparent from magazine ads from the war years. At their most basic, these ads advertised "the American way," eulogizing America as a land of opportunity and freedom. As one ad for Republic Steel phrased it: "Red-blooded, hard-working, risk-taking Americans have built this country—the greatest in the world." Yet, as Philip Soffer has shown, the "durable imagery" of wartime advertising displayed an increasingly consumerist spin and became more and more concrete as the country inched closer to war. The shift in advertising by the Nash Kelvinator Corporation, which produced refrigerators and cars in peacetime and airplane engines and propellers during the war, mir-rored this trend. In 1943, one ad featured an airman who openly reflected on his wartime experiences and postwar vision: "I know now that there's only one decent way to live in this world—the way my folks lived and the way I want to live. When you find a thing that works as that— brother, be careful with that monkey-wrench." Through 1944 and 1945, the narrative focus shifted to the airman's wife, who expressed their common vision in an ad headlined "We'll Live in a Kingdom All Our Own":

When you come home to stay . . .
We'll live in a kingdom all our own. . . .
A kingdom just big enough for three . . . with a picket fence for boun-dary.[. . .]
And we'll follow our noses to the kitchen door. It will be like no kitchen you've ever seen before. It will be an enchanted place. . . .
There'll be the very newest refrigerator, bigger and roomier, with gleaming shelves chockfull of cheeses and cold cuts and steak . . . and salad and greens that sparkle with dew with magical compartments of glass. And right behind it another kind of fabulous chest . . . a home freezer, something brand new. [. . .][66]

Jackson Lears has argued that advertising provided "the 'soft' side of ideological mobilization" during World War I. In World War II, this

process repeated itself—only on a vastly intensified scale. It is difficult
to find hard evidence to measure this soft mobilization. But it coincided
to a large degree with Americans' own immediate aspirations and desires, even if they eventually got more than they had bargained for.

Radio entertainment played a crucial part in this wartime process.
Like no other medium, radio entertainment merged the various layers
of wartime culture into one: advertising as the selling of the product;
advertising as selfless wartime service, with official government sanction
no less; and, finally, advertising fused with radio entertainment and
closely connected with the favorite radio stars of the American people.
Despite persistent criticisms and controversy over specific radio advertisements or the amount of advertising on the air, and despite Americans' continued skepticism toward advertising and propaganda, it was
a winning combination for business.

The war had added an important new layer of communication to
radio advertising. By associating American businesses and their trademarks with patriotism, sacrifice, and victory, these companies reaped a
"wartime dividend" that was largely denied other groups, most notably
labor unions. The role of the government was essential in this development. For a number of reasons, government partially retreated from
the public sphere, leaving the field wide open for corporate interests and
their privatized, consumerist vision. This provided advertising a semiofficial status, with government sanction. The next chapter will carry
this discussion further by providing an in-depth analysis of the creation
of an ingenious radio propaganda apparatus and the seamless integration of these messages into the most popular broadcast genre—the radio
comedy programs.

CHAPTER 5

"Radio Propaganda Must Be Painless"

The Comedians Go to War

For a jittery radio industry concerned about the future of American broadcasting in the early months after the nation's entry into World War II, William B. Lewis was a godsend. As head of the Domestic Radio Bureau of the Office of Facts and Figures, and later the Radio Division of the Office of War Information, Lewis, a former vice president of CBS, reassured the industry that the commercial structure of American radio would remain unchanged. In his first meeting with network executives and radio sponsors and advertisers in January 1942, he outlined his pragmatic approach to radio's war effort. As he argued, "radio [was] valuable only because of the enormous audiences it has created." During wartime, his government office planned to make use of radio's popularity without unnecessarily disrupting its structure and schedule: "Let's not forget that radio is primarily an entertainment medium, and must continue to be if it is . . . to deliver the large audiences we want to reach."[1]

As described earlier, Lewis and his fellow "dollar-a-year men" were very successful in pushing through his pragmatic approach for radio's war effort. Lewis was instrumental in filling the Radio Division of the OWI with men and women from radio stations, the networks, and advertising agencies. He was a charismatic, well-liked person who quickly developed a reputation for getting things done. By January 1943, he was promoted to assistant director of the OWI's Domestic Branch, extending his influence to other media such as motion pictures, graphics, and magazines. In the case of commercial radio, Lewis's office, in collaboration with the radio industry, developed a simple yet effective plan for radio's participation in the war. According to this Network Allocation

Plan (NAP), as it became known, radio programs would integrate war messages on a rotating schedule—roughly twice a month for weekly shows and once a week for daily programs. Radio's war programming would be superimposed on the existing schedule, thus minimizing disruptions of Americans' listening habits and maximizing the effect of the messages. The plan adhered to a simple premise shared by Lewis and radio representatives alike: "Radio propaganda must be painless."[2]

The NAP became the master schedule for the government's war effort through commercial broadcasting because it combined two crucial imperatives. It demonstrated that a free media could effectively execute its war effort on a voluntary basis, adding credence to the conviction that democracy was a viable and preferable alternative to totalitarian fascist regimes. In addition, the plan caused minimal disruption to the established broadcasting schedule and thus, at the same time, assured comfortable profit margins for the radio industry, securing radio sponsors' and advertisers' continued interest in the swift, effective execution of radio's war effort.

In contrast to this amicable relationship between radio and the OWI, Clayton Koppes and Gregory Black have described a rather contentious relationship between Hollywood and the OWI during the war. The Bureau of Motion Pictures, which was established to collaborate with the film industry, at times intervened in a heavy-handed fashion, asking to review film scripts and demanding major plot changes. Even after the bureau's director, Lowell Mellett, was forced to resign in 1943 because of his "left-liberal leanings," the government review did not end but moved to the Overseas Branch of the OWI, which had escaped the conservative backlash of 1943 unscathed. What ensured the government's continued leverage over the industry was the fact that the Overseas Branch had censorship rights over American cultural expression abroad, which included the foreign release of films. Since the release of Hollywood films in other countries often determined the difference between financial success and failure, and since this market had already shrunk because of the war, Hollywood was very responsive to government wishes. As Koppes and Black have characterized this relationship: "[The] OWI in Hollywood represents the most comprehensive and sustained government attempt to change the content of a mass medium in American history. . . . [It] not only told Hollywood what should be excluded but what should, in fact, be included." Thomas Doherty, who has studied the same issue, has captured the outcome of this government intervention in more sanguine terms: "Hollywood was constrained but not unduly stifled by the wartime regulators. . . . [The censorship] restrictions were insufferable but not insurmountable."[3]

Radio experienced very little of this acrimony and tension. Since everybody in the Radio Division of the OWI had prior radio or advertising experience, they went to great lengths not to disrupt the existing radio schedule. The transition from peacetime to wartime broadcasting was smooth and fluid. Moreover, because radio had a well-established schedule and institutionally was organized along clear hierarchical lines, its propaganda effort was also steady and predictable, permeating every aspect of the business.

Radio was the primary communication medium during World War II in the United States: 110 million Americans, or 90 percent of the population, listened to an average of four hours daily.[4] Late in 1942, Lewis argued that radio's execution of the war effort made it the most pervasive and persuasive propaganda instrument in the country: "As 1943 dawns, American radio—of the free will of all its component parts—is coordinated to do a more effective job in the dissemination of war information than any other radio system in the world, or than any other medium of communication in this country."[5]

I agree with Lewis that American radio presented a formidable propaganda medium and here will analyze radio's war effort through three of the most popular comedy programs of the 1940s: *The Jack Benny Show, Fibber McGee and Molly,* and *Bob Hope.* Radio comedy was in the vanguard of radio's efforts to supply propaganda through entertainment. It was the most popular radio genre and thus reached the greatest number of Americans on a regular basis. Even during the war, it maintained its transgressive and carnivalesque function by turning accepted norms upside down and pushing against the boundaries of what was deemed acceptable. Most important, these comedy shows simultaneously informed and inspired their listeners through a steady stream of well-dosed and well-orchestrated propaganda campaigns.

Commercial Radio Propaganda

> *Fibber McGee:* I tell you it ain't fair, Molly, they can't do this to me—four gallons a week. Why, that's ridiculous.
>
> *Molly:* I think so, too.
>
> *Fibber:* You do?
>
> *Molly:* Yes, you don't need four gallons!

> *Fibber:* Doggone it. I do, too. Four gallons is outrageous. Where can I go on four gallons of gas?
>
> *Molly:* Where do you wonna go, dearie?
>
> *Fibber:* Well. . . . Gee, whiz. . . . What if I did want to go some place? Even in an emergency or something. . . .
>
> *Molly:* You mean like running out of cigars?[6]

On December 1, 1942, gas rationing went into effect nationwide. It was a Tuesday, and at 9:00 P.M. on the very same day thirty million Americans tuned in to their favorite comedy couple, Fibber McGee and Molly. Gas rationing had also come to the residents of 79 Wistful Vista of a fictional midwestern town, and Fibber McGee loudly expressed his dislike of the new measure.

> *Fibber:* Ah, forget my cigars. I'm talking about this mileage rationing. I think it's a dirty deal. The whole thing is silly! It's going to make everybody stay at home. Why, in two years a guy from Indiana won't gonna know what a guy from Kansas is talking about.
>
> *Molly:* Where are you from?
>
> *Fibber:* Illinois.
>
> *Molly:* Then it's happened already. I don't even know what you're talking about.
>
> *Fibber:* I'm talking about giving all the car owners a measly medicine drop full of gasoline. It's an infringement on private rights, that's what it is!
>
> *Molly:* Look, dearie, look. The main reason they're rationing gasoline is to save tires. Don't you know if we keep driving like we have been a majority of automobiles will be off the road by next year?
>
> *Fibber:* Good! There's too much traffic anyway! Too crowded. Get the cars off the road. That'll be fine. That's swell.
>
> *Molly:* Well, I'm glad you feel that way, because yours would be one of them.
>
> *Fibber:* What?!! Me? Give up my car? Oh, no I don't. I paid for my tires and by the hind leg of Leon Henderson I got a right to drive it! . . .

As Molly went on to explain, Leon Henderson, the director of the Office of Price Administration, had taken this step not because of a shortage of fuels. Instead, the Roosevelt administration had decided that the only way to safeguard the precariously low rubber supply was to ration gasoline and thus curtail driving. Gas rationing had started on the East Coast in May 1942. Over the summer and fall, the administration had also ordered a ban on pleasure driving and imposed a thirty-five-mile-per-hour speed limit on all of the nation's highways.

As part of its rationing order, the government issued A, B, and C stickers, which indicated how much gasoline individuals could obtain. Holders of A stickers received four gallons per week (later three). Those with B stickers, including war workers, were given additional gasoline for essential driving. C stickers were issued only to people who needed their cars for work-related driving, for example, doctors and businessmen. This rationing became a contentious issue because the respective stickers, which were issued by local rationing boards, indicated a person's social status and standing in his community. As one historian has put it: "Obviously, if you were an A card holder, you were a nobody—a nonessential who puttered about in his car on insignificant little errands while cars packed to the roof with joyriding war workers or large sedans driven by powerful men with mysterious connections blew carbon monoxide in your face." Nationwide gas rationing cemented Henderson's reputation as the most unpopular man in America and eventually cost him his job.[7] Like most Americans, Fibber McGee had received only an A sticker, which added to his frustration over the new policy:

> [Enter Mr. Wilcox, one of McGee's neighbors]
>
> *Fibber:* This mileage rationing has gotten me disgusted.
>
> *Molly:* You know, he's been raving about it all day, Mr. Wilcox. He thinks the OPA is trying to make an A-P-E out of him.
>
> *Fibber:* And they are, too! A citizen of my standing, trying to get along on an A-A-A [stuttering] book. It's a lot of foolishness. I've got business to take care of.
>
> *Wilcox:* What business, pal?
>
> *Fibber:* Well, in the first place, I'll. . . . Well, gee whiz. I've got responsibilities.
>
> *Molly:* Oh, he really has, Mr. Wilcox.
>
> *Fibber:* [feebly] Yes.
>
> *Molly:* You know, he's the sole supporter of three pinochle players at the Elks Club.
>
> *Wilcox:* Fibber, you talk like a chump. . . . If you had the brains of a seahorse, you'd realize the spot this country's in regarding rubber. Why, England has no civilian driving and Canada has had mileage rationing for months. So has our eastern seaboard.
>
> *Fibber:* What's that got to do with . . . [interrupted]

Wilcox: And you stand there and squawk, putting your petty little private life against the importance of winning this war.

Fibber: I still don't get . . . [interrupted]

Wilcox: Get wise. Only a monkey could expect to do business as usual. And we haven't got time for monkey business!
[Exit Wilcox under loud applause]

Fibber: You know, Molly, m-m-maybe I was wrong.

Molly: Well, for goodness' sake, at last you've begun to realize it.

Fibber: As he says, only a monkey could. . . . Hey! Was that guy calling me a monkey? Why that . . . just because I think I got a right to more than four gallons a week. A guy of my standing in the community . . .
[Fade into song by Kingsmen Quartet]

Like much of the nation, Fibber McGee was visibly rattled over the new gas rationing measure. By the early 1940s, Fibber, played by Jim Jordan, was a well-known and well-liked character, who presented an excellent foil for the disgruntled American citizen: Fibber was full of himself, he was a windbag and a braggart, and yet he was a likable neighborhood nuisance. He conducted his friendly rivalries with his neighbors in the open; in fact, the name-calling and utter disrespect for social etiquette was one of the show's distinctive features. Above all, however, Fibber was a bungler and an easy fall guy for his patient and loving wife, Molly (Marian Jordan), and the other frequently intruding friends and neighbors.[8]

The show's writer, Don Quinn, usually left it to Fibber to bring up all the self-serving criticisms against government rationing measures — "They should have foreseen this"; "What in the case of an emergency?"; "It's an infringement of civil liberties" — only to have each of his charges deflated by the show's more respectable and socially responsible characters. Yet Fibber echoed many of the sentiments of actual citizens, who were as dissatisfied as he was about the measure. Like Fibber, these citizens were told through both subtle and more direct means to lighten up and put their petty self-interest aside and focus more on the national interest and the war effort.

Typically, Fibber was put in his place through humorous repartee or quick stabs at his inflated ego. During wartime, however, these exchanges could include a serious note or even harsh reminders of the war that America was engaged in. One of the best examples was the parting scene of Mayor LaTrivia on the same gas rationing show. Gale Gordon, who played LaTrivia, had been drafted into the Coast Guard and was leaving the program; his farewell was included in the December 1 show. Mayor LaTrivia was a serious, respected administrator of the fictional small town. Typically, in exchanges with Fibber, LaTrivia was bogged down by Fibber's quick wit and often illogical and nonsensical wordplay and faux pas. He often made long, dramatic pauses and generally left the McGees' residence befuddled. In his farewell show, however, it was LaTrivia who left Fibber dumbfounded:

> *LaTrivia:* Well, for heaven's sake, [McGee], stop your griping. You're lucky you've got a car at all. Well, excuse me, McGee, but when I get over to Africa or Australia or wherever they send me, I'll be thinking of you, McGee, and all the hardship you're suffering. . . . Good-bye, Mrs. McGee. I'll see you when this is over.
>
> *Molly:* Bye, Mr. Mayor, and happy landing.
>
> *LaTrivia:* Thank you. Good-bye, McGee.
>
> *Fibber:* Good-bye, Mr. Mayor. Don't take any wooden anchors.
>
> *LaTrivia:* I won't. And, McGee, when you drive, if you get up to thirty-five miles an hour, think of somebody who didn't get a rubber lifeboat. Good-bye.
> [Exit LaTrivia under loud applause]

During World War II, Don Quinn was one of the acknowledged masters of the integrated OWI war messages. Quinn had been with Jim and Marian Jordan since the debut of the *Fibber McGee and Molly Show* in early 1935. By 1940, the program was one of the top comedy broadcasts in the country. From 1942 to 1946, it alternated with Bob Hope's show as the top-rated comedy program, with each of them attracting an average weekly audience of thirty million Americans.[9] When asked about the success of his "propaganda shows," Quinn argued that he was simply following established rules for comedy writing. Listeners were already interested in these war-related topics, which made it easier for the writer: "We have better audience reaction, we get more fan mail, our Crossley [listener rating] goes up." In fact, to test the effectiveness of popular radio programs, the OWI agreed to give *Fibber McGee and Molly* the exclusive rights to one OWI plug, an appeal for merchant seamen. On the day after the program was aired, according to the War Shipping Administration, the number of people who signed up to be merchant seamen doubled.[10]

Quinn and *Fibber McGee and Molly* were part of a highly effective and efficient propaganda effort. In radio circles the master schedule for this propaganda became known as the Network Allocation Plan. This plan was instituted in April 1942 and from then on ran parallel to noncommercial government propaganda; by 1943, the NAP was the only game in town. It was frequently discussed in the trade magazines, but the general public remained largely unaware that American radio was organized into an extremely powerful propaganda medium. The NAP grew out of an intimate collaboration between the Radio Bureau of the OFF, network executives, and radio advertisers, who met repeatedly in the early months of 1942 to discuss how radio could contribute to America's war effort. And if these months were any indication, the biggest fear was not radio's apathy but its overzealous and uncoordinated participation.

Immediately after the bombing of Pearl Harbor, radio writers and advertisers on both the national and the local level seized the opportunity to exhibit their patriotism and tried to outdo each other in appeals for sacrifice and national unity. Moreover, government requests for airtime increased even further after December 7. In a first assessment of radio's war effort a little more than a month after America's entry into the war, national advertisers criticized what they called "the present hit-and-miss system" of radio's effort and openly wondered whether the overall result of the time contributed was worthwhile. They especially objected to the incessant "plugging" of war messages and the "canned material" disseminated by government agencies.[11]

The Hooper polling firm issued an equally critical report on radio's 1942 springtime programming. As the report indicated, the regular drop in listeners in the first months of a new year was especially pronounced in 1942. The researchers wondered whether radio's uncoordinated and overzealous approach to the war effort was to blame for listeners' abstention.[12]

These were not the only criticisms. In fact, the assessment of the advertisers echoed the sentiment of the leading officials in the Radio Division of the OFF. After all, only a few months earlier, William Lewis and Douglas Meservey had held leading positions at CBS and NBC, respectively. Lewis had become head of the Radio Bureau of the OFF in October 1941; Meservey was recruited as deputy chief one month later. They understood the challenges ahead of them as well as anybody else in the industry. In mid-December 1941, Meservey, in a departmental memorandum, summarized what had to be done. First of all, it was important to remember that to the American listener "radio is primarily an entertainment medium." Consequently, radio had a natural saturation point in terms of informational and educational material. "The problem," as Meservey described it, was "to make the best possible use of radio for the war effort while still maintaining the tremendous audience which [made] the medium so valuable." The radio industry was ready to do its part. But advertisers and writers needed "curbing as well as direction." The key points for Meservey were selectivity, coordination, and allocation.[13]

Lewis fully agreed with this assessment. When the leading officials in charge of radio at the OFF and at other government agencies met with representatives of the Association of National Advertisers on January 20, 1942, Lewis presented Meservey's proposal for overall radio coordination. As he emphasized, the main problem facing radio was one "of skillfully superimposing the war effort on the existing structure," which needed the concerted collaboration of government agencies and the entire radio industry.[14]

The radio industry concurred with this call for coordination. The National Association of Broadcasters, for its part, had founded the Broadcasters' Victory Council as the central liaison between the radio industry and the various government war agencies. The networks created the Network Relations Committee for the same purpose. The advertisers, finally, had established the War Advertising Council to assess the new challenges coming in the wake of America's entry into the war. Its Radio Advisory Committee was charged with handling radio's cooperation with the government's war effort.

Radio became one area of intricate government-business cooperation that characterized America's privatized war effort. The industry accepted the Radio Division of the OFF—and finally the OWI—as the main clearinghouse for their collaboration. The plan that coordinated radio's war effort, on the other hand, was conceived of by the Radio Advisory Committee of the WAC. It was simple and yet effective, in essence asking government agencies to provide every national advertiser with a definite schedule of war messages to be covered. The schedule was to be presented well ahead of time, and it would then be up to a program's writer or producer to incorporate the government message in the most effective manner.[15]

The Network Allocation Plan was inaugurated on April 27, 1942, and dealt solely with sponsored shows carried over one of the three networks—NBC, CBS, or the Blue Network (later ABC). It asked sponsors and advertisers of weekly programs to include a war message on every fourth show. Network programs that aired more than once a week, for example, news broadcasts or soap operas, were asked to include OWI messages on a biweekly schedule.[16]

The OWI also drew up four-week plans to give sponsors and advertisers adequate time to prepare their shows. It selected three or four topics per week and ranked them according to their respective importance. Then the Radio Bureau, in connection with network executives and the WAC, matched the topics with the networks' weekly radio schedules: the highest-rated show dealt with the most important topic, the second most popular show treated the second most important theme, and so on. (Table 1 presents one such four-week plan, showing the allocation of themes for specified time slots, networks, and shows on Tuesday nights.)

The Radio Bureau of the OWI, again in connection with network representatives and the WAC, prepared a similar schedule for daytime and nighttime radio for every day of the week. As Seymour Morris, the chief of the Allocation Division of the Radio Bureau, rightly argued, it was "the largest advertising campaign that has ever been attempted in this country." When Archibald MacLeish, director of the OFF, informed FDR about the NAP, he was equally enthusiastic: "I think the plan offers potentially the most powerful weapon of communication on government information ever designed in any country."[17] Through the NAP, the OWI messages reached ninety million Americans every day of the week. At least as important, however, was the fact that radio had become a part of everyday life and radio characters were as familiar to listeners as friends or neighbors.

From May 15 through June 15, 1942, *Variety* and the OFF Radio Bureau worked together to monitor the network allocations. They discovered that, despite some glitches, the Network Allocation Plan was catching on fast. Robert J. Landry, the editor of *Variety* who wrote the reports on "radio's showmanship," especially praised shows that integrated allocated OWI messages into the plot rather than delivering straight messages.[18]

Landry and the OFF highlighted examples of shows that introduced war-related topics without missing a beat. The first *Fibber McGee and Molly* program under the NAP received wide attention as a model for other shows. Broadcast on May 5 under the title, "Sugar Substitute," it was part of the OFF's effort to register Americans for sugar rationing. In the episode Fibber McGee had set his mind on helping the government by developing a chemical sugar substitute. As he explained his reasoning to Molly, "Hitler got a substitute for everything." "Yes," re-

TABLE 1. Radio Network Allocation Plan for Tuesday Nights
(April 27–May 24, 1942)

First Week: (April 27–May 3, 1942)

7:30 NBC-Red	8:00 CBS	9:00 Blue	10:00 CBS
Burns & Allen	*Missing Heirs*	*Jury Trials*	*Glenn Miller*
22.1 rating*	13.0	7.1	3.4
War bonds	Marines	Need for nurses	Scrap metal

Second Week (May 4–May 10, 1942)

8:00 Blue	8:30 NBC	9:00 CBS	9:30 NBC
Cugat	*Treasure Chest*	*Duffy's Tavern*	*Fibber McGee*
3.3	14.4	6.4	40.8
Sugar rationing	War bonds	Price control	Sugar rationing

Third Week (May 11–May 17, 1942)

7:00 Blue	7:30 CBS	9:00 NBC	10:30 NBC
Easy Aces	*Second Husband*	*Battle of Sexes*	*Red Skelton*
6.1	8.5	15.3	22.6
Price control	Need for nurses	War bonds	USO

Fourth Week (May 18–May 24, 1942)

6:15 CBS	8:00 NBC	8:30 CBS	10:00 NBC
Voice of Broadway	*Johnny Presents*	*Bob Burns*	*Bob Hope*
3.7	12.9	16.7	34.3
Car pooling	War bonds	War bonds	USO

*CAB ratings of April 1942, as given in the OWI outline; obviously these ratings changed over time, but they presented general estimates of the program popularity. The themes reflect the priorities of the OWI for the first four weeks after the inauguration of the Allocation Plan on April 27, 1942.

torted his wife, who frequently topped him in her repartee: "And do you know that they'll soon need a substitute for Hitler."

The entire show focused on the government sugar rationing drive. Mayor La Trivia dropped by to make sure that Molly had signed up for the sugar campaign and also presented the official line for the drive, which was that this was the largest registration drive ever undertaken to ensure that everyone got their share of sugar for the duration. In the end, Fibber's experiment to ease the shortage of sugar was exposed as a hoax: he had simply roughed up the bottom surface of teacups. All of the McGees' regularly intruding neighbors and friends had believed that the substance was sugar, however; indeed, they complained that Fibber had given them too much of it.[19]

Another show Landry cited favorably was *Easy Aces,* a long-running comedy program starring Goodman and Jane Ace, which broadcast three times a week for fifteen minutes over the Blue Network. The comedy largely built on Goodman playing the straight man to his dim-witted wife, Jane. In one episode, Ace was discussing a new war or-ganization called the USO, which he had just read about in the paper:

Ace: I see here where they're starting a big campaign to raise thirty two million dollars between May 11 and July 14. . . . There's an organiza-tion [called] the U.S.O.

Jane: U.S.A. you mean.

Ace: No. U.S.O.

Jane: Now wait a minute, dear. . . . Don't start telling me they've changed the name of this country. . . . I know the U.S.A. as well as . . .

Ace: I'm talking about the U.S.O.

Jane: United States of, and nothing else?

Ace: It's not the United States. . . .

Jane: Dear, don't let anybody hear you talk like that. . . .

Ace: Like what. . . . I said U.S.O.

Jane: U.S.A. . . . United States of America. You can't say United States of . . . and leave it dangling there in the air. . . . Can't you admit when you made a mistake. . . . I won't tell anybody, Dear!

Ace: Seven, eight, nine, ten.

Jane: What?

Ace: Look, Jane, there's an organization known as the U.S.O. The United Service Organizations. . . . It's a very important outfit. . . . It makes the leisure time the boys in the army have pleasant . . . and they even perform personal service for the men in the Army. . . . They give them movies . . . radio entertainment. . . . they entertain the men in the camps . . . even on the firing lines. And they need money to carry on this wonderful work . . . thirty-two million dollars to be exact.[20]

Whether its task was to familiarize Americans with new war organi-zations, to inform them about rationing measures, or simply to reinforce the general sacrifices that were necessary for the war effort, radio was the primary medium to deliver these OWI messages. As Landry em-phasized, the NAP and the *Radio War Guide,* which were published regularly to inform sponsors, writers, and advertisers of the government messages to be covered, came as close to a "master morale plan" as the United States ever developed.[21]

Hand in hand with the NAP, the OWI started to undertake weekly public opinion surveys through its Intelligence Bureau. These surveys helped the planners in the OWI prioritize their themes. To be sure, some themes presented themselves quite naturally after America's entry into the war: the OWI responded to the need for army recruits, the need for nurses, the shortage of some key natural resources, and the fear of runaway inflation. Yet through the Intelligence Bureau surveys, OWI officials found out which measures were well received and well understood, and which ones encountered resistance. At times they discovered contentious issues they had not yet considered.

The official task of the Intelligence Bureau, then, was to provide the Domestic Branch of the OWI with "sound facts to further its effective relations with [the] press, radio, magazines and book publishers." It began its work in April 1942 and worked through a number of channels: it collaborated with existing polling institutes and undertook polls independently; it conducted man-on-the-street surveys; it solicited hundreds of case histories by social workers, psychiatrists, psychoanalysts, ministers, priests, and rabbis in order to analyze the impact of the war on the American home front. In the name of the war effort, everybody was eager to help, which left the OWI as well informed as it possibly could be.[22]

Participation in the NAP was voluntary, but the Radio Bureau did not sit idly by when it found an agency or sponsor that was not in compliance. In these few cases, the resistance generally was due to company presidents' dislike of the Roosevelt administration and the OWI. The staff of the Radio Bureau usually worked through the advertising agencies to coax radio sponsors into compliance, sometimes reminding the agencies that the OWI had not taken over radio, as feared by some in the industry, or referring to contributions and patriotic sacrifices made by the sponsor's competitors. Most often, however, they used their connections and friendships to apply subtle pressure, as in the following letter from Seymour Morris of the Allocation Division. In this instance Morris wrote to a friend at Procter and Gamble, a radio sponsor, and asked for his help with another program sponsor:

Here is a little confidential matter which I would like to drop in your lap. Of all the agencies in the country, the one which is doing the poorest job for us on the Allocation Plan assignments is the Biow Company [*Ginny Simms Show,* NBC]. . . . The situation was unfortunate enough when it was simply a case of doing a poor job for us on every message they delivered. . . . They now want to be excused altogether from any cooperation on this program. . . .

Therefore, it occurred to me that you as an individual could be extremely helpful to us if—when a convenient occasion arises—you could drop into Mr. Biow's ear a few of the opinions which your Company has about the Network Allocation Plan and the job it has done to date.

A week after he sent the letter, Morris received assurance from W. M. Ramsey, general manager of Procter and Gamble, that he personally would take care of the problem: "I should be very glad to take this matter up with him [Milton Biow] at the first convenient opportunity. I shall also consider the matter as off the record by destroying the letter as you suggest."[23]

Morris's request had to be off the record because the OWI had no authority to enforce the NAP. Yet, for the most part, the Radio Bureau did not have to apply pressure to get compliance from radio sponsors and advertisers. In fact, the radio industry's cooperation was driven as much by self-interest as by patriotism. First of all, voluntary collaboration had ensured that the government would not take over radio broadcasting. In addition, as Quinn indicated and most advertising agencies and writers agreed, "When they use war themes and use them well, their Crossleys go up."[24] Finally, as the army recruitment campaigns intensified throughout 1942, making radio shows that were essential to the war effort provided an "insurance policy," protecting stars and writers from the draft and keeping popular shows on the air, to the financial benefit of everyone involved.

By August and September 1942, the draft had become the biggest concern of the entertainment industry, as the call went out to every able-bodied man between the ages of eighteen and thirty-eight to serve his country. Of the twenty-five most popular radio stars, slightly more than half were of draft age:

Abbott and *Costello	Eddie Cantor	*Andre Kostelanetz
*Goodman Ace	*Bing Crosby	*Harold J. Peary
Fred Allen	*Nelson Eddy	Edward G. Robinson
*Amos and Andy	*Clifton Fadiman	*Lanny Ross
Jack Benny	Jean Hersholt	[Kate Smith]
Major Bowes	*Bob Hope	*Red Skelton
Bob Burns	Jim Jordan	*Fred Waring
George Burns	*Kay Kyser	

[* indicates being of draft age]

It is true that all of them probably made more valuable contributions to the overall war effort on radio than they would have in battle fatigues.

On the other hand, it was not difficult to see through the scheme of the WAC, whose head, Chet LaRoche, suggested to the OWI in August 1942 that the Radio Bureau was not making enough use of the commercial programs. As Nat Wolff, the Hollywood representative of the Radio Bureau, argued, the advertisers were scared of losing their radio talent, a fear that could simplify the enforcement of the NAP through the OWI:

Let's not kid ourselves about Chet La Roche [*sic*]suddenly practically demanding that commercial radio be used more importantly by the government.

Chet has already lost Ezra Stone of the *Aldrich Family;* Reber [another advertiser] is worried about losing Crosby; Lord & Thomas [advertising agency] is just as worried about losing Hope as well as Kyser. And it is quite obvious that if we can use commercial programs more effectively by using more of their time, that the agencies will have very little trouble selling the ideas to their clients because the alternative is that they will lose their top stars altogether.[25]

Thus, while cooperation in the NAP was voluntary, wartime circumstances almost guaranteed the radio industry's full and swift collaboration. The Radio Bureau did not need legal jurisdiction to enforce the radio propaganda effort: most shows participated willingly and eagerly. The dissenting minority was for the most part coaxed into compliance by the collective pressure of radio sponsors and advertisers, who feared nothing more than bad publicity or being deemed nonessential to the country's war effort.

Radio Comedy, Humor, and Wartime Unity

Wilson: And now, Ladies and Gentlemen, from Williams Field near Chandler, Arizona, we bring you a man who after a week under the blazing Arizona sun no longer looks like a frog belly in the moonlight. . . . Jack Benny!

Benny: Thank you, thank you. . . . Hmmm. . . . Frog belly in the moonlight? Jell-O again. This is Jack Benny speaking. And, Don, although you put it rather crudely, there's no question about it. . . . I do look much better with my desert tan.

Wilson: Yes, Jack, you certainly do.

Benny: Why not, I was outdoors all the time—horseback riding, swimming. . . . I tell you, Don, I feel like a million dollars. . . . I mean twenty-five thousand, yet I *can* feel like a million.
[Loud laughter][26]

Jack Benny was America's most popular tightwad and fall guy. In fact, he is credited both by radio historians and by fellow comedians with building the first radio comedy based on the idea of the fall guy. The comedian Fred Allen has argued, "Practically all the comedy shows owe their structure to Benny's conceptions. . . . He was the first comedian in radio to realize you could get big laughs by ridiculing yourself instead of your stooges." Or, as Benny himself put it, "The minute I come on, even the most henpecked guy in the audience feels good."[27]

At the time of America's entry into World War II, Benny's show already was a national institution. He started his radio program in 1932, and after five years on the air had become the most popular radio comedian. His trademark greeting, "Jell-O again," quickly became part of everyday language, and his legendary stinginess turned all Scotsmen into his relatives. When a national magazine conducted a poll in 1944 to determine who had the best-known radio voice, Benny finished first, followed by Franklin D. Roosevelt, Bob Hope, and Bing Crosby.[28]

Jack Benny was the best-developed radio character on the air. Equally well known was his radio "gang," the key members of which appeared with him for nearly two decades (on radio and, for the most part, television): Don Wilson, the big, jolly announcer; Phil Harris, bandleader, southern playboy, and reputed drunkard; Dennis Day, the show's singer, who also played the silly, polite, and stupid "kid"; Eddie Rochester, Benny's skeptical and, at times, disrespectful black valet and butler; and, finally, Mary Livingstone, Benny's wife in real life, who played a variety of roles. Other well-known features of the show included props like Benny's violin and the continuous joking about his poor playing, the vault in the basement of his house (where he hid his money), and his 1924-model car, his beloved "Maxwell." On October 18, 1942, Maxwell became the first war casualty of *The Jack Benny Show.*

> *Wilson:* And now, Ladies and Gentlemen, I have an important announcement to make. . . . Last Monday afternoon Jack Benny went to an official automobile graveyard in Los Angeles and contributed his famous Maxwell to the [War] Salvage Drive.
>
> *Benny:* Yup, little Maxie has gone to do her bit in the war effort.
>
> *Wilson:* So at this time, folks, we would like to reenact for you all that took place on that historic occasion. . . .
> [Whole cast riding in Maxwell—sound of an *old* car]
>
> *Benny:* Oh, just imagine. Imagine turning a car like this into the junk pile. While the motor is in a wonderful condition. . . .

Rochester: Wonderful condition?

Jack: Yes.

Rochester: I lifted up the hood yesterday, and the spark plugs were playing "Reel Down the Fan Belt."

Benny: That's a lie, because I'm wearing the fan belt. . . . You know, fellows, I realize I should give my car to the Salvage Drive. . . . But you can't blame a fellow for being blue and all choked up.

Dennis: Did the laundry shrink your collar, Mr. Benny?

Benny: No! Pay attention! . . . I'm sentimental.

Benny's show was part of the October 1942 scrap metal drive. Scrap metal, especially steel, was one of the scarcest raw materials during World War II. The OPA hoped that five million of the thirty million tons of steel scrap needed to maintain steel production would be furnished through the recycling of old automobiles. Benny's Maxwell was the best-known old car in the country, and the show was therefore ideally suited to carry the government appeal to the American people.

As the show continued, Benny returned home with Rochester after delivering his car to the junkyard. But he was still mourning the loss of his dear "Maxie":

Benny: How can I sleep with my Maxwell all busted up in that junkyard I don't know.

Rochester: Boss, why don't you look at it this way? . . . Before you know it, the scrap from your car is gonna be part of a battleship . . . or a tank . . . or an airplane.

Benny: Gee.

Rochester: I tell ya, boss, if everybody in the country turned in their old junky cars and dug up all the scrap they could, there wouldn't be no shortage of nothin' . . . specially Victory.

Benny: You're right, Rochester. . . . Absolutely right. . . . [Yawns]. . . . Well, goodnight. . . . No wonder I'm tired [Yawns]. . . . Gee, I practically helped Henry Kaiser build a ship today. . . . Gosh, just think. . . . Little Maxie's gonna be a ship . . . or a tank . . . [Yawns].

Even as "straight" integrated messages, the OWI plugs could have a certain appeal when phrased in the right way: "Donate your old jalopy to the war effort and bring the boys home faster. Did you know that one-sixth of our steel production is dependent on scrap automobile metals? Contact your nearest automobile graveyard and bring in your old cars, so that we can keep the steel mills rolling and provide our boys with the materials they need to win this war for us!"[29]

Yet the government had been conducting scrap metal drives since early 1942. As the Radio Bureau officials well understood, there was a danger that the public would tire of repeated appeals for rationing, as it had for other drives. Periodic reports by the Special Service Division of the OWI Intelligence Bureau showed that this was indeed the case.

The Special Service Division undertook its first major radio listening survey in December 1942 and found that the radio war effort was generally well received by the public. Between December 1 and 5, 1942, OWI investigators interviewed 518 people, a cross section of Philadelphia residents, and conducted longer interviews with 45 additional people. A parallel group of researchers monitored the city's four radio stations over a two-week period to determine the amount and types of war messages they broadcast.[30]

The monitoring report showed that approximately one-fifth of all radio time in Philadelphia was used for presenting war-related material, which indicated that local programs were following their special Local Allocation Plan, which the OFF had modeled after and synchronized with the Network Allocation Plan. Like the NAP, the Local Allocation Plan specified that approximately every fourth show should present a war message. The OWI interviews indicated that three-fourths of Philadelphia residents listened to as many radio programs, or more, as they had a year earlier, and 62 percent agreed that there was about the right number of war-related shows on the air. The most disliked shows were serials about the war, war dramatizations, and some talks by government officials. The least criticized programming, as the report emphasized, were special messages such as those asking people to save tin or to have their tires inspected in order to save rubber. One man's comment captured the tenor of the report concerning war messages: "I think it [everybody's contribution to the war effort] should be called to the public's attention a lot. . . . Some need an awful lot of prodding. I didn't save at first, and I think it was the radio that got me started."[31]

As the war wore on, however, listeners became less sympathetic to the "prodding" by government agencies. The OWI Intelligence Bureau learned this in a study conducted in December 1943, a year after the first survey, in which thirty-five hundred people nationwide gave their opinion of radio's war effort. The researchers found that many listeners were fed up with war appeals but hesitated to express such an unpatriotic sentiment. Clearly, the war was one year older, and some appeals had been repeated hundreds of times during that year. In fact, 60 percent of listeners disliked some specific appeals, including salvage drives. The criticism of listeners was not always a reflection of the radio propaganda effort but could reveal the poor execution of certain drives: half of the people who were tired of scrap drives, for example, argued that tin cans and waste paper were not collected anyway.[32]

More important, however, the study showed that listeners increasingly viewed straight appeals as just another type of "commercial." As the researchers found, one-third to one-half of the respondents disliked commercials. Straight government messages eventually met the same resistance as did commercials; in fact, they contributed to listeners' impression that there were too many commercials on the air. As individual survey responses indicated, straight government messages between programs or at the beginning or end of radio shows were often tuned out just like commercials; people simply did not listen to these fillers anymore. One person expressed this sentiment both for himself and for other people he knew: "Lots of people don't listen to the announcements between programs because they are fed up on [sic] silly, sentimental commercials."[33]

Radio comedy programs sometimes resorted to straight announcements when their writers failed to come up with a funny way to integrate the allocated OWI message. For the most part, however, these announcements were delivered in the middle of the program, when listeners were less likely to stop listening or turn off their radio sets. On *The Jack Benny Show,* these appeals were generally read by the announcer, Don Wilson, often instead of the scheduled commercial, as was done with the following message on rationing delivered on April 4, 1943:

> *Wilson:* And now, Ladies and Gentlemen, before Dennis sings his song, I have a message of importance for all of you. Tomorrow your "B" ration stamps . . . that is, the red ones . . . may be used for purchasing meat, cheese or fats. This is your second set of stamps . . . the "B" stamps in ration book two. You have a whole row of them to use this week in eight-, five-, two- and one-point values, totaling sixteen points in all for each person. Spend your stamps wisely and supplement them as much as you can with the plentiful, nourishing, un-rationed foods.[34]

Plugs like these were not uncommon, even in the best-written and most popular comedy programs. Yet, for the majority of their shows,

Benny's writers did not lack ideas for integrating OWI themes, especially on rationing. Benny's renowned stinginess presented the ideal foil for discussing savings of any kind. Early in 1942, when the country went on "war saving time" and turned back the clocks to save electricity, Benny was the first to use the "loss" of one hour to his advantage—by cutting his cast's pay.[35] When the OPA announced a flurry of rationing measures toward the end of 1942, Benny just as easily became the butt of the cast members' jokes, as in the following exchange, in which they commented on Jack's hospitality:

> *Wilson:* Well, Jack, gas isn't the only thing being rationed nowadays.
>
> *Jack:* No, there are a lot of things, Don, . . . A half-pound of sugar a week . . . *no* whipped cream . . . *one* cup of coffee a day . . . a meatless Tuesday. . . . But we'll just have to get used to it.
>
> *Mary:* Get used to it. . . . You've been rehearsing for this all your life.[36]

As some excerpts show, not all of the integrated OWI messages were ingenious works of radio comedy writing: some fell flat, some were predictable, and some were uproariously funny—like radio comedy in general. What made them so important for the OWI propaganda effort was that they provided a steady, well-dosed, and well-monitored stream of official reminders, government messages, and appeals for sacrifice to 70 percent of the American people *every single day of the week.*

Moreover, these messages were delivered by comedians and entertainers Americans had come to love. As Benny argued, the most important aspect of any comedian's success was whether the audience liked him or her: "In the first place, to become real successful they [the listeners/audiences] must like you very much on the stage. They must have a feeling like: 'Gee, I like this fella.'" After that, he went on, everything else was secondary. A comedian could develop a character comedy, a situation comedy, or a straight gag routine, as long as he or she was well liked and recognizable. Once this basis was established, listeners forgave comedians if they had occasional bad shows.[37]

Clearly the delivery of messages through humor and by likable comedians was far preferable to straight propaganda programs. Yet at least one further element made the radio comedy programs of the 1940s particularly suited for the execution of these propaganda campaigns. This was the formula of the fall guy, which had become a dominant feature of radio comedy in the early 1940s.

Critics of humor have generally applied three overarching theories in their discussions of laughter and joking: laughter to express superiority, jokes as subversion, and laughter as relief. The superiority theory is based largely on Thomas Hobbes's account of laughter, which claims that people generally laugh at other people, thereby setting themselves apart from and above them. The notion of joking as subversion is drawn from Sigmund Freud's and Henri Bergson's frequently quoted observations on humor. Freud emphasized the importance of joking as a release from control and rigid standards of behavior; Bergson similarly emphasized humor as the assault of the living, lively spirit on encrusted norms and institutions. Finally, and most widely accepted, is the notion of laughter as relief, in which humor is seen as a distraction from personal problems and fears or as a temporary escape from real life.[38]

Undoubtedly, radio comedy in the 1940s contained all three of these elements, yet most important in the context of the war was the comedians' ability to *unite* the public behind America's war effort. Whereas laughter and comedy can be contentious and even vindictive, wartime radio comedy overwhelmingly followed a different route: it provided laughter as a means for achieving social cohesion and cross-cultural and cross-class harmony. John Morreall has best summarized this social function of humor: "Laughter is contagious, but in spreading from person to person, it has a cohesive effect. Laughing together unites people. . . . To laugh with another person for whatever reason, even if only at a piece of absurdity, is to get closer to that person. . . . Sharing humor is in this respect like sharing an enjoyable meal."[39]

This cohesive role was one of radio comedy's main functions during World War II. People laughed with each other at home and with the live audiences, and listeners knew there were millions of people tuned in to the same program that they were hearing. The likable fall guy provided the ideal foil for this kind of humor, allowing everyone to laugh at the same thing or the same person, knowing full well that the comedian could take it and would even come back for more. At the same time, through characters such as Fibber McGee, listeners could be subtly reminded of their own foolishness, yet without having a finger pointed at them.

The fall guy was the creation of a medium apprehensive of public criticism and concerned about offending somebody—anybody. Compared with today's comedy style, the social satire and political criticism of radio comedians in the 1940s were often quite tame. Don Quinn once remarked, "Any radio show with a rating of 0.01 or more will have enough trouble with pressure groups and self-appointed guardians of public morals without begging for more with offensive material."[40] Especially during World War II, comedy writers, entertainers, and sponsors were even more careful not to attract bad publicity or cross the OWI. The convention of the fall guy, which had developed as a successful protection for the sponsor in the early days of radio by uniting the listening public, was ideally suited as cohesive humor for wartime America.

It is important to recognize, however, that while this technique was the dominant trend, no comedy program abided by it exclusively. Comedy has to be critical in order to stay credible. Despite censorship by the networks, sponsors, and the OWI, comedy writers did insert critical and irreverent comments that reflected the American public's growing disgruntlement with government measures. For example, in the spring of 1942, the U.S. military imposed a ban on radio weather reports because of the widespread fear of Axis bomber attacks on American cities. Initially the American public had supported the ban, but people complained when it was still in effect a year later, even though it was then clear that the chances of bombing attacks were virtually zero. In a show in May 1943, Jack Benny expressed the widespread ridicule of the ban on weather reports in the following exchange with Don Wilson:

> *Jack:* Anyway, Don, here we are at Gardner Field [California]. . . . If I was in the Air Force, this is where I'd like to be stationed. I mean the climate is so cool and refreshing.
>
> *Wilson:* Cool? . . . I stepped outside a few minutes ago and the thermometer said—
>
> *Jack:* Huh uh, Don, that's a military secret!
>
> *Wilson:* But these fellows in the audience are all soldiers, can't we tell them?
>
> *Jack:* No, no Don. . . . And stop perspiring, that's a clue.[41]

Writers considered it a great feat if they were able to outsmart the censors, even in what nowadays might seem like relatively minor issues. Milt Josefsberg, one of Benny's writers, recalls with great relish how the show's team of writers got around the NBC censors during World War II. In the following program, performed for sailors at a navy base, Benny showed off his knowledge of naval military history by listing naval heroes:

> *Jack:* . . . and then of course there was Admiral Stephen Decatur, who earned immortality when in the face of overwhelming enemy odds he uttered those fearless words, "Full speed ahead and 'oh fudge' to the torpedoes."

Mary: Jack—in the middle of a battle, Stephen Decatur said, "Oh fudge to the torpedoes"?

Jack: Well, Mary, he wanted to say something stronger, but he couldn't because the Shore Patrol was standing next to him.
[Loud laughter]

As Josefsberg explained, the phrase "damn the torpedoes" was well known, especially among sailors. By using the dainty "oh fudge," Benny was playing on his slightly effeminate radio character and sharing a laugh with the sailors at the censors' expense: the Shore Patrol was fair game for sailors' ridicule because it frequently spoiled their fun, much as the network censors did for radio.[42]

The Network Allocation Plan prescribed only the minimum of co-operation expected by the OWI. By the fall of 1942, most shows were actually integrating war-related topics far more frequently than was originally planned under the network schedule. To catch up with this trend and avoid a return to radio's uncoordinated participation, the OWI doubled the assigned allocations for network shows in September 1942. For one comedian in particular, these assignments presented a springboard for dedicating his shows completely to America's war involvement.

Patriotism and Pleasure

Bob Hope: How do you do, Ladies and Gentlemen, this is Bob "Army" Hope telling you soldiers whether you're generals or top sergeants, if you use Pepsodent your teeth will never be loose-tenants. . . .

Well, here I am at March Field . . . and what a scene when I arrived. . . . All the men threw their hats up in the air, but they couldn't get them into the propeller and I landed safely. . . . The boys were mad because I didn't get down here yesterday . . . the tar hardened. . . . And you know they give twenty-one-gun salutes to all the famous people that visit camp. . . . Well, for me, two guys on K.P. [kitchen patrol] came out of the kitchen and broke a paper bag. . . . I got a really military welcome. . . . the soldiers lined up in two rows, and you know how they hold their swords up while the honored guests walk under them? I wonder what gave them the idea I was four feet three.[43]

In 1942, at the age of thirty-nine, Bob Hope was one of the youngest radio comedians. His career in broadcasting started in September 1938, when Pepsodent offered him his own radio show after his great movie success of the same year, *The Big Broadcast of 1938*. This was indicative of Hope's coming stardom: other radio stars appeared in their own movies in the late 1930s and throughout the 1940s, but Hope's movie career eclipsed those of all other radio entertainers. In January 1942, Hope won both *Motion Picture Daily*'s "Champion of Champions" award and *Radio Daily*'s "No. 1 Entertainer" honor, which for the previous two years had gone to *The Jack Benny Show*.[44]

In radio, Hope pioneered a new kind of comedy show. He became known for the rapid-fire delivery of jokes in his opening monologues: within four minutes (which included time for laughter), Hope told thirty jokes, one every two lines or one every ten seconds, which was half as many as Jack Benny tried to include in his whole thirty-minute program. The rest of Hope's show moved along at a similar speed. Because Hope consumed jokes faster than other comedians, he also had the biggest stable of writers, which has led some radio historians to criticize his program as an example of a "slick, assembly-line" approach to comedy. He started with eight in 1938 and increased the number to twelve throughout the war years, whereas Benny still worked with two to four writers, and Don Quinn worked alone or sometimes with the help of one other writer on *Fibber McGee and Molly*.[45]

During World War II, Bob Hope became the quintessential GI comedian. Starting on January 27, 1942, and continuing for the duration of the war, he broadcast almost all his shows from army and navy bases. He became the GI's unofficial spokesperson and earned a reputation as "radio's No. 1 soldier in greasepaint."[46] Hope engaged in the same self-deprecating humor as Fibber McGee and Jack Benny. The "welcomes" to military bases became a standard routine of Hope's opening monologue. So, too, did his supposedly weak physique, which time and again deflated his stage ego, as in the following dialogue with his steady companion, the lush-voiced movie star Frances Langford:

> *Hope:* Well, Frances—how do you like it down here at March Field?
>
> *Frances:* Great, Bob . . . but don't you feel odd among all these young men?
>
> *Hope:* Whaddaya mean by that?
>
> *Frances:* Well, Bob . . . you look weak and puny compared to the soldiers here.
>
> *Hope:* Wait a minute. . . . Look at those soldiers in the audience. . . . now look at me. . . . who looks bigger and tougher?
> [Long pause]

Well, I eat wheaties! But seriously, Frances, I have a real soldier's physique.

Frances: Yes, but your chest looks as if it obeyed a command to fall in while your stomach is still at ease! . . . [47]

Like other comedy programs, the Pepsodent program worked with a regular cast and followed a fairly standard routine. After Hope's monologue and a song by Langford, Hope usually engaged her in an "intimate dialogue," in which they discussed relationships, soldiers, kissing—or Hope's physique. Or Hope might get into a verbal fistfight with Jerry Colonna, who played the absent-minded "professor" with a complete disregard for logic; Colonna played any number of roles, all based on incongruous, nonsensical humor. After another song by a guest star, Hope played a sketch either with Vera Vague, the middle-aged, man-chasing maid, or with Skinny Ennis, an anemic, weakly youngster who did justice to his name.[48]

The Bob Hope Show cooperated in the Network Allocation Plan, but as Hope's reputation as the GI's comic grew, his writers geared the program increasingly toward soldier audiences, and the OWI allocation became secondary to Hope's wartime role as a comedian. He became the commentator on life on military bases, a sounding board for soldiers' disgruntlement, and a mediator between the civilian population and America's men and women in uniform. To be sure, all big-name radio shows traveled to military bases and brought entertainment and distraction to soldiers, but nobody became as closely identified with this mission during World War II as Bob Hope.

As the war progressed and more and more men were called into the army, Americans were eager to learn about life on the bases and, starting in late 1942, in the European and Pacific theaters. One of the best-selling books of 1942, *See Here, Private Hargrove,* humorously described Private Marion Hargrove's experiences during military training. Excerpts of the book were reprinted in *Reader's Digest* and *Life;* by 1945, the publisher had sold two and a half million copies.[49]

Trade magazines originally criticized Hope for playing largely to his military audiences and ignoring civilian listeners.[50] Indeed, his material violated one of the established tenets of comedy writing: in order to be funny, comedy shows had to take on topics that were relevant to listeners' lives or that played on familiar characteristics and circumstances. As the war progressed, however, the American public seemed to become accustomed to the military slang and Hope's style of humor.

As other comedians discovered as well, it was difficult to find a compromise between soldier and civilian audiences. In early 1942, Jack Benny was also playing camps and experimenting with his comedy material. Benny finally decided, however, that he could not please both civilian and military audiences at the same time. Starting in April 1942, Benny and his writers decided to play two shows every Sunday, the regular network program plus a show for servicemen, which would not be broadcast. The only exceptions were Benny's occasional visits to camps, when the show was broadcast live.[51]

Yet Americans liked Hope's comedy because it provided them with an all-important link with husbands, friends, sweethearts, sons, or daughters who were in the service. Hope frequently said that one of the reasons he continued to play for the soldiers was that he received many letters from parents, thanking him for making the lives of their sons happier and a bit easier. Wives and fiancées could feel closer to their loved ones by listening to Hope's shows. As one woman wrote to her boyfriend, "I listened to Hope tonight which was broadcast from a base somewhere. Hope was really a scream. How I wish I could be with you. I love you."[52]

The contents of Bob Hope's shows were not prescribed by the NAP or any other government agency, although the shows were produced under the auspices of the USO, the entertainment branch of the military services. Yet the comedian's war effort proved invaluable to the government's propaganda effort, keeping Americans in touch with their fighting men and women and pulling the country together behind the armed forces. These comedy programs and other entertainment shows reminded listeners over and over again of the lonely, brave soldiers who might be their husband, boyfriend, or neighbor's son.

Hope's wartime broadcasts also were highly popular because he seemed to understand soldiers' emotions better than most comedians and took aim at the often mundane and frustrating routines they had to endure:

Bob Hope: Well, here I am at Camp San Luis Obispo, San Luis Obispo, that's Spanish for roll 'em out again boys, I'm two bucks behind. . . . And you should see the young couples in love out driving in their cars. . . . The fellow with his arm around the girl . . . and the guy from the draft board with his arm around the fellow. . . . Spring has really affected the soldiers, too. . . . While I was here, I saw two big soldiers take some shovels and rakes and go out into a little garden behind their tent, and tenderly plant an M.P. . . . I saw one soldier taking all his clothes out of his barracks and he kept handing them to another soldier. . . . I asked, "spring cleaning?", and he said, "Nope, . . . crap game."[53]

Like other comedians who visited the camps, Hope talked about the things that most directly affected soldiers' lives: romance, local bars, or crap games on the base. Moreover, he poked fun at all those superiors the soldiers loathed yet had to put up with, especially sergeants, overly eager second lieutenants, or the military police. As Hope himself argued, the real enemies of these soldiers often were not the Germans or the Japanese, at least not as long as they remained stateside: "It took me a long time to realize that all the rules of comedy were going to be changed [for camp shows]. We represented everything those new recruits didn't have: home cooking, mother, and soft roommates. Their real enemies . . . were never just the Germans or the Japanese. The enemies were boredom, mud, officers, and abstinence. Any joke that touched those nerves was a sure thing."[54]

What Hope was saying applied equally to soldiers and civilians: comedy and satire depended on "resistant humor." Recently, media scholars and cultural theorists have used the term "carnivalesque" to describe this resistant tradition inherent in much of popular culture, especially humor and comedy. This notion was advanced in a highly influential book by Mikhail Bakhtin, who described the openness and subversive nature of the novels of the French writer Rabelais as being similar to the burlesque traditions of medieval carnival. Like the medieval carnival tradition, he argued, Rabelais's novels resisted the dominant ideology and turned the existing social and economic order upside down through the use of laughter and satire. As Bakhtin put it, "One might say that carnival celebrated temporary liberation from the prevailing truth and from the established order; it marked the suspension of all hierarchical rank, privileges, norms, and prohibitions."[55]

There is no doubt that radio comedy contained strong elements of this carnivalesque tradition. Hope's jokes about "tenderly planting an M.P." and subverting army discipline are very much in this vein. They helped soldiers let off steam and vicariously express their pent-up frustrations. Benny's references to the Shore Patrol and petty wartime censorship rules worked in the same way. Even Fibber's rantings over government rationing measures were open to negotiated or resistant readings, even though, as I argued earlier, their intended purpose was to ridicule the offenders.

This critical slant of radio comedy applied even more so to radio's master of political satire and irreverent wit, Fred Allen, who was the most censored radio comedian during the 1930s and 1940s. To be sure, Allen, who was sponsored by Texaco, collaborated with the OWI to promote civilian cooperation in rubber salvage drives and other automobile-related campaigns. He was also particularly effective in ridiculing hoarders and ration-book cheaters. Yet he simultaneously delivered some of the most stinging criticisms of government measures during World War II. In 1943, one of his radio characters, Mrs. Nussbaum, explained the point rationing system to her audience through a practical example: buying coffee.

> *Mrs. Nussbaum:* You are pointing to the coffee grinder.
>
> *Allen:* Yes.
>
> *Mrs. N.:* The grocer is pointing to an empty shelf.
>
> *Allen:* Yes.
>
> *Mrs. N.:* You are pointing to your rationing book.
>
> *Allen:* And?
>
> *Mrs. N.:* The grocer is pointing to the door.
>
> *Allen:* That's all there is to the point system?
>
> *Mrs. N.:* You are getting the point.[56]

While Allen's battles with network vice presidents over censorship issues were legendary, many other comedians and comedy writers also routinely complained about the petty restrictions under which they were working. Every script had to be sent to the Continuity Acceptance Division of the network, where censors checked the material for decency, possible offenses, and sponsor concerns. To start with, all swearing, even relatively harmless words like "darn," was out. Next, as Allen emphasized, when the scripts returned from the network censors, jokes had to be deleted because of "mention of competitive products and networks, . . . and political references were banished lest they stir up somebody in Washington."[57]

Soldiers and civilians responded to, indeed demanded, this kind of comedy. Rowdy soldier audiences that welcomed Hope with howls and screams testified to the degree with which the comedian connected with them. Yet sometimes there was a cutting or unsavory side to this kind of humor, especially when the discussion turned to matters of the heart—and groin.

Under the motto "Boys Will Be Boys!" off-color jokes invaded all comedy programs, but nobody excelled at this type of humor more than Hope.

> *Bob Hope:* Well, here I am, still in Georgia . . . And it's almost harvest time here. . . .

> The farmers are looking over the peach crop . . . and the sol-
> diers go to town every weekend and do the same thing. . . .
> Most of the soldiers in Camp Wheeler go to Macon when they
> get a three-day pass. The three-day pass is just right. . . . Half a
> day to get there and half a day to get back . . . and two days in
> the hotel lobby waiting for a room.[58]

Sherwood Schwartz, one of Hope's prewar writers, recalled that it
was not difficult for the Hope show to adjust to this shift. Even before
the war, Hope's writers had included what they referred to as "intimate
spots," in which Hope and Frances Langford discussed matters of the
heart or aired Hope's failed exploits. Hope had aimed his comedy pre-
dominantly at younger audiences and continued to do so in the early
1940s. His repertoire also included derisive and misogynist "girl jokes,"
which were pervasive in all wartime comedy. Hope's "She was so
fat . . ." jokes were not new, but during the war years they became increasingly popular, especially with soldiers.[59]

> *Bob Hope:* Last week when I was in Camp Roberts, [California,] I went out
> on a date with four soldiers. . . . Three of them had six-hour
> passes and the other one had the sentry by the throat. . . .
> You should see the girl they got for me. . . . Boy, was she fat.
> . . . She was so fat, you couldn't dance with her, when the music
> started . . . you just did sentry duty. . . . To give you an idea how
> fat she was. . . . Well, they got up a big conga line . . . and she
> was both the front and the rear ends of it.[60]

Nothing more excited the young, sex-starved recruits than "girl talk,"
and nothing provided easier laughs. Interestingly enough, though, in
Hope's shows it was frequently a man-chasing woman who presented
an excellent foil to receive this abuse. Among Hope's cast, Vera Vague,
the middle-aged maid, filled this role. As conveyed in numerous
sketches, she preferred action over talk and glossed over derogatory
barbs, as in the following example, in which Hope introduced her to a
soldier who was part of the show:

> *Hope:* James is a soldier, not a sailor. Look at his uniform.
>
> *Vera:* What for? I don't want a branch of service. I want a man! [Turning
> to James] You know, sergeant, I may not look too well under these
> awful spotlights . . . but why don't you come for a walk with me
> outside? . . . You know . . . moonlight becomes me!
>
> *James:* Yeah, and a blackout wouldn't hurt any either![61]

Throughout the war, the networks and army representatives tried to get shows to cut back on what they called "risqué humor." In August 1942, the U.S. Army Bureau of Public Relations, concerned about the reputation of the armed services, called a conference with radio representatives to discuss the comedy material being presented to camp audiences. The conference participants agreed that it had to be curtailed. In December 1943, the networks again publicly warned comics to quit "wandering" into off-limits material and cut out the profanities. The yearly admonitions became as routine as the comedy material itself.[62]

Conclusion

Most Americans who lived during World War II were not even aware that there was such a thing as a master propaganda plan for radio. Unless they read one of the trade journals or were involved with the field, there was no reason they should have. The radio propaganda effort was a well-tempered campaign, steady and pervasive. It ensured that the uncoordinated, loud appeals of the first war months, which had quickly oversaturated Americans with patriotic appeals, would remain an exception. Moreover, radio's hands were never tied. As Hope's comedy programs demonstrated, the Network Allocation Plan was only a blueprint; it did not stifle the medium's creativity or limit its expansion into new territory. During World War II, radio comedies were indeed able to do it all at once: they continued to entertain their audiences and sell products for their clients while simultaneously informing the public and uniting Americans behind the war effort.

Hope's case again is instructive in this respect because it showed that patriotism and public relations for both the entertainer and the product went hand in hand. In the spring of 1942, for example, when Paramount released Hope's movie *My Favorite Blonde,* the comedian arranged to premiere the film on the military bases where he was scheduled to broadcast his radio show—with references to the movie included in the scripts. Hope was equally successful in promoting his book *I Never Left Home,* a humorous account of his first trip to the European theater in the summer of 1943. In late spring of 1944, the comedian and the USO announced that Hope was going on another trip to the South Pacific war zones during July and August. In July, the Sunday supplement of the *New York Herald Tribune* published an article by Hope, "Sure Fire Gags for the Foxhole." Both the announcement and the article were part of a larger publicity campaign promoting the sale of Hope's book, which was published in July 1944. By September, half a million copies had sold. A year later, sales had reached a million and a half, making it one of the best-selling wartime books. Finally, as Hope's star rose, so did the market share of his sponsor's product, Pepsodent.[63]

Another indication that radio's propaganda effort was good not only for the country but also for business was the unanimous approval and numerous accolades received by the officials in charge of the Network Allocation Plan. Only two weeks after the plan was initiated, as one leading advertiser stated, this "splendidly coordinated job" had calmed the field and put the medium on the right course. Harry Dwight Smith of the U.S. Tobacco Company concurred, saying he had "only praise and commendation for the way in which the plan has been worked out."[64] Indeed, the Network Allocation Plan was to stay for the duration. Even on the occasion of its two-year anniversary in 1944, advertisers recalled how they had welcomed the plan in 1942 as a "relief from [the] confusing and conflicting method of spotting messages as requested by many and various government agencies" and judged its success as "highly satisfactory."[65]

But comedies and nighttime radio were only two of the areas that did their part during the war. Writers and entertainers in daytime radio were just as eager as their evening colleagues to demonstrate their importance to the war effort. Indeed, the Network Allocation Plan was implemented in the daytime programs as well. Yet unlike the OWI's easy relationship with the comedians and their writers, its cooperation with daytime serials was more tenuous, and it created significant controversy.

CHAPTER 6

"Twenty Million Women
Can't Be Wrong"

Wartime Soap Operas

When the United States entered the war in December 1941, daytime radio was dominated by soap operas: between 9:00 A.M. and 6:00 P.M., 75 percent of broadcasting consisted of serial drama. The listeners had a choice of sixty-two serials, fifty-six of which ran in the usual fifteen-minute, five-times-a-week format. Every day these programs attracted an overwhelmingly female audience of approximately twenty million listeners, the vast majority of whom were housewives. One-third of total radio revenue in the early 1940s came from the sponsors of daytime serials, and because most sponsors advertised household or cleaning articles, these programs acquired the label "soap operas." In the early months of 1942, this programming, like other forms of cultural expression, faced the litmus test of wartime America: How does it help win the war?[1]

The person who brought this question to the forefront of public awareness in the early stage of the war was Louis Berg, a New York psychiatrist and prolific fiction writer. In March 1942, he warned the Buffalo Advertising Club that listening to soap operas not only caused mild physical symptoms such as increased blood pressure and profuse perspiration but also could lead to serious psychosomatic illnesses such as "nocturnal frights, vertigo, and gastro-intestinal disturbances." Berg published two pamphlets, one of which was ominously entitled "Radio and Civilian Morale." As he preached in this brochure, working himself into an emotional frenzy all of his own making, listening to soap operas could have truly frightening emotional consequences: "What if the line between fantasy and fact is obliterated and what appears as escape becomes a retreat, a flight of the neurotic, a frantic, backward parade of the emotionally damned?"[2]

Berg's broad incrimination of soap operas was based on very flimsy evidence: he had merely administered a blood pressure test to his assistant and himself before and after listening to two daytime serials. That his reports nevertheless ignited a major debate involving professionals and cultural critics from various walks of life was due mainly to the United States' inadequate and inefficient preparation for war. Soap operas, as their critics claimed, were partially responsible for this lack of will and determination.[3]

Radio network executives immediately took up the challenge and hired their own team of medical researchers, headed by Morris Fischbein, editor of the *Journal of the American Medical Association,* to study the effects of listening to serials. These researchers agreed that daytime serials could use improvement, yet they disagreed with Berg's damning conclusions. In fact, they believed that these serials could provide comfort and help to their listeners and generally presented ethically acceptable solutions to human problems.[4]

This episode as a whole is both intriguing and instructive. It fed into the notion that radio shows had a direct, immediate effect on their listeners, reinforcing the "hypodermic needle theory," which was being disproved in the field of communication studies at the time. Moreover, it clothed in medical language what cultural critics had been saying for years and would repeat for decades, that is, that this kitsch could not possibly have any positive effects. Yet these critics believed that the serials wielded a strong influence upon their listening audiences, which was why some of them hoped to turn the programs into a positive influence that would help America win the war.

This chapter focuses largely on the serials of Irna Phillips, one of the most prolific and successful serial writers from the early 1930s until her death in 1973.[5] During the period of World War II, she had between three and five serials on the air. An analysis of Phillips's wartime shows in conjunction with her papers and correspondence allows a unique glimpse behind the scenes of soap opera writing and production during these years. It also addresses some of the key charges raised by critics of the genre: How realistic were the shows? How did writers and producers respond to changes in the external environment, in this case, the relatively sudden change from a peacetime to a wartime society? And, finally, how would these programs address some of the highly controversial topics of the war years, especially the concerted propaganda campaign to entice women into the workforce and the related shifts in traditional gender ideology that this entailed?

Wartime Soap Operas

By the time the United States entered World War II, radio daytime serials had been on the air for about ten years. It is difficult to pinpoint the beginning of daytime serial drama or to identify one person who originated it. In the early 1930s, the idea was in the air, so to speak, spurred by two developments: the radio industry was trying to duplicate the unprecedented success of the nighttime serial *Amos 'n' Andy,* and radio executives and sponsors were starting to realize the potential selling power of daytime radio.

Irna Phillips came to radio in 1930. For the previous five years, she had been a schoolteacher in Dayton, Ohio, yet had filled in at WMAQ of Chicago during her vacations. In 1930, she was hired as an actress by WGN of Chicago, occasionally writing sketches and small pieces as well. The station manager soon discovered that she had a knack for writing, and that same year Phillips was commissioned to write a serial drama, *Painted Dreams,* a story about Mother Moynihan and her grown children. *Painted Dreams* did not take hold with the audience, however, and was discontinued after the first season.[6] In 1933, Phillips introduced her first successful serial, *Today's Children.* Only a slight variation on *Painted Dreams, Today's Children* centered on Mother Moran, who raised a family without her husband. The story was a tribute to Phillips's mother, who, after the death of her husband, had brought up ten children; Irna was the youngest. Phillips's parents had immigrated to the United States from eastern Europe and settled in Chicago, where they operated a small grocery shop in a Jewish neighborhood. Her deeply personal feelings about the show became evident in 1938, when, in an unprecedented move, she pulled the successful serial off the air because her mother had died a few months earlier.[7]

In 1937, she started two other daytime dramas: *The Guiding Light* and *Road of Life.* The former followed the life of nonsectarian minister Dr. John Ruthledge and his community in the small town of Five Points; *Road of Life,* the first soap opera set in a hospital, presented the story of surgeon Dr. Jim Brent. Following up on this success, Phillips premiered *Woman in White* in 1939, another hospital plot, this time from the perspective of nurse Karen Adams. Finally, also in 1939, she started one additional serial, *The Right to Happiness,* a spin-off from *The Guiding Light,* which centered largely on the many marriages of Carolyn Allen, the daughter of a magazine editor.[8] Phillips was one of the few writers who dominated the daytime serial genre in the early 1940s. The most prolific writers in this small group were Frank and Anne Hummert, who daily put between ten and twelve serials on the air during the war years. Elaine Carrington wrote three, and Phillips generally had four on the air simultaneously. Phillips's approximate yearly income in the early 1940s was $250,000, and her serials frequently emerged as trendsetters in the field, emulated by other serial writers.[9]

Irna Phillips's participation in the early war effort was probably typical for the soap opera genre. As early as July 1941, Phillips incorporated plugs for defense bonds in her programs. By late December 1941, one of her characters, a physician, had been called to serve his country, and another, Jim Brent of *The Road of Life,* planned to enlist as soon as possible. Conveniently, Brent, a central character of the show, was rejected by the draft board and ended up serving the "Home Defense Program." From early on, Phillips also used every possible opportunity to emphasize that "all races and creeds can live as neighbors" in melting-pot communities like Five Points of *The Guiding Light.*[10]

In a letter to an advertising executive a few days after the attack on Pearl Harbor, Phillips summarized her immediate response to the outbreak of the war and its impact on her serial writing. She emphasized that the wartime changes would be incorporated into the programs, yet not to the extent that they would override everything else:

I know and you know and millions of other people know that we are faced with a very grave situation—that living and life for years to come are going to be difficult at best. Ideals will be smashed to hell—homes will be broken up—casualties will be listed; but each one of us is still a human being. . . .

We still have our own little world—if we didn't, God help us. Life goes on in one way or another. We make our adjustments, we still have our petty little hatreds and jealousies—we still have our ambitions—we must know some moments of happiness. . . .

The characters in our serial stories of course must be aware of what's going on—must attempt to do their bit to help; but their lives must go on—their problems still exist, still must be met and possibly solved. What seems petty to you might be very important to me.[11]

In the immediate months after America's entry into the war, this general point was widely accepted: daytime serials would expand their plots to incorporate war themes and the changes that everyday people

TABLE 2. Irna Phillips' Daytime Serials during World War II

The Guiding Light (January 25, 1937; aside from a three-month interruption in 1941–42, it ran under Phillips's supervision until her death in 1973): Until the late 1940s, followed the ministry of John Ruthledge and his nonsectarian congregation in the small, melting-pot town of Five Points.

The Road Of Life (September 13, 1937; sold in 1943): Focused on the private and professional life of Dr. Jim Brent, surgeon at City Hospital.

Woman in White (January 3, 1938; discontinued in 1942; returned with a new cast in 1944): Centered on life and career of nurse Karen Adams. After 1944, the main character was Eileen Holmes.

The Right to Happiness (October 16, 1939; sold in late 1942): Revolved around the married life of Carolyn Allen.

Lonely Women (June 29, 1942–December 1943): Portrayed the life of a number of single women, who lived in The Towers hotel in New York.

(New) Today's Children (December 13, 1943–50; developed from *Lonely Women*): Story about Mama and Papa Schultz and their children, Marilyn (Maggie), Bertha, Elizabeth, and Otto. Marilyn, one of the lonely women in The Towers, provided the bridge between the two serials.

encountered. As George A. Wiley has argued, most of the serials applied a "khaki tint to the dramatic structure."[12]

Soon the problems facing soap opera characters replicated or even anticipated those facing many American households. When the War Advertising Council submitted a report on the integration of war themes in soap operas to the Office of Facts and Figures in early March 1942, the OFF was largely satisfied with the results thus far. Even before the inauguration of the Network Allocation Plan one month later, most of the nine serials the WAC had monitored had incorporated war-related changes. Phillips's *Road of Life* was mentioned as one of the favorable examples. The show's central character, Dr. Jim Brent, was on call for the Medical Corps as part of the Home Defense Program. The characters frequently referred to buying defense bonds or mentioned other characters who had already enlisted in the armed forces. Moreover, women in the show knitted sweaters for soldiers, prepared gift boxes, and emphasized the sacrifices everybody had to make to win the war. In another soap opera by the Hummerts, *Young Dr. Malone,* the central character was sent to England, underscoring Anglo-American friendship and affinity. While he cared for the wounded members of the armed forces abroad, his wife, Ann Malone, became involved in war work on the American home front.[13]

The WAC report stressed one of the most important adjustments made to the soap opera plots. Expendable male characters joined the armed forces, their memories kept alive by the concerns expressed by mothers, wives, and girlfriends they had left behind. Off in Europe or the Pacific, they participated in the major campaigns of the war, providing an easy bridge for continuous updates on the actual fighting. They would be missing in action and, occasionally, die in battle. Central male characters, on the other hand, usually did not fight in the war. Some, like Superman, would fail the physical exams. (Superman had peered through a wall and mistakenly read the eye charts in the next room, thus failing his exam.) No matter what the reason, the circumstances of every male character of draft age had to be explained to listeners.

When the OWI's Bureau of Intelligence checked up on radio soap operas over a period of three months from June to August 1942, after the initiation of the NAP, its report noted only one serial out of a total of thirty-six that had made no mention of the war during this time. The researchers reported that 90 percent of the serials monitored (fifteen shows on CBS and twenty-one on NBC) had scheduled their messages for broadcast once per week, following the recommendations of the NAP. Notably, 60 percent of the daytime serials provided additional time for war plugs above and beyond the amount allocated.

The authors of the OWI report noted with satisfaction that a number of soap operas furthered their listeners' understanding of the nature of the enemy and the Allies' fighting objectives by dealing with such issues as the Nazi invasion of Denmark, the forced deportation of French labor to the Reich, and life in a Nazi concentration camp. The daytime serials also provided an invaluable contribution to the war effort through their portrayal of home-front issues such as rationing, conservation, and salvage. The OWI report praised shows in which the war dominated the lives of the characters. In *Pepper Young's Family,* for example, seventeen-year-old Pepper Young's desire to enlist provided the basis for a long-lasting argument between his father, who objected to Pepper's enlistment, and his pregnant stepmother, who favored it because "it would help make the world safe for her unborn child." When Pepper finally enlisted, he was turned down because of "an athletic heart" and instead went to work in his father's war factory. His sister, whose fiancé had been reported missing in action, soon joined him. OWI officials liked the show because the war theme completely dominated the plot. Moreover, it dispelled women's fears about war work by describing the smooth integration of Pepper's sister into the workplace.

The OWI researchers praised shows like *Stella Dallas,* in which the central character used simple, everyday terms to explain the Four Freedoms to a friend in the munitions plant where she worked: "Why, you know what those Four Freedoms are? Just little things like whether you're gonna eat today or you ain't gonna eat, whether you're gonna go to church Sunday or you ain't gonna go 'cause the Nazis say you can't go."[14]

Overall, OWI officials and daytime serial writers thus saw eye to eye. Yet the collaboration hit its first snag in the fall of 1942 in connection with a special weeklong propaganda fair suggested by the OWI. In the so-called Victory Parade of daytime serials, each serial would present a complete story during a single week to highlight one of the key goals of the propaganda effort. As proposed, the story would "feature the principal characters from the regular serial, showing how these characters are coping with the problems the government wants the audience to know about."[15]

When Irna Phillips was informed about the OWI's plan by her advertising agency, her response was immediate and unequivocal: "Personally, I think it stinks. It just doesn't make sense. . . . Whoever got up this new idea for using the daytime serials should know a little more about daytime serials, and you can tell that to Bill Lewis of the OWI for me." She proposed that rather than follow the OWI plan, she would prefer to have each of the main characters in her four shows then on the air take up one of the proposed topics. Yet the OWI was not asking for proposals; it went ahead with its Victory Parade for daytime serials in October 1942, and Phillips had to go along.[16]

Anybody familiar with soap operas would agree with Phillips that the Victory Parade was a ludicrous plan. It was anomalous to daytime serial writing in a number of important ways. For one, soap operas are not completed stories. The lack of ultimate closure is one of the defining elements of soap opera writing. Certainly subplots are resolved, but never within the span of a week. Usually this takes weeks or even months, and most often it turns out to be a temporary rather than a final closure. In addition, soap opera characters cannot be lifted out of their natural environments, so to speak, without losing the very essence of what they stand for. They are defined by their role in their families or communities. Like many of their listeners, they have long histories and long memories of both painful and joyful relationships.[17] This scuffle over the Victory Parade was only the first of a number of instances to demonstrate that the largely male staff of the OWI viewed the soaps as clearly inferior to the evening programs. Throughout the war, they asserted their government-backed authority much more vigorously during the daytime than they would have dared to do in connection with the prime-time shows.[18]

Among the sore spots for the OWI were the daytime serials that did not mention the war at all or referred to it only in passing (approximately one out of ten programs). While the researchers in the OWI would have liked to believe otherwise, it was much more risky for a serial to *completely* focus attention on the war than to go to the other extreme and largely ignore it. Sandra Michael's serial, *Against the Storm,* was unusual because it focused almost exclusively on the war in Europe ever since the German invasion of Poland. The plots revolved around Professor Allen and his family. Allen taught at fictional Harper University on the East Coast and proved to be a staunch opponent of Hitler. Professional media critics loved the program, but listeners were only lukewarm about it. Half a year after winning the Peabody Award for radio drama in 1942, the first and only time such an honor was bestowed upon a daytime serial, the show went off the air because of low ratings and waning listener interest.[19]

On the other hand, serials that largely ignored wartime issues could do well in the daytime market. One such show was Phillips's *The Right to Happiness*. To be sure, even before the bombing of Pearl Harbor, Phillips included plugs for defense bonds in the show, and she continued to do so throughout 1942. Yet throughout that year, the program's plot centered on the marital problems of Carolyn Allen. Pearl Harbor would find Carolyn in continual emotional agony, tortured by her self-centered ex-husband, Bill Walker, who was trying to destroy her newfound happiness with her second husband, Dwight Kramer. By the spring of 1942, Carolyn ended up in prison for having murdered her first husband in what she claimed was an accident. While in prison, she conceived the son of her second husband. By the beginning of the new season in September 1942, the Kramers were in strife over the custody of their son, which temporarily ended with Dwight leaving Carolyn and taking their son, to be raised by his parents. By December 1942, Carolyn's innocence was finally proven, and she won the custody battle and was reunited with her child.

Obviously, as with the comedy programs, escape remained one of the reasons for tuning in to serials. Yet during the early 1940s, daytime serials that largely ignored the war remained the exception rather than the rule. The overwhelming majority of programs squarely addressed the social issues of these years. Moreover, serial writers continued their cooperation with the OWI for the duration by providing fast means of communication with vast, largely female audiences, informing them of their part in the war effort, both through straight messages and through dramatic incorporation of war themes. Yet this collaboration was not always a smooth one, as the episode of the Victory Parade indicated. And no single issue would eventually strain it more than the government campaign of recruiting women and mothers as war workers.

The Womanpower Campaign

When the womanpower campaign got under way in September 1942, a number of soap operas supported the change in policy—at least on the surface. As an OWI report showed, a number of central and secondary soap opera characters had already taken jobs in the defense factories by this time. Stella Dallas had signed up for work in a war factory and, aside from working her shifts, continued to expend her motherly ministrations to fellow workers. In *Bachelor's Children* a woman physician replaced a male colleague after he was called for active duty. The heroine of *Joyce Jordan,* a doctor in a Washington hospital before the war, suffered a major blow when her husband, a war correspondent, was killed in the Far East.[20]

Many of these adjustments were very much in line with accepted standards of soap operas because single women had been portrayed as professionals—as nurses, doctors, or magazine editors—long before the war. It is important to realize that although the serials were listened to primarily by women who worked in their homes, they went well beyond the mere reflection of the lives of housewives. Yet the new emphasis of the OWI womanpower campaign hit a sensitive nerve with many soap opera listeners. The general wisdom in these shows was that mothers cared for their children when they were young. To propose otherwise, as the OWI policy requested, suggested a drastic break with accepted, traditional gender ideology—an ideology that remained one of the mainstays of wartime serial writing.

Following OWI instructions almost to a word, Phillips introduced the issue of women workers into one of her shows, *The Guiding Light,* in early October 1942. In the program, Dr. Ruthledge, the minister of the community of Five Points, approached a successful artist, Ellis Smith, to ask him to help build an urgently needed day care facility for the children of working women. Ruthledge described the great need for more child care facilities, since so many women were needed in the factories. The critical issue, as the minister elaborated further, was that mothers with small children would be needed as well. It was at this point that Smith, although not always a model of moral rectitude on the show, voiced his reservations about this new policy:

> *Dr. R.:* And from present indications a great many more will be needed. . . . The children of these mothers who have taken jobs must be looked after.
>
> *Ellis:* Wait a minute. Let me get this straight. How old are these children?
>
> *Dr. R.:* Anywhere from two years old on up.
>
> *Ellis:* But why should it be necessary for anyone to leave their children? Certainly there are enough unmarried women—girls—enough women without children. Those with children ought to stay at home. That's their first duty.
>
> *Dr. R.:* It might look that way, but let me explain. In the first place, there actually aren't enough women to fill our war requirements without calling on everybody who's able and willing. In the second place, there's the economic consideration. A great many of these mothers must work in order to support their children. . . .
>
> *Ellis:* But Dr. Ruthledge, you can't deprive young children of their mother's care.
>
> *Dr. R.:* I won't say that I'm entirely in favor of it. . . . But if we can enlist the proper people—if we can assure the mothers that their children will have the right kind of supervision, we'll be doing a great service.[21]

Soap operas thus collaborated with the OWI in disseminating the new policy. For a majority of housewives and soap opera listeners, this was probably the most unsettling policy supported by the government during the war years. As Maureen Honey has rightly argued, even though the OWI assumed that the change was only temporary, it reversed the traditional notion that the employed, married woman was an aberration. Now, instead, the housewife and homemaker had to explain herself: "The woman who did not enter the labor force had to assume the burden of proof that what she was doing was socially useful."[22]

It was in this context that a new show originated by Phillips in early July 1942 took on specific meaning. *Lonely Women* portrayed the lives of a number of young women who had come to the city in pursuit of work. They had left behind parents and families (interestingly enough, none of them seemed to have any hometown friends) and come to live in The Towers, an elegant women's hotel in midtown Manhattan. The central character was Marilyn Larimore, a beautiful and successful model. In time, listeners would discover that Marilyn Larimore was actually Maggie Schulz, daughter of the lower-class Schulzes.

Read in the context of the OWI womanpower campaign, which significantly increased the pressure on women to leave their homes for the workplace, this serial provided a powerful antidote to the official government propaganda. Hand in hand with the new economic opportunities went a new cultural image and reality: women out on the town, enjoying their newfound economic and personal freedom. What Phillips was telling her audience in these tumultuous and unsettling months, however, was that their lives as housewives and homemakers were at least as essential to the war effort as those of working women—and certainly more happy and fulfilled.[23]

Phillips left no doubt about the thrust of her story. In the lead-in to the very first program, broadcast on July 2, 1942, the narrator clearly spelled out the premise of the serial:

This story of ours is one to make you cease to envy glamour girls—or career women whom you might imagine only as excitingly in touch with the outside world—where things are going on—where things are happening. You'll come to see that you who feel that yours is the hum-drum existence—you who only rear a family—who prepare three meals a day—who sit at home and wait for husband and children—you are the lucky one! You're the one who eats the meat of life—you grasp the things that make the world go 'round! Oh yes, we grant there is a glamorous side—but so is there the frosting on a cake. And yet we must get down to what's inside![24]

Phillips gradually uncovered the miserable lives of the women in The Towers, all of whom were running away, or hiding some secret, or unhappily in love with an ambitious man unwilling to commit to marriage. The listeners met Jean Evans, a salesgirl, who had been fired from her job because she had dated one of the floor men. She had been reported to her boss by another salesgirl, who had her eyes on the same man. To make matters worse, her family asked her to repay a loan they had given her because they desperately needed the money. All that Jean really wanted, the listener learned as the story continued, was to marry and be taken care of, to have a house and family. Yet the best she could do was find work with a couple of architects, where the model penthouse in which they and Jean worked became her "real imitation home."

Then there was "Fairlee," Mrs. Alfred J. Jones, divorced and living on alimony. She was the quintessential busybody, the channel through whom all hotel gossip flowed. Another central character was Mary Collins, the hotel's middle-aged manager, who made The Towers her permanent home. More important, she was the woman behind the telephone switchboard—as Phillips envisioned it, the "secret ear of the hotel." And because the telephone was the lifeline of the characters living in the hotel, Collins held the keys to all these lives.[25]

Most of the women at The Towers had had an unhappy and frustrating love affair. One of the best-developed relationships in the early shows was that between Judith Clark and George Bartlett. At first this relationship was presented as a healthy, long-lasting love affair that would eventually end in marriage. Yet over the weeks listeners learned that all was not well between Judith and George. Judith had increasing doubts about George's love and sincerity and, in an episode that brought this subplot to a climax, discovered that George's ambition superseded any love he had for her:

> *George:* The other night you tried to force an issue. You might just as well have said: "Either we get married or we stop seeing each other." [Pause] If that's the way you want it, there's nothing I can do.
>
> *Judy:* Nothing you can do?
>
> *George:* Except let it go at that.
>
> *Judy:* I see. [Pause] Is that the way you want it too?
>
> *George:* I want nothing more than—than for us to go on as we have in the past.
>
> *Judy:* You leave very little for me to say.
>
> *George:* But I won't ask you to—to go on—and have you feel that I'm being unfair to you. . . . My work—the legal profession—and the future that's beginning to open up for me in politics—well, it's my whole life.
>
> *Judy:* It's what you want more than anything else?
>
> *George:* Yes.
>
> *Judy:* And—marriage doesn't enter into the picture?
>
> *George:* Not at present.
>
> *Judy:* But not ever, George? [Pause] [Very low] Not ever?
>
> *George:* Who can say? I don't know.[26]

On the surface the women in The Towers lived the life that most housewives and mothers dreamed of. They had few responsibilities, worked their jobs, had time and money to spare, and lived in one of the most exciting cities imaginable, right in downtown Manhattan. Yet their lives were miserable, reclusive, and lonely.

To be sure, none of the women living in The Towers worked in the defense industry. The image of Rosie the Riveter was the one that most directly challenged accepted gender ideology, but most of the six million additional women who went to work during the war actually entered clerical positions—what more recently have become known as "pink-color" jobs.[27] Many of Phillips's "girls" in The Towers would have easily fit this description.

In none of her shows in late 1942 and early 1943 did Phillips directly challenge established OWI policies. Rather, she had to camouflage her "counterpropaganda" in order not to be censored. What makes such an interpretation persuasive were the problems she encountered in late 1943, when her show took aim at the women defense workers themselves and the official OWI propaganda line. This turn of events was introduced in November 1943 while the show *Lonely Women* was undergoing a major overhaul. Starting on December 13, 1943, it was broadcast as *Today's Children*. This shift had been prepared throughout the fall, as the show's emphasis turned increasingly to the Schulz family: Mama and Papa Schulz, their three daughters—Elizabeth (the defense worker), Maggie, and Bertha—and son, Otto, who had joined the army. The bridge between the plots of the two shows was provided by the double life of Maggie Schulz, also known as Marilyn Larimore, the beautiful model of *Lonely Women*. As a matter of fact, for the time being she still kept her room at The Towers as well as her profession, yet she now spent most of her time at home with her family.

To understand the show's presentation of Elizabeth, the sister who was working in a defense plant, it is necessary to understand the circumstances within the Schulz household. Elizabeth was actually Elizabeth Austin, married to Frank Austin, who was off in Alaska helping to build the Alaska highway. They had two children, Danny and Bess, aged six and eight. Because of the wartime housing shortage, Elizabeth and her children had moved in with her parents, and despite their objections, she had taken a defense job, leaving her children with her mother during the day. Maggie (alias Marilyn Larimore) was still on call with a modeling agency, and Bertha, who had been helping out at home, was scheduled to start her new job as a salesgirl at a fancy store in a few days. It was in this context that Phillips first introduced Elizabeth to her listeners, in a conversation between Maggie and Bertha. They were in the kitchen, doing the dishes, before the family gathered to discuss some important matters.

> *Bertha:* Maggie, I still don't see what we're going to do about Mama. I'll be gone all day—and you'll be on call at the agency.
>
> *Maggie:* Well, it looks like Elizabeth will have to stay home.
>
> *Bertha:* You know she won't do that.
>
> *Elizabeth:* [Calling] Hey, Bertie—aren't you two nearly finished?
>
> *Maggie:* [Down] Speaking of . . .
>
> *Elizabeth:* Maggie, come on—we're waiting for you.
>
> *Maggie:* Be with you in a minute, Liz—we're almost through.
>
> *Elizabeth:* Mom says to leave the dishes—she'll do them later.
>
> *Bertha:* [Up] All right, we'll be there. [Down] I notice she didn't offer to help.
>
> *Maggie:* Yeah, she's always "just changed her polish." Somebody ought to give that young lady a good spanking.[28]

Elizabeth, as listeners quickly surmised, was a rather egoistic woman, who enjoyed her job and especially the money she made. She also was determined to keep it—even at the expense of neglecting her children and overburdening her mother. Yet she knew how to turn the right phrases. Listeners encountered her again on November 23, a day before Thanksgiving. Elizabeth had taken a day off—to do some shopping for herself—when her mother had her sit down to talk things over.

> *Elizabeth:* I know what you're leading up to, Mom—and I'm not going to give up my job—no matter what you . . .
>
> *Mama Schulz:* Look, liebling, I ain't scolding you. I don't blame you for wanting to make a little money.
>
> *Elizabeth:* It's not only that—it's—well—Mom, it may not be much but I feel as if I were doing my bit, helping out with the war.
>
> *Mama S.:* . . . I ain't able no more to run the house, cook for seven— and look after your kids.
>
> *Elizabeth:* But, Mom, they mind so well. They're not really any trouble.
>
> *Mama S.:* No! You stay home one week, Elizabeth, and see . . .
>
> *Elizabeth:* You don't just give up a defense job, Mom. I—I'd feel like a slacker if I sat home—when I know how much they need workers.

Mama S.:   Danny and Bess need you too, liebling. Ain't there plenty of single girls who can do your job? It don't seem right to me— married women leaving their homes and kids for someone else to look after.[29]

The first thing that is remarkable about the show as a whole, unrelated to the womanpower campaign, is that the main characters are a German-American family and that the dialogue even included German words such as *Liebling*. This is a telling reminder of the different attitudes Americans harbored toward their respective enemies. It is hard to imagine a serial focusing on the Japanese-American Kaizuka family from 1943 through the end of the war. Yet neither listeners, the networks, nor the OWI objected to Phillips's choice, and the serial ran right through D-Day and the Battle of the Bulge and past the end of World War II. When one listener finally objected in a letter to her choice of setting in July 1945—after photographs and films from the liberated concentration camps had been widely disseminated in the United States—Phillips responded that her show served a didactic purpose: "We think it is important to remind them [Americans critical of Germans and, by association, German Americans] through our radio dramas that our enemy is not German blood but the philosophical and political traditions which have dominated German educational and social institutions for more than a century." In short, it was not the Germans who were to blame, and the overwhelming majority of her listeners seemed to agree.[30]

The other striking feature of *Today's Children* is its unequivocally negative portrayal of Elizabeth's defense work. Part of a soap writer's acumen was to anticipate changes as much as to reflect new developments, yet on this issue Phillips—as she soon discovered—had pressed too far ahead. A number of listeners balked at this negative portrayal of working women. As Mildred Olbenburg from Bozeman, Montana, asked rhetorically in a letter to General Mills, the sponsor of Phillips's show: "Are we to infer that all women who are spending their days at hard, dirty factory work are impelled purely by selfish motives instead of honest patriotism?" She added, referring to the work done by Elizabeth's sister Bertha: "Oddly enough, in the very next breath, Bertha talks of getting a very genteel job of selling high-priced dresses in an ultra-fashionable shop. In other words, it is perfectly all right for women wealthy enough not to have to work in dirty defense plants to buy clothes."[31]

Criticism also came from the OWI and NBC, as indicated in letters from Phillips's advertising agency and her agent. The agency reminded Phillips that the womanpower shortage was the number one problem facing the war effort and sent along official OWI guidelines on the issue. Phillips's agent, Carl Wester, was more explicit in his letter, telling Phillips that General Mills was nervous about challenging an important government policy and indicating that there were real reasons to be cautious: "NBC has called us about the Austin story, so if we want to keep peace with OWI, I guess we will have to be careful."[32]

Phillips got the message. She dropped this subplot from the script—at least for the time being. She returned to Elizabeth Austin's story almost a year later, in October 1944, when Frank Austin returned from his war-related work in Alaska. By this time, the OWI itself was winding down its womanpower mobilization, and advertisers across the country were voicing a new female obligation: planning for the return of the soldiers. As one Mobil Oil ad trumpeted, "Yes—your job is waiting for you, Soldier!" Yet, in Phillips's shows, Elizabeth was still not ready to retire to her former roles. Again, she employed all the standard patriotic reasons for staying on the job—pseudo-reasons, in her case—but her husband proved unbending. As he told his wife, "You've got to shoulder your own responsibilities, my dear—you've got to tend our home and take care of our children. That's something no one should have to do for you."[33]

Remembering the intervention by the OWI and NBC a year earlier, Phillips's advertising agency cautioned her to make some concessions or "the wrath to come might take the form of NBC, the OWI, or even General Mills." Phillips's liaison in the ad agency had done some investigations of her own and found that the womanpower situation was actually somewhat confused. While critical shortages still existed in some geographic regions of the United States, other regions actually had a surplus of workers. Phillips thus agreed to make a few revisions in the scripts to indicate that Elizabeth lived in a region with a labor surplus.[34] A few weeks later, the Austins moved out of the Schulzes' house to set up their own homestead. As the moving van pulled out of the driveway, Elizabeth's parents approvingly discussed their move, which ended this subplot:

Papa Schulz: Elizabeth is happy, Mama. Frank's back, the family's together—what woman that can call herself a wife and a mother wouldn't be happy?

Mama Schulz: That's just what I'm saying. . . .

> *Papa S.:* But you ain't forgetting, Mama, that Elizabeth worked for a
> long time while Frank was gone. Maybe she's going to be
> missing the working—maybe she's going to be—restless?
>
> *Mama S.:* No—no, Friedrich. She's got the two children—she's got the
> housework, the marketing, the meals to get, the P.T.A.'s to
> go to—a little Red Cross she's doing—she's got a man com-
> ing home to her every night for supper . . . Restless? Ach,
> such talk from men.[35]

The overall significance of Phillips's serial *Lonely Women* and the sequences in *Today's Children* involving Elizabeth Austin becomes clear
only if juxtaposed against the pressing need for women workers and the
high priority the OWI gave this campaign. From the fall of 1942 until
mid-1944, the OWI and some of the popular media produced a "heroine
of a new order," emphasizing that "housekeeping as usual ended in
America on the day of Pearl Harbor." The predominant motto of these
years was "One woman can shorten this war!" Consequently, any
woman who decided to stay home found herself on the defensive, needing to justify her choice to herself and to others.[36]

Phillips's advertising agency made it a point to relay every letter—by
listeners, the network, or the OWI—to her and usually discussed these
matters in ensuing correspondence. The fact that she received only one
letter of protest during the time that the Elizabeth subplot unfolded
suggests that her instincts were right. In these unnerving and unsettling
months, Phillips stuck with her audience, reaffirmed their values, self-
respect, and belief in a traditional gender ideology. She did so even at
the risk of being censored by the OWI and alienating her sponsors.
Phillips followed her own agenda and addressed social issues from her
vantage point rather than the propaganda directives of the OWI. While
the OWI did prevent Elizabeth's return to the home in 1943, it could
not change the basic assumptions of the genre or the eventual resolution
of this subplot along accepted lines.

Phillips dealt with the womanpower campaign through a narrative
device typical of soap operas: political issues are personalized by being
translated into questions of social morality. Conflicts are contained
within a family, community, or workplace setting, where this morality
can play itself out through personal relationships. Yet characters' personal traits do speak to larger social and political issues. Christine Geraghty has suggested that the question in soap operas is not so much
"What will happen next?" as "What kind of person is this?" People who
listened to *Today's Children* probably disliked Elizabeth Austin both for
the kind of person she represented and, by implication, for the (political)

choice she made.[37] Moreover, as Michele Hilmes has argued, the tension between marriage and a career, as well as between working outside the home and working as a stay-at-home mother, was one of the central struggles in soap opera writing prior to, during, and after the war. And despite multiple, and at times contradictory, narratives, the resolution of the plotline usually "reinforced women's essential domesticity and the idea that their appropriate function of power was within the sphere of home and family."[38]

But soap operas were just one of a number of cultural genres that worked against the portrayal of emancipated women. Radio comedy and Hollywood showed just as little interest in Rosie as did the soaps, and they actively undermined this part of the government propaganda.

Comedians quickly developed a new foil in response to the government propaganda of women in the workforce—especially women who took men's jobs. Mixing the traditions of burlesque and misogynist humor, one image in particular was much lampooned in the comedy routines: that of the woman welder, who was repeatedly caricatured as a mannish amazon. In one of his intimate spots with Frances Langford, Bob Hope was forced to admit that he had been seen in a compromising situation with one member of this species:

Frances: I'll bet these soldiers wouldn't like your type of girl friend . . . the last girl you went out with was a welder at Lockheed!

Hope: She was not!

Frances: Well . . . all I know is . . . when you kissed her, her bridgework fell out, and she riveted it back in.

Hope: Yeah, but she ruined her mustache doing it! . . . [39]

Hope was by no means alone in ridiculing the imagery of working women in traditionally male jobs. Jack Benny also made "Rosie" part of his show, as well as the target of his humor. In November 1942, just as the campaign to entice women into the workplace was getting under way, Benny introduced another of his girlfriends, Maureen Strudelhaven. She was a welder, but as usual Benny couldn't get to first base. In the first segment of the dialogue, Benny tried to explain to Mary Livingstone why they weren't sitting together in the theater: he had only *one* cigar. As the discussion continued, Benny very much tried to keep Maureen's occupation hidden from the rest of the cast. Once it was exposed, his amorous relationship was immediately lampooned in increasingly familiar fashion:

Jack: [picking up on the fact that they were in the movie theater] She's in pictures herself, you know.

Mary: She works in a shipyard.

Jack: She does not.

Mary: I wish I had a nickel for every rivet she's caught in her bucket.

Jack: All right, all right, it's patriotic for women to do work like that nowadays. . . . But she's a beautiful girl and very feminine.

Mary: Feminine? . . . She's got a rattlesnake tattooed on her right arm.

Jack: Well, if you look close, that rattlesnake has a rose in its mouth. . . . It's a two-color job. . . . I held her hand while she got the needle. . . . Anyway, that girl is crazy about me. . . . Did you see those novel cuff links she gave me for a present?

Mary: Novel is right, she bit 'em out of a lead pipe.[40]

Benny's portrayal of working women was part of an emerging routine: they were crude and manlike, boorish and unfeminine. As these shows intimated, this new notion of women was as absurd as the comedy routines themselves. Benny went even further in the show the very next week, when he picked up the theme of the working woman, yet with a slight variation. Now he was the henpecked husband of a working wife in what can only be described as a screwball comedy. As Margaret McFadden has shown, nobody was as precariously situated in the gendered world of radio comedy as Benny. Because of his effeminate and insecure stage persona, Benny could stretch gender boundaries farther than anybody else in the business.[41] In an episode of November 1942 that was built on this premise, listeners encountered Mr. and Mrs. Oglethorpe J. Twink. Benny is Mr. Twink, usually referred to as "Twinky," and the show opened with him anxiously awaiting the arrival of his dear working wife:

Jack: [a la housewife] Oh dear . . . [clicks tongue]. . . . Seven a.m. and Clarabelle isn't home yet. . . . It's payday too, I hope she didn't get into a crap game with some of the girls. . . . Oh well, she works hard and she's entitled to a little fun I guess.

[*Sound:* Knock on the door]

Jack: I wonder who that is. . . . Come in.

[*Sound:* Door opens]

Jack: Why, it's the ice girl. . . . Hello Gloria.

Gloria: Any ice today, Twinky?

Jack: Darn you, Gloria, for the third time today, *no* . . . . I'm a married man.

Gloria: Oh come on, don't you want a cake of ice, sweetie?

Jack: No and take your foot out of the door . . . . If my wife finds you here, Heaven knows what will happen. . . . Now scram.

Gloria: Okay cutie, see you tomorrow.

Next Jack had to get their twin children changed. Finally, Clarabelle arrived, and he nagged her for being late. Not ready to eat breakfast, she first demanded a kiss, and after a little scuffle, Benny complained: "Oh darn it. . . . Don't be so rough, Clarabelle. . . . You broke the clasp on my slave bracelet. . . . Look!" After Mr. Twink and Clarabelle finally sat down for breakfast, Gloria returned, looking for her ice tongs. Since she addressed Benny as "Twinky," Clarabelle suspected that the two of them had an affair and let Twinky have it: "Clarabelle . . . put me down . . . Clarabelle . . . ouch, ouch."[42]

This show is open to a wide variety of readings, but clearly the inverted gender roles of Twinky and Clarabelle lampooned the very notion of working women. It is also interesting that neither Benny's nor Hope's show was censored. Benny was even allowed to do a sequel at the very height of the first concerted womanpower campaign. If anything remotely similar had occurred in Phillips's soaps, the officials of the OWI most certainly would have come down hard on her. This double standard applied throughout the war.

Elaine Tyler May has suggested that Hollywood also only paid lip service to the womanpower campaign. Films of the 1940s did not portray the imagery of Rosie in any significant way; instead, they actually turned back the clock as far as women's equality was concerned. In the 1930s, Hollywood had featured brash, autonomous, and sexually liberated actresses and screen characters. But in a complete turnaround from that decade, the movie industry during the early 1940s applauded women who gave up their careers to become mothers and housewives. Also, in contrast to their well-publicized independent and daring lifestyles of the 1930s, during the war female film stars "were suddenly featured in popular magazines chiefly as wives and mothers." Finally, as in the country at large, marriage and birth rates were on the rise in Hollywood as well, leading to one of the most curious phenomena in the midst of this tumultuous war. As Tyler May has charged, "By 1943, babies had taken center stage." The sex symbols of the 1930s, like Lana Turner and Joan Crawford, were featured as doting mothers in the popular magazines of the war years. And Betty Grable pinups, which were already popular and hard to obtain in 1942, became even more popular *after* she married Harry James in 1943 and had a child later that year.[43]

Radio soap operas were thus no exception. More accurately, they were part of the dominant and expanding trend, especially in the later war years. Yet, I do not want to leave the impression that wartime soap operas were simply one-dimensional stories in defense of this traditional gender ideology. Similarly, it would be a mistake to characterize the genre as conservative or even reactionary. Soap operas, including Phillips's serials, represented a highly varied genre. In many respects, Phillips probably brought more personal commitment to presenting a wide variety of women's experiences than other writers because her own life was very nontraditional. Phillips never married and never bore a child. She did, however, adopt two children, the first one in 1942 when she was forty-two, the second a year and a half later, and raised them on her own.[44] Phillips repeatedly introduced the issues of illegitimacy, adoption, and single motherhood into her shows, especially into her favorite serial, *The Guiding Light*. She was proud of the fact that she created the first illegitimate child of radio in 1941, the product of an adulterous relationship between Rose Kransky and a married man, Charles Cunningham, of *The Guiding Light*. Two years later, after Phillips adopted her first child, she introduced another single mother, Clare Marshall, into the same show. Clare adopted the child of a broken-up marriage between a serviceman and a neighborhood woman.[45]

Even though these issues were to become standard fare in daytime serials in the 1940s, Phillips frequently had to defend her shows against critics who saw these plot developments as unsavory and immoral. Especially after America's entry into the war and after Louis Berg had ignited the great soap opera debate, serials had come under increased public scrutiny. In early March 1942, Phillips had to defend her serials *Road of Life* and *The Right to Happiness* against the criticism of Josephine Quirk, the associate editor of *The Catholic Boy*. Quirk's criticism reached Phillips via Procter and Gamble, which, like any sponsor, took seriously any criticism of shows connected with its name. From Phillips's response it was clear that Quirk had attacked the serials as morally licentious, specifically their portrayal of divorce, illicit love, and illegitimate children. As Phillips wrote in very conciliatory language:

We recognize, as does Miss Quirk, that divorce, illicit love [and] illegitimate children are facts of life, they exist. Perhaps we have been remiss, and I think we have, in not pointing up [*sic*], blue printing, that although they do exist, these things definitely violate every code of decency in human conduct and human relationships—they violate the fundamental beliefs of not only one Faith, but of all Faiths.

As Phillips continued to explain in her letter, Quirk could rest assured that none of this behavior would be condoned in her soap operas. As a matter of fact, for the thirteen years she had been in radio, Phillips had always faithfully abided by a philosophy she called "the Law of Compensation." Any character guilty of such a sin or transgression would ultimately be brought to justice. Or, as the opening lines to *The Guiding Light* announced, "All that we send into the lives of others comes back into our own."[46] Quirk's letter of protest is a reminder that Phillips and other serial writers had to perform a careful balancing act: satisfying their listeners but also avoiding criticism from the public and sponsors, as well as OWI censorship during the war. It also highlighted Phillips's savvy in deflecting protests and potential censorship.

During the war, soap operas provided the same satisfactions to their audiences as at other times. On the most basic level, they provided distraction and a break from routine schedules. One listener probably spoke for many when she explained, "They make time pass so pleasantly, you just forget that you're all alone in the house." When told about Dr. Berg's criticism of the serials, she responded, "Those professors! They never had a cranky baby to manage or the washing to do."[47] Moreover, as many contemporary listener surveys indicated, most women felt that they learned something by listening to serials: they received advice on how to handle other people, behave in refined society, resolve conflicts with their husbands and boyfriends, and bring up their children.[48] Finally, daytime serials satisfied listeners' curiosity about other women's lives, about the challenges facing professional women and the hardships of single mothers or divorced women. Serials provided vicarious participation through entertainment, plus the suspense of murder trials, the romance of intimate love relationships, or the jealousies and hatred between estranged or divorced partners.

None of this changed during World War II. Nor did the desire of serial listeners to have their own choices reaffirmed through the serial stories. Phillips made room for straight allocated messages and even incorporated some of the necessary changes into her subplots, like the establishment of a day care center in *The Guiding Light*. Yet in her central plots and through her main characters she continually challenged the

OWI womanpower drive and the implied break with traditional gender assumptions. The image and ideology of "Rosie the Riveter" might have been eagerly snapped up by a number of popular cultural genres, but soap operas wanted no part in it. Consequently, when the need for women workers decreased in 1944, Phillips did not have to do an about-face like other cultural creators. Instead, on issues such as juvenile delinquency and rehabilitation, which directly tied in with the "problem" of working mothers and women, she would ride the crest of the return to a traditional gender ideology, what Betty Friedan later termed the "feminine mystique."

Juvenile Delinquency and Veteran Rehabilitation

Short of directly attacking women who worked in the defense industry, as Phillips had done in *Today's Children*, a number of soap opera writers soon latched on to another issue that in the minds of many spoke directly to the question of working mothers: juvenile delinquency. Most commentators agreed that juvenile delinquency actually rose during World War II, but there was much less agreement on the main cause of such a development. Family mobility, the absence of many fathers, the lack of playgrounds and recreational activities, and the huge increase in the illegal employment of minors were all mentioned as contributing factors.[49]

Yet for the characters in Phillips's soap operas the case was clear-cut: more children got in trouble because parents, that is, mothers, worked and were not home to supervise them. At the same time that Phillips was asked to drop her negative portrayal of Elizabeth Austin in *Lonely Women* in late 1943, she was introducing the issue of juvenile delinquency in another of her shows, *The Guiding Light*. In mid-November 1943, King Painter of the Knox Reeves Advertising Agency congratulated her on the incorporation of the theme of juvenile delinquency: "We notice in a recent Guiding Light script that you are introducing the matter of child delinquency which, I think, is a swell idea—very timely." Painter informed Phillips that *Ma Perkins*—another daytime serial—was already dealing with the issue as well.[50]

Phillips integrated the topic very gradually into *The Guiding Light*. The story involved Wally Mason and Ralph Dickinson, two teenagers from the Five Point community. Wally was an orphan and was raised by his older sister; Ralph's father was in the military, and his mother was working in a beauty parlor. Wally and Ralph would soon be involved in a car theft ring that was being uncovered. The problem of juvenile delinquency was placed at the center of the show in early 1944, when Dr. Gaylord, the new pastor in town, criticized the increase in juvenile delinquency and related it to the large number of working mothers.

That Phillips was aiming at all working mothers, including those working in defense industries, became very apparent three days after Dr. Gaylord's sermon, when the pastor and his wife, Margaret, discussed the impact of his sermon:

> *Margaret:* You won't find it easy, my dear, to persuade them that you have only their welfare at heart. Not when the issue is one of money—of women giving up non-essential jobs to look after their children.
>
> *Dr. Gaylord:* I urged them only to weigh their need of money against their duties as parents. Many women who might well be contributing to the war programs, Margaret, are shirking their responsibilities. And many of those who are working are doing so for reasons of pure selfishness and might better be spending their time at home with their children. It's a question of adjustment—of a proper balance between the immediate objectives of the community—the country—and its future good and security.[51]

Dr. Gaylord and his wife need not have worried. As it turned out, many of the mothers in the show felt exactly as they did and soon started a successful community organization to battle juvenile delinquency. This community effort closely mirrored suggestions proposed by the American Legion. In fact, one show featured Emma Puschner, director of the National Welfare Division of the American Legion, as a guest of Dr. Gaylord. The show was turned into a straight question-and-answer debate, in which Puschner promoted community councils like the one in Five Points to stop or prevent juvenile delinquency. She emphasized that the crucial aspect of prevention was loving and caring parents and—by implication—mothers who stayed home with their children.[52]

Unfortunately, the community council of Five Points came too late for Wally Mason in *The Guiding Light*. In an effort to escape the police, he tried to jump a rolling train, slipped, and died under its wheels. Yet it was not too late for Ralph Dickinson (and others like him). In fact, nobody was more shaken by Wally's death than Ralph's mother, Elly

Dickinson, who quit her job. When she told her son about her decision, he was a different child almost immediately.

> *Ralph:* Well, don't think I like the way it's been. I don't like a dirty house anymore'n anyone else. But a guy gets used to it, if he has to. I just figured you wanted to work, and that was that. But if you don't want to—well, all right. I think it'd be fine. [Pause] [Wistfully] We could play some checkers in the evening, if you wanted to. Like we used to. . . .
>
> *Ralph:* Have you told Dad?
>
> *Elly:* Not yet.
>
> *Ralph:* Gee, I bet he'll be glad.
>
> *Elly:* Yes.
>
> *Ralph:* Mom?
>
> *Elly:* Yes.
>
> *Ralph:* Could I have Billy Williams come over tonight?
>
> *Elly:* Why—sure.
>
> *Ralph:* I was gonna go out, but—I got some homework to do, and if Billy and I could do it together—I mean, if you aren't too tired to have us around.[53]

To be sure, Ralph still had to face up to his participation in the car theft ring and extricate himself from his social ties connected with the gang activity. Yet, as Phillips emphasized, a mother's decision to stay at home was the initial and most decisive change that could save these boys. Phillips received an unusually large number of positive listener responses to this segment of her show. She was also honored with a special citation by the American Legion at its annual meeting in the fall of the same year.[54]

A final war-related issue, which was soon incorporated into a number of shows, concerned the consequences of reconversion—returning wartime America to a peacetime status—and especially the rehabilitation of returning veterans. Like the concern over juvenile delinquency, it highlighted the traditional image of women: returning veterans needed understanding, nurturing women to ease them back into civilian life. Moreover, in order for veterans to heal completely, both emotionally and physically, women had to relinquish their positions of increased authority—inside and outside of the home.

Again, Phillips was eager to get going on this issue late in 1943. While she was staying home sick late in November 1943, she screened daytime radio to see what the competition was doing. To her surprise, she discovered that at least one program, *Gallant Heart*, an NBC sustaining program, was "doing all the things that we weren't permitted to do—bringing wounded men back, disabled." In a letter to her advertising agent, Phillips went on to express her sincere interest in the issues awaiting postwar America: "The problems that are already casting their shadows on the postwar world are terrifying, and if we can present a few of them delicately and realistically, and of course constructively, we'll be doing a better job than buying another bomb for another bombshell."[55]

When, a month later, Phillips still had not received permission from the OWI to go ahead with her rehabilitation stories, she sent another angry letter to her advertising agency. "How about General Mills going to bat for us once in a while?" she wrote.

Their cooperation with OWI, NBC and Pillsbury is touching. . . . I'm going to write a long letter . . . to General Mills about the problems of rehabilitation and what the newspapers are giving forth—and I will want to know why we can't give forth on the air. Believe me, King [her advertising agent], they will say "no" to us and in two months' time policies will change, everybody else will have the edge on us, and where will we be? . . . Censored.[56]

Phillips was referring to the ratings war and the fact that soap opera writers had to anticipate the major issues months ahead of time. Like news agencies, which competed to be the first to break important political events, soap opera writers were eager to gain an edge over other shows by incorporating important issues as soon as possible. The fear of replication or of coming too late further increased the competition among the serials.

Phillips finally got the go-ahead on the rehabilitation issue in early 1944. Conveniently, she resurrected her show, *Woman in White,* which had been dropped in late 1942, and structured it around the private and professional life of a nurse, Eileen Holmes. The problem of veteran rehabilitation entered the plot in June 1944, when Bill Sommers, a marine who had fought for two years in the South Pacific, entered the Municipal Hospital. Bill had lost a leg in the fighting, and the story revolved around his coming to grips with his disability.

It turned out that caring, loving, and nurturing women would be the key to Bill's successful rehabilitation. The first one was Eileen Holmes herself, who through daily care and numerous talks with Bill helped him feel comfortable about his artificial leg and put his injury into perspective. Moreover, when Bill refused to inform either his family or his girlfriend, Alice Hendricks, about his hospitalization and his lost leg, Eileen secretly cabled Alice and encouraged her to visit Bill. In a cliff-hanging episode, Bill brusquely rejected Alice and told her there was someone else in his life.[57]

When Bill finally returned home, he continued his antagonistic behavior toward his friends, neighbors, and parents. He quickly told his parents that he would not stay long in his hometown; it had gotten too small for him, and he would like to try his luck in the city. Bill, as the listeners realized by now, was still hurting—especially emotionally. The conflict came to a head several weeks later when Alice told him that she would leave town because she could not endure seeing him yet not being with him. Finally, Bill broke down and confessed to Alice why he had been so hostile:

> *Bill:* Don't you see, darling? What was wrong with me physically was only a small part of the greater damage to my spirit, to my way of thinking. I pretended that I didn't even miss not having a leg, but deep down inside, I considered myself just half a man. . . . I had a warped outlook on life—afraid I'd be a burden on everyone and that people would pity me. I even thought you'd only marry me because you felt sorry for me.
>
> *[Music:* Sneak in "I'll Never Smile Again"]
>
> *Bill:* So I was determined you wouldn't be "tied down" for the rest of your life, and that you'd get over me and fall in love with someone else.
>
> *Alice:* Bill . . .
>
> *Bill:* I was afraid to face life with a handicap, and in that fear had doubted those I loved the most. Don't you see, darling, there never has been anyone but you—why, there never could be . . .
>
> *Alice:* Oh, Bill . . . [58]

Phillips stayed in close contact with the Radio Division of the OWI regarding the rehabilitation stories. In fact, she submitted her long-term plot outlines through NBC to the OWI prior to writing the daily shows. Both Phillips and her advertising agency attributed at least part of the success of the resurrected *Woman in White* to its integration of the rehabilitation stories. As King Painter wrote to Phillips, "After having gone through all the trouble of clearing the soldier rehabilitation story with OWI and NBC, I am sure you are happy as I am to see it paying off so well on the air."[59]

The men who had been sent off to fight the war in Europe and the Pacific started to return home in the soap opera plots in increasing numbers late in 1944. By mid-1945, their numbers would be legion. *The Guiding Light* saw the return of Jacob Kransky, a shell-shocked soldier with an honorable discharge from the army, who had to overcome doubts (his own as well as others') about his military record. Then there was Otto Schulz, son of the Schulzes of *Today's Children,* who spent long months in a veterans hospital coming to grips with the loss of his eyesight. In all these cases, women provided the unwavering support necessary for the successful reintegration of the veterans.[60]

The soldiers who faced the most difficult transition were those who returned to working wives, especially if the women refused to give up their jobs. Such was the case of Larry Johnson, the son of the Schulzes' upstairs neighbors. In Larry's absence, his wife, Julie, had become quite an attraction as a singer at a popular nightclub in town. Julie loved her work and brought home a sizable salary. Larry, who had entered the military fresh out of high school, now could not find a job that would bring in nearly as much as Julie's singing. Although the couple had no children, Larry grew increasingly resentful of his wife's work, especially because she earned so much more than he could. In one of the climactic episodes, Larry told Julie that he had started to hate her "for what she's done to him, his self-respect."

The show emphasized that it was Julie's earning "power" that presented the main threat to Larry's "self-respect" and masculinity, eventually leading to the couple's temporary separation. In the weeks to come, Larry resigned himself to the fact that he had to start at the bottom and took a job as a sales clerk. Julie, on the other hand, spent two weeks agonizing over their breakup. On top of it all, her situation was complicated by her boss's declaration of love for her and a job offer from one of New York City's top cabaret clubs. In a sudden turn of events, Julie left it all behind and decided to return to Larry, surprising him one morning with an image he had fancied throughout his time in the military: they would have their own place, and Julie would cook his breakfasts in a fancy little apron.

Julie: Good morning, Larry.

Larry: Julie. What're you doing here?

Julie: Darling—breakfast is almost ready. Better hurry with your shower.

Larry: What's the idea?

Julie: Aren't you going to say good morning to your wife?

Larry: My—my wife?

Julie: Yes. Yes, your wife. I've—I've come home, Larry.[61]

Julie had come home for good. She did not want to work as a singer for the rest of her life, she explained, as she asked Larry for another chance to prove herself as the wife he had always wanted.

Conclusion

Because of Phillips's early and sustained incorporation of social issues such as juvenile delinquency and veteran rehabilitation, she was recognized as a trendsetter in the soap opera genre and received attention beyond daytime radio as well. In the immediate postwar period, Phillips cited with satisfaction the many commendations she had received from social and government agencies. The National Child Welfare Division of the American Legion praised her timely incorporation of the problem of juvenile delinquency. The U.S. Public Health Service lauded her continued effort to publicize the shortage of nurses in civilian hospitals. The Department of Labor thanked Phillips for presenting the womanpower problem and the related issue of day care facilities. And both the National Rehabilitation Committee and the War Department commended her for her realistic portrayal of the rehabilitation of veterans.[62]

When asked what had spawned her social activism through her daytime serials, Phillips responded that this was in fact nothing new as far as her programs were concerned. As she argued in an NBC press conference in May 1945, serial writers would do even more if network and sponsor concerns did not force them to "soft-pedal" their social commitment. She also recalled the difficulties she had encountered with the OWI when she first wanted to include the rehabilitation problem in her plots.[63] Phillips could have underscored her point by mentioning numerous instances of network or sponsor squeamishness, from Procter and Gamble's objections to such apparently innocuous phrases as "Mommy's going to kill me" to deletions of scenes depicting social drinking. As the advertising agency reminded Phillips in the latter case, General Mills generally had no objections to social drinking per se. Yet considering the teetotalers in their audience, why "needlessly irritate at least twenty percent of our audience" for no plot purposes whatsoever?[64]

Wartime soap operas were a highly contested cultural genre and, like radio comedies, served a number of functions. They were escapist, as many of their contemporary critics claimed, but they also exhibited a high degree of realism and provided a strong sense of cultural and political activism. In her wartime serials, Phillips opposed the imagery of emancipated working women. Without sacrificing the wide variety of dramatic representations of women's experiences and without idealizing the lives of housewives, she validated the choices of her audiences. While the government-sponsored image of "Rosie the Riveter" drew millions of women into the workplace and often implied a carefree, exciting social life, in *Lonely Women* Phillips reminded her listeners to look beneath "the frosting on the cake." The propaganda hype, she assured them, hid the miserable, lonely lives of women who had moved to the city and lived in hotels such as The Towers.

In *Today's Children* and *The Guiding Light,* Phillips continued to challenge the image of "Rosie." Enforcing contemporary prejudices, she presented working mothers who shirked their responsibilities and neglected their children for money and clothes, increasing the chances that their youngsters would run with the wrong crowd and turn into juvenile delinquents. The image of "Rosie the Riveter" did not successfully reach into Phillips's soap operas. Instead, her serials reconfirmed her listeners' choice of adhering to a traditional gender ideology, which directly fed into the "feminine mystique" of the postwar years. Combined with other genres and media, which had increasingly privileged images of motherhood, family, and happiness within the nuclear family, radio soap operas facilitated the transition from the war years to the postwar period.

Epilogue

The Privatization of America

The cultural politics of wartime radio propaganda provided a crucial link for the strengthening and relegitimation of the privatized culture of consumer capitalism. This privatization discourse employed neither a new language nor a new ideology. It was and is an ongoing historical project that has its roots in the middle to late nineteenth century, when the birth of the mass media combined with a new consumption ethic revolutionized American society and culture. "The democratization of desire," as William Leach called it, not only eroded the foundation of a Victorian ethic and regional and ethnic differences but also fueled the homogenization of a national culture. Film and advertising emerged as two of the main arbiters of this new culture. But it was not a truly national culture. Instead, what emerged in the new era were two cultures, one "highbrow," the other "lowbrow"—with the latter winning more of the upper hand as the twentieth century progressed.[1]

The democratization of desire and the new culture of the early twentieth century aggressively worked at breaking down the barriers that divided the private and the public spheres. More than that, the public and the commercial spheres increasingly overlapped, with the demands of the latter superseding those of the former. As Charles McGovern has so eloquently put it, "Consumption was the foundation of a distinctly American way of life; this was the new order for the ages."[2]

The key change in the first half of the twentieth century was that American citizens were increasingly defined as consumers. Private consumption was elevated as one of the primary political obligations of citizens and became a vital vehicle for the acculturation of millions of new Americans. There is little doubt that advertisers and business stoked the fires of this drive towards commercialization. In fact, in their "search for a corporate soul," advertisers and publicists embarked on an unrelenting campaign to humanize the face of big business, which intensified as the century progressed. These campaigns not only secured the moral legitimacy of increasingly anonymous and vast corporate enterprises but also elevated corporate concerns to the forefront of what Lizabeth Cohen has termed the development of a "consumer Republic" in the postwar period.[3]

Radio, more than any other medium in the first half of the century, helped to level these boundaries: in the radio set, the private and the public spheres had literally merged. And as it continued its march to the hearths and hearts of the American people in the 1920s and 1930s, radio was quickly absorbed into the dominant ideological matrix that shaped all popular media in the United States: it became commercialized. Thus it became part of the ideology of consumer capitalism—in fact, it emerged as its favorite vehicle for more than two decades. No medium merged entertainment and advertising more effectively than radio, and few did more for the ongoing corporate search to endear both American business and its products to the population at large.

This is the broader context in which World War II propaganda, specifically radio propaganda, was situated. Of course, the first goal of most Americans during this period was to return victorious from the battlefields, and to that purpose they combined their efforts and strengths. But as Americans embarked on this patriotic, national, and public duty, the war rhetoric was increasingly depoliticized at home. Political partisan strife and the takeover of the wartime economy by business signaled a new era of cozy government-business relationships. The shift in the political economy was replicated in the sphere of cultural politics during the war, as the "dollar-a-year men" took over the propaganda apparatus in the United States. As a result, wartime propaganda was increasingly inscribed with an important subtext—a discourse of privatization—that became more evident as victory moved closer. The calls for sacrifice became highly personalized, and the appeals to civic duty were expressed in terms of private obligations. Leading business organizations and conservative politicians, as well as advertisers and media producers, put the ideological struggle into high gear to solidify and expand their vision of a privatized, consumer-oriented postwar America.[4] One of the key arguments of this book is that this critical transition began *during* the war and not after it was over.

This increased political power and moral authority of American business expressed itself in a number of areas in the postwar era. The first area combined the twin legacies of the war: intimate business-government relations and the propaganda battle in support of free enterprise. At the end of the war, another surge in pro-business mobilization still lay ahead. Through well-publicized and generously financed campaigns such as the "Freedom Train," "Our American Heritage," "Confidence in Growing America," and "The People's Capitalism," the Advertising Council—previously known as the War Advertising Council—continued its work of intertwining "commonsense" beliefs and the principles of free enterprise. Moreover, like so much of postwar politics, the council quickly adopted the strident rhetoric of the cold war in order to win Americans' consent or, as one ad asserted, "to strengthen the nation against the poisonous flood of Communist propaganda from within and without." As the country returned to a (cold) war footing, the Advertising Council worked in increasingly close collaboration with the government and once again frequently spoke with the semiofficial voice of a government agency, especially during the Eisenhower era. When the council ran its campaign "The Future of America" in 1954, for example, not only was the Eisenhower staff involved from the very beginning but the government support also ensured that each TV network contributed half an hour for the showing of the campaign's main film in January 1955.[5]

The second element of the political trajectory concerned business-labor relations. The labor movement was one segment of society that had escaped the turn toward a privatized corporate vision during the war years. Indeed, it had been further invigorated, and by the immediate postwar period it was at the height of its power and was confident that the time was ripe for the realization of its dream of an industrial democracy. Between 1933 and 1945, the number of unionized workers had increased fivefold; by the end of the war, fourteen million Americans, or 30 percent of the workforce, were members of unions. Moreover, as a number of labor historians have argued, it was not just the size but also the enthusiasm of the rank-and-file membership that characterized the postwar labor movement. But labor's goals were not realized. It proved unable to maintain the tripartite wartime arrangement in the postwar era, in which labor had bargained for its members on an equal footing with business and government. Its internal problems, such as wildcat strikes and continued tension between the Congress of Industrial Organizations and the American Federation of Labor, hampered its efforts. But more important was the fact that business had the ear of the government, which increasingly diminished labor's chances for a permanent consolidation of its wartime influence. When the Taft-Hartley Act, which through its restrictions on union practices symbolized the end of labor's ambitious postwar dreams, was drafted in the midst of the conservative, antilabor climate of 1947, business representatives sat in on the negotiations. Labor's plans for an expanded federal pension system failed as well. Labor increasingly had to rely on private-sector resolutions, which led to what Nelson Lichtenstein termed a "retreat to a more privatized conception of what labor could accomplish," as well as to "the privatization of the welfare state."[6]

George Lipsitz has demonstrated that one must look beyond the obvious fields of politics and political economy to explain why the labor movement was unable to transform the power and strength at the local base into a concerted national movement. Certainly we cannot ignore the expanding corporate economy, but the deeper reason for the weakening of the labor movement was that dominant business groups and their supporters had reconstituted "U.S. politics and culture along individualistic, private, and materialistic lines." This privatization drive did not just undermine labor's reformist power; its repercussions were felt across the entire social and political landscape: "Postwar corporate-liberal policies undermined the importance of the factory floor, urban inner-city neighborhoods, labor unions, ethnic lodges, public meeting places, day care centers, and public transportation in the U.S. society." In short, this discourse of privatization grew stronger and cast an ever-longer shadow each time alternative visions by reform movements, labor unions, or consumer advocates were defeated or forced to retreat.[7]

It is important to remember that this was a retreat and not a capitulation on the part of those who challenged this corporate hegemony. Strong antiestablishment currents continued to exist: within labor unions and among radicals, in popular music, comic books, science fiction stories, and mainstream films. Equally important, consumption and family "togetherness" could not allay the nagging feelings of insecurity and doubt—especially in the face of the emerging nuclear age. But this general sense of anxiety most likely contributed to the segmentation and individualization of American culture in the 1940s. William Graebner identified the "turn inward" as a natural response, since many Americans in the 1940s abandoned political and broad social solutions to confront their own unease: "Americans were more interested in personal survival than in social progress, more concerned with exorcising demons within than with building a new world without."[8]

Particularly the newest of the mass media, television, felt the increasing pressure of this privatist expansion in the postwar period. The relationship between the Federal Communications Commission and network television in the second half of the 1940s is a good case in point. When James Fly took over the FCC in 1939, he brought the antitrust New Deal impulse with him. Over the next several years he oversaw one of the most radical reforms in broadcast history when he forced NBC to divest itself of one of its networks and freed the stations from exclusive network contracts. After Fly resigned in December 1944, the FCC quickly displayed much greater business acquiescence. The FCC soon deliberated a technical issue that would have wide political and cultural ramifications for postwar America. The question was whether the United States should adopt a very high frequency (VHF) or ultrahigh frequency (UHF) band for its nascent television industry. VHF, which was backed by RCA (NBC), limited the transmission spectrum to a small number of channels; UHF would have allowed for a much higher channel capacity and thus greater potential diversity. In May 1945, the FCC, under its chairman Charles R. Denny, adopted thirteen-channel VHF television, which gave the networks a near monopoly over the new medium—with NBC as the big winner. To cap off a rather dubious and unsavory decision-making process on the part of the FCC, Denny resigned six months later to become an NBC vice president at triple his salary at the FCC. Like so many regulatory government agencies, the FCC loyally backed the TV monopolies over the next fifteen years.[9]

In the context of the conservative political culture of the postwar period, the FCC thus guaranteed that the networks' monopoly would remain unchallenged. In 1945, nearly 95 percent of radio stations broadcast network programs in the prime-time evening hours. Television would be equally dominated by the major networks, a development that was exacerbated in 1948, when the FCC instituted a four-year license freeze, eliminating any possibility for the establishment of competing or alternative networks. At the threshold to the postwar period, the related expansion of commercialization and privatization had shredded the last vestiges of the New Deal impulse in the field of broadcasting, leaving it more than ever in the hands of business, advertising, and monopoly networks. J. Harold Ryan, the new head of the National Association of Broadcasters, best captured the spirit of this corporate resurgence. Like so many other officials, Ryan had made a successful transition from wartime government service to postwar business employment—in his case, from chief of the Radio Division of the Office of Censorship to the chairmanship of the NAB. When broadcasters celebrated the twenty-fifth anniversary of radio in 1945, Ryan gave the keynote address, in which he captured the industry's strutting self-confidence: "American radio is the product of American business!" he exclaimed. "It is as much that product as the vacuum cleaner, the washing machine, the automobile and the airplane."[10]

In terms of the cultural content of postwar television, the development was similar. Hand in hand with increasing commercialization and network control, overall television programming functioned to maintain and strengthen the ideology of the dominant commercial interests. Working classes and urban life were faded out. When they were televised, they were reinscribed with meanings that validated the prevalent consumerist and privatized bias of the dominant culture. Women also played a prominent role in these emerging television discourses, as Lynn Spigel has emphasized. While this public medium penetrated the private space with unprecedented speed and force, TV-related discourses portrayed images of a return to family values and the centrality of the home. In its advertising discourse as well, television tried to mask one of its central functions—the further leveling of the public-private boundaries—instead emphasizing "togetherness" as family cohesion around the TV set. As has occurred so often in the expansion of the privatization discourse, women became the anchors of these discursive strategies through the ideological reaffirmation of a gendered private sphere.[11]

The rhetoric of this privatization discourse worked itself into a fever pitch at the height of the cold war. In his fascinating study on cold war culture, Stephen Whitfield has noted that no aspect of culture remained untouched by the belligerent, pervasive influence of containment and anticommunism. Culture was politicized much as it had been during World War II, and the political and cultural spectrum in the United States narrowed considerably. Liberalism was forced even further on the defensive, and Americanism increasingly became identified with the red-blooded, individualistic, and consumer-driven society business and advertisers had in mind. Television was at the center of this ideological intensity: "Television became a custodian of the cultural Cold War. Its viewers were boxed-in to a tight consensus."[12]

Privatization, commercialization, and the return to a more traditional vision of gender relations—these were the three core discourses of the ideological strategy of wartime and the postwar period. Lizabeth Cohen has analyzed these interrelated strategies in an intriguing study of the postwar shopping center boom. The shift from commercial town centers to shopping malls had tremendous political, social, and cultural repercussions. Not only did these new commercial hubs create public spaces designed to optimize commercial imperatives and continue the "feminization of public space"; they also had a decisive new political dimension. Even though they were categorized as public spaces, the courts repeatedly upheld the restriction of free speech in these public arenas. Shopping malls have always excluded vagrants and panhandlers, as well as legally prohibiting demonstrators and political petition drives. In the battle between two key American principles—the freedom of speech versus the right of private property—the commercial privatization discourse clearly held the upper hand in the postwar era.[13]

Ironically, the resurgence of this intensified drive towards privatization and commercialization was situated within a most civic and public context: World War II. The American war effort, which helped to preserve democracy as a viable alternative abroad, simultaneously weakened the foundation of this very same democratic process within the United States for the decades to come.

Notes

Introduction

1. Outstanding examples of this scholarship are Alan Havig, *Fred Allen's Radio Comedy* (Philadelphia, 1990); Michele Hilmes, *Hollywood and Broadcasting: From Radio to Cable* (Chicago, 1990); Holly Cowan Shulman, *The Voice of America: Propaganda and Democracy, 1941–1945* (Madison, Wis., 1990); Melvin Patrick Ely, *The Adventures of Amos 'n' Andy: A Social History of an American Phenomenon* (New York, 1991); Robert W. McChesney, *Telecommunications, Mass Media, and Democracy: The Battle for the Control of U.S. Broadcasting, 1928–1935* (New York, 1993); and Susan Smulyan, *The Commercialization of American Broadcasting, 1920–1934* (Washington, D.C., 1994).

The most important recent studies are Michele Hilmes's excellent overview of American radio broadcasting, *Radio Voices: American Broadcasting, 1922–1952* (Minneapolis, 1997); Susan Douglas's refreshing and provocative study *Listening In: Radio and the American Imagination* (New York, 1999); and Barbara Divine Savage's fascinating book on black radio, *Broadcasting Freedom: Radio, War, and the Politics of Race* (Chapel Hill, N.C., 1999).

Important earlier studies include the first two volumes of Erik Barnouw's broadcasting history, *A History of Broadcasting in the United States*, vol. 1, *A Tower of Babel. To 1933* (New York, 1966) and vol. 2, *The Golden Web. 1933 to 1953* (New York, 1968); J. Fred MacDonald, *Don't Touch That Dial: Radio Programming in American Life, 1920–1960* (Chicago, 1979); Arthur Frank Wertheim, *Radio Comedy* (New York, 1979); LeRoy Bannerman, *Norman Corwin and Radio: The Golden Years* (University, Ala., 1986).

2. Most important with respect to radio news broadcasting is David H. Culbert's book *News for Everyman: Radio and Foreign Affairs in Thirties America* (Westport, Conn., 1976). See also David H. Hosley, *As Good as Any: Foreign*

Correspondence on American Radio, 1930–1940 (Westport, Conn., 1984); Edward Bliss Jr., *The History of Broadcast Journalism* (New York, 1991), chaps. 7–20; and Douglas, *Listening In,* chap. 7. For an excellent study of noncommercial black radio programs during the war years, see Savage, *Broadcasting Freedom.*

For studies on World War II films, see Colin Schindler, *Hollywood Goes to War: Film and American Society, 1939–1952* (London, 1979); Bernard Dick, *The Star-Spangled Screen: The American World War II Film* (Lexington, Ky., 1985); Clayton R. Koppes and Gregory D. Black, *Hollywood Goes to War: How Politics, Profits and Propaganda Shaped World War II Movies* (Berkeley and Los Angeles, 1990); and Thomas Doherty, *Projections of War: Hollywood, American Culture and World War II* (New York, 1993).

3. Holly Cowan Shulman's book *The Voice of America* is the best study on the wartime propaganda of international broadcasting. Lawrence C. Soley, *Radio Warfare: OSS and CIA Subversive Propaganda* (New York, 1989), covers the covert U.S. radio operations during World War II.

4. The reports of social workers are referred to in Barnouw, *The Golden Web,* 6. For the *Fortune* survey, see *Fortune* 20 (November 1939): 176. The postwar poll is cited in Harry Field and Paul F. Lazarsfeld, *The People Look at Radio* (Chapel Hill, N.C., 1946), 101.

5. Field and Lazarsfeld, *The People Look at Radio,* vii.

6. Hilmes, *Radio Voices,* 22–23. See also Warren I. Susman, *Culture as History: The Transformation of American Society in the Twentieth Century* (New York, 1984), chap. 9; and MacDonald, *Don't Touch That Dial,* esp. chap. 3. This assimilation effect of the commercial mass media, particularly network radio, is also a key argument of Lizabeth Cohen's study, *Making a New Deal: Industrial Workers in Chicago, 1919–1939* (Cambridge, Mass., 1990), chap. 3.

7. While I disagree with both Robert Griffith's and Elizabeth A. Fones-Wolf's interpretations of the wartime period, I have learned a great deal from their very astute and insightful analysis of postwar America: Robert Griffith, "Forging America's Postwar Order: Domestic Politics and Political Economy in the Age of Truman," in *The Truman Presidency,* ed. Michael J. Lacey (Cambridge, Mass., 1989), 63; and Elizabeth A. Fones-Wolf, *Selling Free Enterprise: The Business Assault on Labor and Liberalism, 1945–1960* (Urbana, Ill., 1994), 4.

8. In very significant ways, the thrust of my argument complements the one advanced by George Lipsitz in his groundbreaking studies, especially his book *Rainbow at Midnight: Labor and Culture in the 1940s* (Urbana, Ill., 1994). Chapter 11 deals specifically with the wartime period. See also his study *Time Passages: Collective Memory and American Popular Culture* (Minneapolis, 1990).

9. In terms of World War II, some of the best-known studies of this revisionist trend include Paul Fussell, *Wartime: Understanding and Behavior in the Second World War* (New York, 1989); Michael C. C. Adams, *The Best War Ever: America and World War II* (Baltimore, 1994); and several articles in Kenneth Paul O'Brien and Lynn Hudson Parsons, eds., *The Home-Front: World War II and American Society* (Westport, Conn., 1995), as well as in Lewis A. Erenberg

and Susan E. Hirsch, eds., *The War in American Culture: Society and Consciousness during World War II* (Chicago, 1996).

10. Alan Brinkley, *The End of Reform: New Deal Liberalism in Recession and War* (New York, 1995), 139. For a general discussion of this development, see Richard Polenberg, *War and Society: The United States, 1941–1945* (New York, 1972), chap. 3; and John Morton Blum, *V Was for Victory: Politics and American Culture during World War II* (New York, 1976), chap. 4. For a similar line of argument, see John W. Jeffries, "The 'New' New Deal: FDR and American Liberalism," *Political Science Quarterly* 105 (1990): 379–418.

11. Karl D. Barry, *The Uneasy State: The United States from 1915 to 1945* (Chicago, 1983), chap. 10, 209; and Alan Brinkley, "The New Deal and the Idea of the State," in *The Rise and the Fall of the New Deal Order, 1930–1980*, ed. Steve Fraser and Gary Gerstle (Princeton, N.J., 1989), 102–3.

12. Robert B. Westbrook, "'I Want a Girl, Just Like the Girl That Married Harry James': American Women and the Problem of Political Obligation in World War II," *American Quarterly* 42 (December 1990): 588, 598–600.

13. Frank W. Fox, *Madison Avenue Goes to War: The Strange Military Career of American Advertising, 1941–1945* (Provo, Utah, 1975), 57, 69; Mark H. Leff, "The Politics of Sacrifice on the American Home Front in World War II," *Journal of American History* 78 (March 1991): 1296–318. I also benefited greatly from an unpublished paper by Philip Soffer, "Dreamers, Consumers, Citizens: The Ideology of American Advertising in World War II" (submitted to Larry Levine, May 1994).

14. Doherty, *Projections of War*, 181–83.

15. George H. Roeder Jr., *The Censored War: American Visual Experience during World War Two* (New Haven, 1993), 15 and Visual Essay 1. For a discussion of the wartime black market, see Blum, *V Was for Victory*, 96–97.

16. Roeder, *The Censored War*, 12, 33; Doherty, *Projections of War*, chap. 10.

1. From the New Deal to World War II

1. Kenneth G. Bartlett, "The Social Impact of Radio," *Annals of the American Academy of Political and Social Science* 250 (March 1947): 93–94. For the number of radio commentators, see Irving E. Fang, *Those Radio Commentators!* (Ames, Iowa, 1977), 6; and Dixon Wector, "Hearing Is Believing: How Reliable Are the News Commentators?" *Atlantic Monthly*, June 1945, 54.

2. Paul W. White, *News on the Air* (New York, 1947), 222. That this transformation had begun to take hold as early as 1940 is evident in smaller citywide and statewide polls cited in Paul W. White, "Covering a War for Radio," *Annals of the American Academy of Political and Social Science* 213 (January 1941): 83–92.

3. These quotations are from William E. Leuchtenburg, "The New Deal and the Analogue of War," in *Change and Continuity in Twentieth-Century America*, ed. John Braeman, Robert H. Bremmer, and Everett Walters (Columbus, Ohio, 1972), 105, 121.

4. Elinor Kahn, "The Propaganda of the National Recovery Administration" (master's thesis, Stanford University, 1935), 45; and Andrew Davis Wolvin, "The Blue Eagle Campaign: A Study in Persuasion and Coercion" (Ph.D. diss., Purdue University, 1968), 58. These are the two most comprehensive sources on the NRA propaganda campaigns.

5. Hugh Johnson emphasized in his memoirs that the War Industries Board and the propaganda campaigns of World War I provided "a great schooling for the new national effort of which the NRA was a part." *The Blue Eagle from Egg to Earth* (New York, [1935] 1968), 96, 114, 258.

6. "Mobilizing the Nation to Smash Unemployment," *Literary Digest,* August 5, 1933, 6; and B. P. Draper, "Marching as to War under the Blue Eagle," *Literary Digest,* August 12, 1933, 7.

7. Cedric E. A. Larson, "Found: Records of the Committee on Public Information," *Public Opinion Quarterly (POQ)* 1 (January 1937): 116–18; and Cedric Larson and James R. Mock, "The Lost Files of the Creel Committee of 1917–1919," *POQ* 3 (January 1939): 5–29.

8. Cedric Larson and James R. Mock, *Words That Won the War: The Story of the Committee on Public Information* (New York, 1968), 4, 19, 215.

9. George Creel, "Propaganda and Moral," *American Journal of Sociology* 17 (November 1941): 340–51; and H. C. Peterson, *Propaganda for War: The Campaign against American Neutrality, 1914–1917* (Norman, Okla., 1939), 327.

10. Harold Lavine and James Wechsler, *War Propaganda and the United States* (New Haven, Conn., 1940), 89, 257.

11. Ibid., chap. 4.

12. E. Pendleton Herring, "Official Publicity under the New Deal," *Annals of the American Academy of Political and Social Science* 179 (May 1935): 167, 170.

13. Mitchell Dawson, "Censorship on the Air," *American Mercury* 31 (March 1934): 267. The other article was written by Elisha Hanson, "Official Propaganda and the New Deal," *Annals of the American Academy of Political and Social Science* 179 (May 1935): 178, 185.

14. Winfield, *FDR and the News Media,* chap. 7. She cites the growing discrepancy between popular vote and newspaper support on pages 127–28. For a similar overall argument about the increasing newspaper opposition to Roosevelt, see also Graham White, *FDR and the Press* (Chicago, 1979).

As Winfield has made clear, however, this development did not mean that the newspapers were largely closed to the Roosevelt administration. While the owners and publishers increasingly turned against the New Deal, FDR carefully groomed the White House correspondents in particular and earned the respect, goodwill, and friendship of many journalists. See *FDR and the Press,* chaps. 3 and 4.

15. Jeanette Sayre, "An Analysis of the Radiobroadcasting Activities of Federal Agencies," *Studies in the Control of Radio,* no. 3 (Harvard University, June 1941), 11–12.

16. For discussions of FDR's first fireside chat, see Robert S. McElvaine, *The Great Depression: America, 1929–1941* (New York, 1984), 140–41; and Win-

field, *FDR and the News Media*. The *New York Times* citation is quoted in Winfield's account on page 104.

17. Steven E. Schoenherr, "Selling the New Deal: Stephen T. Early's Role as Press Secretary to Franklin D. Roosevelt" (Ph.D. diss., University of Delaware, 1976), 67–69; *Variety,* February 12, 1936, 1.

18. Sayre, "An Analysis of the Radiobroadcasting Activities of Federal Agencies," 22, 81–83. For an in-depth analysis of another important Office of Education program, "Americans All, Immigrants All," see Savage, *Broadcasting Freedom,* chap. 1.

19. James L. McCamy, *Government Publicity: Its Practice in Federal Administration* (Chicago, 1939), 54–55.

20. On Long's and Coughlin's respective use of radio, see Alan Brinkley, *Voices of Protest: Huey Long, Father Coughlin, and the Great Depression* (New York, 1983), esp. chaps. 4 and 8. For a discussion of business publicity and propaganda in the 1930s, see Richard S. Tedlow, *Keeping the Corporate Image: Public Relations and Business, 1900–1950* (Greenwich, Conn., 1979), chap. 3. For an argument that complements Tedlow's, see Roland Marchand, "The Fitful Career of Advocacy Advertising: Political Protection, Client Cultivation, and Corporate Morale," *California Management Review* 29 (winter 1987): 2.

21. Quoted in Barnouw, *The Golden Web,* 43.

22. Milton Wright, *Public Relations for Business* (New York, 1939), 126–27; Tedlow, *Keeping the Corporate Image,* 64–65.

23. Wright, *Public Relations for Business,* 126.

24. "The Public Is not Damned," *Fortune* 19 (March 1939): 83.

25. For a fascinating discussion of this ongoing public relations campaign, see Roland Marchand, *Creating the Corporate Soul: The Rise of Public Relations and Corporate Imagery in American Big Business* (Berkeley, 1998), chap. 6.

26. Gordon Carroll, "Dr. Roosevelt's Propaganda Trust," *American Mercury* 17 (September 1937): 6–16.

27. For one of the best studies on this general trend, see William Stott, *Documentary Expression and Thirties America* (Chicago, 1986). See also Milton Meltzer, *Violins and Shovels: The WPA Arts Projects* (New York, 1976); Roy Rosenzweig et al., eds., *Government and the Arts in Thirties America: A Guide to Oral Histories and Other Research Material* (Fairfax, Va., 1986); and Barbara Melosh, *Engendering Culture: Manhood and Womanhood in New Deal Public Art and Theater* (Washington, D.C., 1989).

The one issue that has received much scholarly attention in this connection is the post office murals. See Karal Ann Marling, *Wall-to-Wall: A Cultural History of Post-Office Murals in the Great Depression* (Minneapolis, 1982); Marlene Park and Gerald E. Markowitz, *Democratic Vistas: Post Offices and Public Art in the New Deal* (Philadelphia, 1984); Sue Bridwell Beckham, *Depression Post Office Murals and Southern Culture: A Gentle Reconstruction* (Baton Rouge, La., 1989); and Richard B. Megraw, "The Writing on the Wall: Treasury Section Murals in New Deal Louisiana," *Prospects: An Annual of American Cultural Studies* 21 (1996): 327–46.

28. Sayre, "An Analysis of Radio Broadcasting Activities of Federal Agencies," 33.

29. For a general discussion of these events and the novelty of steady, around-the-clock radio news coverage of foreign events, see Barnouw, *The Golden Web*, 78–83; and Richard Ketchum, *The Borrowed Years, 1938–1941: America on the Way to War* (New York, 1989), chap. 5.

30. For an in-depth analysis of H. V. Kaltenborn's background and career, see Culbert, *News for Everyone*, chap. 3; and Fang, *Those Radio Commentators!* chap. 2. See also H. V. Kaltenborn's account of the event, *I Broadcast the Crisis* (New York, 1938).

31. Letters to H. V. Kaltenborn: the first one was from a woman listener in Los Angeles, September 27, 1938; the second one came from Rosalie Roberts in Texas, September 26, 1938; Kaltenborn Collection, State Historical Society of Wisconsin [hereafter SHSW], Box 31.

32. Letters to H. V. Kaltenborn, Kaltenborn Collection, SHSW, Boxes 31 and 32.

33. Ibid.

34. *Nation*, October 1, 1938, 285; Rorty's article is printed in the October 15 issue of the magazine, pp. 372–74. For another congratulatory response, see *Variety*, September 21, 1938.

35. White, *News on the Air*, 1–13.

36. Paul F. Lazarsfeld, *Radio and the Printed Page: An Introduction to the Study of Radio and Its Role in the Communication of Ideas* (New York, 1940), 145.

37. Ibid., chap. 4. For a discussion of this same issue, see also Hadley Cantril and Gordon W. Allport, *The Psychology of Radio* (New York, 1935), chap. 9.

38. For a compelling analysis of the impact of radio news during World War II, see also Douglas, *Listening In*, chap. 7.

39. For the Roper poll, see *Fortune*, August 1939, 70. The results were broken down even further in the survey: radio press bulletin, 22.7 percent; radio commentator, 17.6 percent; an authority you heard speak, 13 percent; an editorial in the newspaper, 12.4 percent; a news item in the newspaper, 11.1 percent; a columnist in the newspaper, 3.4 percent. For an interesting discussion that emphasizes the documentary nature of the radio medium, see Stott, *Documentary Expression and Thirties America*, chap. 5.

40. Hadley Cantril and a team of researchers conducted the most in-depth study of this event, titled *The Invasion from Mars: A Study in the Psychology of Panic* (New York, 1940).

41. Ibid., 70.

42. Mitchell V. Charnley, *News by Radio* (New York, 1948), 8.

43. Hosley, *As Good as Any*, 14–17.

44. Sammy R. Danna, "The Rise of Radio News," in *American Broadcasting: A Source Book on the History of Radio and Television*, ed. Lawrence Lichty and Malachi C. Topping (New York, 1975), 341–42.

45. Sammy R. Dana, "The Press-Radio War," in *American Broadcasting: A Source Book on the History of Radio and Television*, ed. Lawrence Lichty and Mal-

achi C. Topping (New York, 1975), 344–50; see also Barnouw, *The Golden Web*, 18–22; and Charnley, *News by Radio*, 15–25.

Charnley provides a very telling table that points to the steadily increasing number of radio stations subscribing to one or more of the four major news services between 1936 and 1948 (p. 25):

1936 — 325 radio stations	1941 — 843	1945 — 1,105
1937 — 443	1942 — 956	1946 — 1,146
1938 — 541	1943 — 983	1947 — 1,389
1939 — 611	1944 — 1,024	1948 — 1,783
1940 — 743		

46. Bliss, *Now the News*, 31–35, 74–75; Hosley, *As Good as Any*, 26–27.

47. Hosley, *As Good as Any*, chap. 2; Stanley Cloud and Lynne Olson, *The Murrow Boys: Pioneers on the Front Lines of Broadcast Journalism* (Boston, 1996), chap. 2.

48. William Shirer, "'Berlin Speaking,'" *Atlantic Monthly*, September 1940, 308–11; Cloud and Olson, *The Murrow Boys*, 34–37.

49. Shirer, "Berlin Speaking," 311; Bliss, *Now the News*, 86.

50. Charnley, *News by Radio*, 46.

51. Letter from the Leo Burnett advertising agency to the Pure Oil Company, May 13, 1939, Kaltenborn Collection, Box 150, Folder "Pure Oil Correspondence, May 1939–April 1941," SHSW.

52. "U.S. Radio at War," *Time*, December 15, 1941, 48. Several other writers commented on this practical dimension of news broadcasts: see Rorty, "Radio Comes Through," 310; and Charnley, *News by Radio*, foreword.

53. For a discussion of Hollywood's interventionist bend, see Koppes and Black, *Hollywood Goes to War*, chap. 2; and Doherty, *Projections of War*, 39–41.

54. For an excellent summary of Culbert's argument, see *News for Everyone*, 5–7; quotation on p. 204.

55. Richard Steele, *Propaganda in an Open Society*, chap. 5; quotation on p. 130.

56. On Kaltenborn's political stances and his news programs, see Giraud Chester, "The Radio Commentaries of H. V. Kaltenborn: A Case Study in Persuasion" (Ph.D. diss., University of Wisconsin, Madison, 1947), chap. 6; and Fang, *Those Radio Commentators!* 35. For an insight into his dealings with his sponsor, see Kaltenborn Collection, Box 150, Folder "Pure Oil Correspondence, 1939–April 1941," SHSW. The quotation is from a letter by the Leo Burnett Co. to Kaltenborn, January 27, 1941.

57. Earl Sparling, "Let's Listen to Swing," *Current History and Forum*, August 1940; Swing's comment is quoted on p. 25. See also Fang, *Those Radio Commentators!* 158–60.

58. Culbert, *News for Everyone*, 110–19; quotation on p. 118.

59. The radio commentary is quoted in Culbert, *News for Everyone*, 139; for another good discussion of the evolution of Davis's interventionism, see Fang, *Those Radio Commentators!* 181–88.

60. Quoted in R. Franklin Smith, *Edward R. Murrow: The War Years* (Kalamazoo, Mich., 1978), 56. The literature on Edward R. Murrow is richer than on any other single news commentator of the time. For two relatively recent book-sized biographies, see Joseph E. Persico, *Edward R. Murrow: An American Original* (New York, 1990) and A. M. Sperber, *Murrow: His Life and Times* (New York, 1986).

61. Edward R. Murrow, *This Is London* (New York, 1941), 167. For a discussion of the increasing censorship in Germany, see Cloud and Olson, *The Murrow Boys,* 98–101.

62. Quoted in Fang, *Those Radio Commentators!* 315. On the daredevil attitude of Murrow and LeSueur, see Cloud and Olson, *The Murrow Boys,* 94–95.

63. Eric Sevareid is quoted in Smith, *Edward R. Murrow,* 107; for a discussion of Murrow's interventionist politics, see Culbert, *News for Everyone,* chap. 7.

64. Quoted in Cloud and Olson, *The Murrow Boys,* 97–98.

65. For a discussion of these policies, see Barnouw, *The Golden Web,* 135–37; and Fang, *Those Radio Commentators!* 7.

2. Government Radio Propaganda

1. For a good discussion of these issues, see Richard W. Steele, "The Great Debate: Roosevelt, the Media, and the Coming of the War, 1940–1941," *Journal of American History* 71 (June 1984): 69–92. On the creation of a central propaganda agency, see his article "Preparing the Public for War: Efforts to Establish a National Propaganda Agency, 1940–1941," *American Historical Review* 75 (October 1970):1640–53. See also Margaret Hicks Williams, "The President's Office of Government Reports," *Public Opinion Quarterly (POQ)* 5 (1940): 548–59.

2. Edward Kirby, *Star-Spangled Radio* (Chicago, 1948). The two main functions of this new public relations section of the War Department were the production of informational and "inspirational" series and special events broadcasts in cooperation with the networks, as well as the clearance of all national shows dealing with the military. The National Broadcasting Company (NBC) cooperated in the production of *Wings of Destiny,* which dramatized stories of the U.S. Army Air Corps, and *Defense for America,* which presented talks on the national defense effort and featured defense factory pickups. The Columbia Broadcasting System (CBS) sponsored *Report to the Nation,* a series that outlined the work of major federal departments. In June 1941, CBS added two further shows: *Spirit of '41,* which dramatized historical episodes from the army, navy and marines, and *Proudly We Hail,* which introduced the contributions of national defense workers by broadcasting from defense factories and featuring guest star performers. The Mutual Broadcasting System (Mutual) sponsored similar shows, such as *Your Defense Reporter, At Home in the Army.*

After December 1941, the War Department continued a number of these shows and added several more. Most successful of all was *The Army Hour,* which provided live, on-the-spot broadcasts from various branches of the armed forces. It played from training camps, battle cruisers, and bombers; like live news coverage, it brought the war home to the American people.

3. William A. Bacher, ed., *The Treasury Star Parade* (New York, 1942), foreword.

4. For a general overview of the creation of the Office of War Information, see Allan M. Winkler, *The Politics of Propaganda: The Office of War Information, 1942–1945* (New Haven, Conn., 1978). On government defense agencies, see George E. McMillan, "Government Publicity and the Impact of War," *POQ* 5 (1940): 383–98.

5. Quoted in memorandum by William B. Lewis to the Radio Bureau Division, summarizing a number of weekly intelligence surveys, June 11, 1942; National Archives, Record Group 208, Entry 93, Box 607 [hereafter cited as, e.g., NA 208–93–607], folder "Intelligence Bureau, OWI."

6. Quoted in Polenberg, *War and Society,* 184.

7. Bannerman, *Norman Corwin and Radio,* 74–75. See also *We Hold These Truths,* in *More By Corwin: 16 Radio Dramas by Norman Corwin* (New York, 1944), 88–96.

8. Corwin, *We Hold These Truths,* 73.

9. Joseph Julian, *This Was Radio: A Personal Memoir* (New York, 1975), 73.

10. Corwin, *We Hold These Truths,* 77.

11. For a detailed discussion of this series, see especially Sherman H. Dryer, *Radio in Wartime* (New York, 1942), chap. 8; and Bannerman, *Norman Corwin and Radio,* 93–101.

12. Norman Corwin, *This Is War! A Collection of Plays about America on the March* (New York, 1942), 5.

13. Ibid., 11–15.

14. Ibid., 87–88.

15. "Hoover Special Reports," March 7 and March 28, 1942, NA 208–93–607, folders "Surveys General" and "Hooper."

16. Corwin, *This Is War!* 288–98.

17. Ibid., 8.

18. Ibid., 28–29, 43. See also Blum's discussion of this series, *V Is for Victory,* 25–30.

19. "The Audience of the Government's 'This Is War!' Radio Program, Survey # 108," April 6, 1942, NA, 44–164–1796, folder "Intelligence Bureau."

20. Norman Corwin, "Radio Drama in Wartime," in *Education on the Air: Thirteenth Yearbook of the Institute for Education by Radio* (Columbus, Ohio, 1942), 88.

21. Arch Oboler, *Plays for Americans: Thirteen Non-royalty Plays by Arch Oboler* (New York, 1942), 93.

22. Arch Oboler, "Hate," in ibid., 23–43.

23. "Survey of Intelligence Materials No. 12," OFF, Bureau of Intelligence, March 2, 1942, Personal Subject File [hereafter PSF], Box 155, folder "OWI, Survey of Intelligence, February–March, 1942," FDR Library.

24. Ibid., especially 7–9.

25. For a discussion of the tense relationship between the FDR administration and the isolationist press, see David Brinkley, *Washington Goes to War* (New York, 1988), 175–84.

26. Winfield, *FDR and the News Media,* chap. 9, "The Office of Censorship." For a discussion of domestic wartime censorship, see especially pp. 178–80.

27. Fireside chat on the progress of war, February 23, 1942, *The Public Papers and Addresses of Franklin D. Roosevelt,* ed. Samuel I. Rosenman (New York, 1938–50), 1942 volume, 107–8.

28. Letters to FDR, February 24, 1942, President's Personal Files [hereafter PPF] 200B, Container 109, Folder "Public Reaction—February 24, 1942," FDR Library.

29. Speech by Archibald MacLeish, March 19, 1942, Office File 4619, Box 2, folder "OFF, January–March, 1942," FDR Library.

30. Doherty, *Projections of War,* 3. On the censorship of photographs, see Roeder, *The Censored War.*

31. Ranald R. MacDougall, "Documentaries for Civilians: The Man behind the Man behind the Gun," in *Off Mike: Radio Writing by the Nation's Top Radio Writers,* ed. Jerome Lawrence (New York, 1944). The example is quoted on p. 155.

32. Norman Rosten, "The Ballad of Bataan," *The Treasury Star Parade,* 18–19.

33. Interview with Jerome Lawrence by the author, July 27, 1992.

34. For a discussion of the production of the *Why We Fight?* series, see Koppes and Black, *Hollywood Goes to War,* 122–25.

35. On the Atlantic-First strategy, see James MacGregor Burns, *Roosevelt: The Soldier of Freedom, 1940–1945* (New York, 1970), 179–80. For the survey, see "Survey of Intelligence Materials No. 21," April 29, 1942, PSF, Box 155, folder "OWI: Survey of Intelligence, 1942," FDR Library.

36. See John Dower's brilliant study, *War without Mercy: Race and Power in the Pacific War* (New York, 1986), especially chaps. 3 and 4.

37. Both examples are drawn from Neal Hopkins, "A Lesson in Japanese," *The Treasury Star Parade,* 358, 363–64.

38. "Report from the Nation," December 7, 1942, OWI Bureau of Intelligence, PSF, Box 156, folder "OWI, Survey of Intelligence, December 1942," 27, FDR Library.

39. Douglass Miller, *You Can't Do Business with Hitler* (Boston, 1941), 219.

40. The whole set of English-language scripts of this series has been preserved in the OWI Records at the National Archives: NA 208–146–765, folder "You Can't Do Business with Hitler." It was also transcribed in a number of foreign languages for domestic use.

41. *Variety,* April 15, 1942, 28.

42. See "Beast of Burden" and "The Sell-Out," Episodes 31 and 32, NA 208–146–765.

43. Surveys of March 29, 1944, and April 5, 1944, NA 208–118–706, folder "Surveys Division, Bureau of Special Services, OWI."

44. *This Is Your Enemy,* NA 208–146–761–763.

45. The letters are excerpted in the OWI records; they did not include the dates: NA 208–93–604, folder "Radio Bureau–General."

46. This cumulative effect is discussed in the summary of the Intelligence Bureau survey: "American Public Opinion since Pearl Harbor," September 11, 1942, NA 208–93–607, folder "Intelligence Bureau, OWI." The quotation is from the same report.

47. Quoted in MacGregor Burns, *Roosevelt: The Soldier of Freedom,* 213.

48. Boris Grabatov, "A Letter from a Red Army Man," in *The Treasury Star Parade,* 171, 175.

49. See Gregory and Black, *Hollywood Goes to War,* chap. 7; Agee's remark is mentioned on p. 208.

50. "Report from the Nation," December 7, 1942, 33–35, PSF, Box 156, "OWI, Survey of Intelligence, December 1942," FDR Library.

51. Ibid.; see also OWI Intelligence survey, March 2, 1942, 3–4, PSF, Box 155, folder "OWI, Survey of Intelligence, February–March 1942," FDR Library.

52. Norman Corwin, *Untitled and Other Radio Dramas* (New York, 1945), 160. See also Bannerman, *Norman Corwin and Radio,* chap. 7; and Sperber, *Murrow: His Life and Times,* 212–14.

53. Bannerman, *Norman Corwin and Radio,* chap. 7.

54. MacDougall, "Documentaries for Civilians," in *Off Mike,* 152.

55. The OWI records in the National Archives contain a large number of these usually monthly reports; see, e.g., NBC War Effort Report, February 1–29, 1944, NA 208–103–649.

56. Carl Hovland et al., *Experiments on Mass Communication,* vol. 3 (Princeton, N.J., 1949), chaps. 2 and 3.

57. For detailed discussions of various aspects of this new paradigm, see Wilbur Schramm, ed., *The Process and Effects of Mass Communication* (Chicago, 1954), especially the sections "Getting the Meaning Understood" and "Modifying Attitudes and Opinions." For a succinct summary of the emergence of this new communications model, see Shearon Lowery and Melvin L. De Fleur, *Milestones in Mass Communication,* 2d. ed. (New York, 1988), chap. 5, "Experiments on Mass Communication: Persuading the American Soldier in World War II."

58. Corwin, *More by Corwin* (New York, 1944), 51; and Corwin, *Untitled* (New York, 1945).

59. See Winkler, *The Politics of Propaganda,* chap. 2, "Propaganda at Home."

3. Domestic Foreign-Language Radio

1. *Variety,* May 20, 1942, 1, 31–32; May 27, 1942, 26. See also letter to F. H. Peter Cusick, May 15, 1942, NA 208–233–1117, folder "Censorship."

2. See, for example, Hadley Cantril's public opinion survey, "America Faces the War: A Study in Public Opinion," *Public Opinion Quarterly* 4 (September 1940): 387–407.

3. See Harry N. Scheiber, *The Wilson Administration and Civil Liberties, 1917–*

1921 (Ithaca, N.Y., 1960), chap. 3; and David Kennedy, *Over Here: The First World War and American Society* (Oxford, 1980), chap. 1.

4. "Functions of the Foreign Language Division," undated, NA 208–232–1115, folder "General Memos." For information on staff size, see undated memo, "Staff of the Foreign Language Division, 1942—Slash or Expand?" NA 208–222–1079.

5. Brett Joseph Gary, "American Liberalism and the Problem of Propaganda: Scholars, Lawyers, and the War on Words, 1919–1945" (Ph.D. diss., University of Pennsylvania, 1992), chaps. 4 and 6.

6. "Sixteenth Census of the United States: 1940," NA 208–232–1114, folder "Statistics on Enemy Aliens." For the number of newspapers, see NA 208–222–1079, folder "Foreign Language Division—Objectives."

7. "Ban on Broadcasts by Aliens Discussed," *New York Times,* February 18, 1940, IX, 12:5; "FBI-FCC Mull Propaganda," *Variety,* February, 21, 1940, 24. On the continued debate of this issue during 1940, see "FCC Head Cold on Foreign Lingo Ban," *Variety,* September 18, 1940, 26.

8. "Report of Meeting of Representatives of Stations Broadcasting Foreign Language Programs, New York, July 25, 1940," NA 208–233–1117, folder "Cox Committee"; "Suggest It Helps Democracy to Use the Italian Language," *Variety,* June 26, 1940, 36; and "Precautions on Linguals," *Variety,* July 17, 1940, 23.

9. FCC, *Analyses and Tabulation of the Returns of the Commission's Questionnaire Concerning Broadcasts by Licensees in Languages Other Than English* (Washington, D.C., 1940); "57 Drop Foreign Lingo: FCC Checks U.S. Alien Programs," *Variety,* December 18, 1940, 29.

10. Rudolf Arnheim and Martha Collins Bayne, "Foreign Language Broadcasts over Local American Stations: A Study of a Special Interest Program," in *Radio Research 1941,* ed. Paul F. Lazarsfeld and Frank N. Stanton (New York, [1941] 1979), 3–64.

11. Ibid., 8–13. The percentages for musical items on other foreign-language programs were Yiddish, 68.1 percent; Polish, 73.3 percent; Lithuanian, 55.8 percent; and Spanish, 88.1 percent.

12. Arnheim and Collins Bayne, "Foreign Language Broadcasts," 25.

13. For the report on the German propaganda film, see *Variety,* July 24, 1940, 2; on WBNX, see *Variety,* June 26, 1940, 1. The reporter's observation on Italian Americans is quoted in Blum, *V Was for Victory,* 147.

14. For general discussions of the Italian and German antifascist refugees in the United States, see, respectively, John P. Diggins, *Mussolini and Fascism: The View from America* (Princeton, N.J., 1979); and Joachim Radkau, *Die deutsche Emigration in den USA. Ihr Einfluss auf die amerikanische Europapolitik, 1933–1945* (Düsseldorf, 1971). For the ongoing debate over banning foreign-language programs, see "Radio Safeguard Asked," *New York Times,* August 26, 1940, 17:3; and "Legion Stand Protested: Broadcasters Defend Foreign Language Programs," *New York Times,* September 28, 1941, 31:2. Also see "FCC Head Cold on Foreign Lingo Ban," *Variety,* September 18, 1940, 26; and "Government Still

Skeptical about Foreign Language Broadcasts But Accepts Thesis of Usefulness," *Variety,* December 24, 1941, 27.

Salvemini's article was published under the headline "Salvemini Study," *New York Times,* October 13, 1940, 5:1. Two days later the *Times* printed an article which reported that WOV had taken "vigorous exception" to Salvemini's charges. See "Propaganda Charge Is Denied by WOV," *New York Times,* October 15, 1940, 5:4.

15. *Aufbau,* December 12, 1941, 6.

16. *Neue Volkszeitung,* October 20, 1941.

17. "Report on German- and Italian-Language Programs in New York City," undated, NA 208–233–1113, folder "WBNX." Cranston's comment is taken from his memorandum to William B. Lewis, March 20, 1942, NA 208–233–1117, folder "Cox Committee."

18. The decision to clean up the New York City stations first is presented in "Activities of the Foreign Language Division—Report No. 5," March 17, 1942, NA 208–232–1115, folder "Foreign Language Division."

19. "Report on the German Language Broadcasts of Station WBNX in the Period December 11–18, 1941," NA 208–233–1117, folder "Cox Committee."

20. Dorothy Thompson, *Washington Evening Star,* February 28, 1942. See also Charles R. Olift, "German and Italian Language Personnel, Station WBNX, New York, N.Y.," undated, NA 208–233–1117, folder "Censorship."

21. FCC, "Foreign Language Broadcasts, WBNX—German Language," January 19, 1942, NA 208–233–1117, folder "Cox Committee"; and "German and Italian Language Personnel, WBNX," NA 208–233–1117, p. 1.

22. Letter by Rudy R. Strauss to Lee Falk, June 1942, NA 208–233–1117, folder "Censorship"; Lee Falk's actions are discussed in a memo written by him to Elmer Davis titled "Foreign Language Radio," July 29, 1942, NA 208–232–1116, folder "Special Personnel."

23. On the creation of the Foreign Language Radio War Committee and the code ratified, see memorandum by Lee Falk to Alan Cranston, May 14, 1942, NA 208–233–1115, folder "Office Memorandums"; and circular by A. Simon, Chairman of the FLRWC to Station Managers, July 21, 1942, NA 208–233–1117, folder "Censorship."

24. "Program Machinery for Regulation and Improvement of Domestic Foreign Language Programs," memorandum by Robert D. Leigh (FBIS), September 8, 1942, NA 208–233–1117, folder "Cox Committee."

25. "Foreign Language Radio Programs," memorandum from Alan Cranston to William B. Lewis, January 27, 1942, NA 208–232–1115, folder "Foreign Language Division."

26. Lee Falk to Alan Cranston, "German Language Radio," March 17, 1942, NA 208–6A-1, folder "Foreign Language Division, Memoranda"; Alan Cranston to Ulric Bell, "Activities of the Foreign Language Division—Report No. 5," March 17, 1942, NA 208–232–1115, folder "Foreign Language Division."

27. The only existing recordings I have come across were the first two

and the final two German-language episodes kept in the NA, Motion Picture, Sound and Video Branch (NARA). The examples mentioned here are quoted from the first two shows broadcast in March 1942, NARA, 208–10 and 208–10A.

28.   Listener response to WGES, February 24, 1942, NA 208–233–1119, folder "WGES."

29.   I found five recorded programs of *We Did It Before:* No. 5, NA, Motion Picture, Sound and Video Branch, 208–20; and Nos. 13, 17, 32, and 37, Library of Congress, Recorded Sound, LWO 6920, German OWI Recordings, Group II.

30.   Exchange of letters between Joseph Lang and Lee Falk, NA 208–233–1118, folder "WHOM," July 14, 1943, and July 27, 1943.

31.   "Report on Foreign Language Radio," November 16, 1942, NA 208–232–1115, folder "Office Memoranda."

32.   In all, I came across three programs of the *We Fight Back* series. Episodes 1, 2, and 20 are kept in the National Archives, Motion Picture, Sound and Video Branch, 208–18, 208–18A and 208–19.

33.   Lee Falk to Alan Cranston, "Weekly Report on Foreign Language Radio," October 5, 1942, NA 208–6A-1, folder "Foreign Language Division Memoranda." On the voluntary work of the stations, see, for example, Falk to Cranston, "Weekly Report on Foreign Language Radio," July 15, 1942; NA 208–6A-1.

34.   From a number of editorials, especially in the *Chicago Abendpost,* it becomes evident that many writers for German-language papers resented the fact that they were under suspicion once again. In an editorial titled "Duties and Rights," the author emphasized that German Americans had always fulfilled their duties toward their adopted country. Therefore, as he argued, "they do not need to prove their loyalty through flowery speeches or ostentatious celebrations"; instead, they should be able to expect the protection of their rights due to them. *Abendpost,* July 2, 1942, 4:1.

35.   For a detailed description of this episode, see NA 208–221–1073, folder "Gerhart Seger." Leicht's comments to Seger are quoted in Seger's letter to Cranston, same folder, August 5, 1942.

36.   For a partial list of these replacements, see "Monthly Report of the Foreign Language Division," October 5, 1942, NA 208–6A-1, folder "Foreign Language Division Memoranda," 3. On WTEL, Philadelphia, see letter by Robert M. Kempner to T. J. Slowie, Secretary of the FCC, April 24, 1942, NA 208–233–1117, folder "Censorship"; and "Anti-Nazi Germans Take Over Show Once Featuring Convicted Nazi Agent," *Variety,* September 9, 1942, 24:1.

37.   For a general discussion of the licensing power of the FCC and the development of this prerogative since 1934, see Charles A. Siepmann, *Radio's Second Chance* (Boston, 1947), chap. 1.

38.   United States, Congress, House, Select Committee to Investigate the Federal Communications Commission, *Study and Investigation of the FCC: Hearings before the Select Committee to Investigate the Federal Communications*

Commission, House of Representatives, Seventy-eighth Congress (Washington, D.C., 1943–45), vol. 1, 351, 380, 833, 1008.

39. Ibid., 494–95.

40. Letters of Arnold Hartley to Lee Falk, September 22, 1942, and November 3, 1942, NA 208–233–1119, folder "WGES." For a listing of the foreign-language programs sponsored by the Foreign Language Division, see "Foreign Language Operations of 118 Stations," September 1942, NA 208–232–1113, folder "Foreign Language Radio Study," 2.

41. *Study and Investigation of the FCC,* 480.

42. "Summary of Cox Committee Charges," NA 208–222–1078, folder "Cox Committee Hearings."

43. Letter by Alan Cranston to Lee Falk, August 11, 1943, NA 208–222–1078, folder "Cox Committee Hearings."

44. Letter by Alan Cranston to George Lyon, July 19, 1943; undated memo, "Staff of Foreign Language Division: Slash or Expand?"; and memo, November 2, 1943; all in NA 208–222–1079, folder "Foreign Language Division."

45. On the rejection of a government propaganda agency before the war, see Steele, "Preparing the Public for War," and Winkler, *The Politics of Propaganda.*

46. This discussion is heavily based on Sydney Weinberg's excellent account of this struggle within the OWI: "What to Tell America: The Writers' Quarrel in the Office of War Information," *Journal of American History* 55 (June 1968): 75–84.

47. For Weinberg's quotation, see "What to Tell America," 83. See also Harold F. Gosnell, "Obstacles to Domestic Pamphleteering by OWI in World War II," *Journalism Quarterly* 23 (December 1946): 4; and Blum, *V Is for Victory,* 31–45.

48. Printed in Weinberg, "What to Tell America," 85 n. 55.

49. See George E. Pozzetta, "'My Children Are My Jewels': Italian-American Generations during World War II," in *The Home-Front War: World War II and American Society,* ed. Kenneth Paul O'Brien and Lynn Hudson Parsons (Westport, Conn., 1995), 63. Richard Steele discusses job discrimination against ethnic Americans in his essay "'No Radicals': Discrimination against Ethnics in the American Defense Industry, 1940–1942," *Labor History* 32 (1991): 66–90.

50. For statistics on radio stations broadcasting in foreign languages, see FCC, *Questionnaire Concerning Broadcasts by Licensees in Languages Other Than English;* "Foreign Language Radio Study," September 1942, NA 208–232–1113; and *Study and Investigation of the FCC,* 376. On the decrease of foreign-language programs in 1944, see two articles in *Variety,* November 15, 1944, 26; and November 22, 1944, 22.

51. Cohen, *Making a New Deal,* especially chap. 3.

52. Letter by Lee Falk to the author, May 28, 1992. Alan Cranston expressed the same sentiment to me in a telephone conversation, October 14, 1992.

4. Rewards of Radio Advertising

1. Field and Lazarsfeld, *The People Look at Radio,* 5.

2. Ibid., 5–6, 82, 101.

3. Fox, *Madison Avenue Goes to War,* 19. For the quotation by Benson, see *Printer's Ink* (*PI*), April 21, 1944, 78. See also Marchand, *Creating the Corporate Soul,* chap. 6.

4. For two editorials that reflect the fears of advertisers concerning Arnold and Henderson, see *PI,* October 17, 1941, 11; and *Advertising Age,* July 21, 1941, 12.

5. *PI,* November 21, 1941, 9–12.

6. Ibid., 15.

7. This founding process is recalled in a speech by Paul West before the ANA meeting in March 1943: "Report of a Meeting on the Rationing of Meat, Cheese, Canned Fish, Fats and Oil," March 16, 1943, Thomas D'Arcy Brophy Papers, Box 7, folder "AAAA 1943 Correspondence," SHSW.

8. "American Trade Association Executives [ATAE] News Bulletin," July 19, 1943, Brophy Papers, Box 4, folder "War Advertising Council, 1943," SHSW; see also Fox, *Madison Avenue Goes to War,* 49–50.

9. "ATAE News Bulletin," July 19, 1943.

10. "The Advertising Council. A Six Months Record," October 2, 1942, Brophy Papers, Box 4, folder "The Advertising Council, Reports and Meetings," SHSW.

11. "Facing Realities," talk by Paul B. West, November 11, 1942, NA 208–93–602, folder "ANA."

12. *PI,* November 20, 1942, 17.

13. *PI,* January 16, 1942, 40; *PI,* April 10, 1942, 14.

14. Fox, *Madison Avenue Goes to War,* 68ff.

15. In real advertising dollars, radio still remained second behind newspapers during the war. In 1942, for example, total advertising expenditure for the media listed as followed: newspapers, $580 million; radio, $245 million; magazines, $170 million; *PI,* March 26, 1943, 18–19. For the average yearly advertising revenues during the war, see *PI,* January 25, 1946.

16. *PI,* December 17, 1943, 35, 39.

17. *Variety,* September 15, 1943, 35.

18. *Variety,* November 11, 1942, 25.

19. "The Pepsodent Show," February 3, 1942, LC Manuscript Division, 79271.

20. "Kraft Music Hall," January 7, 1943, J. Walter Thompson Archives, Reel no. 204.

21. "Standard Brands Show," December 21, 1943, J. Walter Thompson Archives, Reel no. 204.

22. See, for example, "Fibber McGee and Molly," February 24, 1942, LC, LWO 12875, 65A1.

23. "Shell Sunset Valley Barn Dance," April 9, 1942, J. Walter Thompson Archives, Reel no. 202.

24. For a survey on service advertisements, see *PI*, January 5, 1945; the general appraisal of radio commercials and the quotation are taken from Lazarsfeld, *The People Look at Radio*, 21–22.

25. News Program over WEAF, New York, sponsored by Planters Peanut Company, December 17, 1943, J. Walter Thompson Archives, Reel no. 202.

26. For polls on service advertisements, see *PI*, June 2, 1944, 21; *PI*, January 5, 1945, 90. The new war slogans are discussed in *PI*, April 16, 1943.

27. The first two examples are quoted in Lingeman, *Don't You Know There's a War On?* 231; the last one is discussed in *Time*, December 29, 1941, 38. Network executives' opposition to "war realism" is discussed in *Variety*, December 24, 1942, 25. A driving force behind this concern was the memory of the "Invasion from Mars" broadcast from 1938.

28. Fox, *Madison Avenue Goes to War*, 37. For the soldier's complaint, see Raymond Rubicam, "Advertising," in *While You Were Gone: A Report on Wartime Life in the United States*, ed. Jack Goodman (New York, 1946), 432.

29. Rubicam, "Advertising," 431.

30. "Swan Song for Singing Commercial," *PI*, August, 1943, 20; see also Norman Corwin, "The Radio," in *While You Were Gone: A Report on Wartime Life in the United States*, ed. Jack Goodman (New York, 1946), 385.

31. *Radio Life*, June 7, 1942, 2. For the second quotation, see Ernest Dichter, "On the Psychology of Radio Commercials," in *Radio Research, 1942–43*, ed. Paul F. Lazarsfeld and Frank N. Stanton (New York, 1944), 478. For a much fuller elaboration of this issue, see Lawrence W. Levine, "The Folklore of Industrial Society: Popular Culture and Its Audiences," *American Historical Review* 97 (December 1992): 1369–99.

32. "Radio's Plug-Uglies," *Reader's Digest*, August 1942.

33. Ibid., 4.

34. Fox, *Madison Avenue Goes to War*, 51; Soffer, "Dreamers, Consumers, Citizens," 14.

35. The framework established in Guy Cook's study, *The Discourse of Advertising* (London, 1992), proved very helpful in organizing my discussion in the following section.

36. One of the best discussions of radio and radio listening is presented in Cantril and Allport's study, *The Psychology of Radio*, 4, 15, 157.

37. Ibid., 241.

38. Marchand, *Advertising the American Dream*, 88, 93.

39. Siepmann, *Radio's Second Chance*, 13.

40. Jack Benny Collection, UCLA, Special Collections, Box 88, folder "American Tobacco Co., 1944–1946."

41. Ibid.

42. Fox discusses Hill's advertising approach in *The Mirror Makers*, chap. 3; quotation on p. 154. For the Benny-Hill correspondence, see UCLA, Special Collections, Jack Benny Collection, Box 97, folder 6.

43. They published their findings in *Mass Persuasion: The Social Psychology of a War Bond Drive* (New York, 1946).

44. Ibid., 27.

45. Ibid., 82, 87.

46. Gordon Kinney to Joseph Ecclesine, May 12, 1944, NA 208–103–647, folder "Memoranda—Allocation Plan," 3.

47. *PI,* July 23, 1943, 26.

48. Barnouw, *The Sponsor,* 39.

49. Wertheim, *Radio Comedy,* 141.

50. "The Jack Benny Show," March 8, 1942, Jack Benny Collection, UCLA, Special Collections, Box 25.

51. "Fibber McGee and Molly," December 26, 1944, LC, Manuscript Division, 91954.

52. Dichter, "On the Psychology of Radio Commercials," 477.

53. Field and Lazarsfeld, *The People Look at Radio,* 27.

54. "The Pepsodent Show," June 16, 1942, LC, Manuscript Division, 81132.

55. "Fibber McGee and Molly," April 27, 1943, SHSW, Division of Archives and Manuscripts, Micro 474, Reel 10.

56. "Testimony in Matter of Transfer of Blue Network," September 10, 1943, 8–10, Lowell Mellett Papers, Box 7, folder "Fly, James Lawrence—Chair, FCC," FDR Library.

57. Paper Draft of James L. Fly, March 15, 1944, Lowell Mellett Papers, Box 7, folder "Fly, James Lawrence, Chair, FCC," FDR Library.

58. Field and Lazarsfeld, *The People Look at Radio,* 18.

59. Ibid., 17, 22, 87.

60. Ibid. 23–24.

61. For a discussion of reasons that listeners disliked commercials, see, for example, Dichter, "On the Psychology of Radio Commercials," 466–72.

62. Field and Lazarsfeld, *The People Look at Radio,* 21, 28.

63. "Democracy's Newest Weapon," address by Charles G. Mortimer, Jr., October 27, 1947, Brophy Papers, Box 1, folder "Advertising Council—Correspondence, 1947," SHSW.

64. James W. Young, "What Advertising Learned from the War," December 11, 1945, Thomas D'Arcy Brophy Papers, Box 3, folder "Advertising Council, Miscellaneous, 1943–1945," SHSW.

65. Paul B. West, "Something New Has Been Added to Advertising," *Advertising and Selling,* May 1945. The sense that government was more appreciative of advertising runs through all the advertising correspondence and memos of the war years (Brophy Papers, for example). The historic meeting in March 1944 is discussed in *W.A.C. Newsletter* of March 18, 1944, Brophy Papers, Box 5, folder "War Advertising Council, 1944–45," SHSW.

66. For the Republic Steel ad, see Fox, *Madison Avenue Goes to War,* 71; Soffer, "Dreamers, Consumers, Citizens," 29, 48–49.

5. The Comedians Go to War

1. Speech by William B. Lewis, January 20, 1942, NA 208–93–602, folder "Association of National Advertisers."

2. Ibid.

3. Koppes and Black, *Hollywood Goes to War,* 111, 139, 324; Doherty, *Projections of War,* 59.

4. Field and Lazarsfeld, *The People Look at Radio,* vii.

5. William B. Lewis, Meeting of Regional Consultants, December 28–30, 1942, NA 208–93–599, folder "Regional Meeting."

6. "Fibber McGee and Molly," December 1, 1942, SHSW.

7. Lingeman, *Don't You Know There's a War On?* 238–39.

8. For a good discussion of the show's history and characters, see Charles Stumpf and Tom Price, *Heavenly Days! The Story of Fibber McGee and Molly* (Salinas, Calif., 1987).

9. Ibid., 45, 165; McDonald, *Don't Touch That Dial!* 132–45.

10. *Time,* June 4, 1945, 60. Quinn's comments are quoted in the same article.

11. Report of letter by Paul B. West, president of the Association of National Advertisers, to large radio sponsors entitled "Cooperation of Commercial Radio Users with Government," January 12, 1942, NA 208–93–602, folder "Association of National Advertisers."

12. Hooper Report quoted in OWI Intelligence Report, "Surfeit with War on the Radio," January 13, 1943, NA 208–103–643, folder "Meetings."

13. "Proposal for Radio Coordination," Douglas Meservey to William Lewis, December 17, 1941, NA 208–93–596, folder "Douglas Meservey."

14. Speech by W. Lewis, January 20, 1942, NA 208–93–602, folder "Association of National Advertisers."

15. Radio's approach did in fact mirror that of the government's cooperation with America's industrial manufacturers. Donald Nelson, director of the War Production Board, outlined the same collaboration between the WPB and private industry in a speech in January 1942: "We are going to have to rely on our great mass production industries for the bulk of our increase under the war program. Wherever we can we must convert them to war production, and convert them quickly. . . . All the government would do was tell the business what it wanted. The question of *how* it would be produced was left up to business." Quoted in Lingeman, *Don't You Know There's a War On?* 107.

16. "How Government Messages Will Be Allocated," April 1942, NA 208–93–598, folder "Allocation Plan."

17. Seymour Morris to Stuart Sherman, October 22, 1942, NA 208–103–645, folder "Policy"; Archibald MacLeish to F.D.R., April 8, 1942, NA 208–93–598, folder "Allocation Plan."

18. *Variety,* May 13–June 17, 1942.

19. "Fibber McGee and Molly," "Sugar Substitute," May 5, 1942, Recorded Sound, LC, LWO 15731, 18A1.

20. Quoted in *Variety,* June 3, 1942, 35.

21. *Variety,* June 17, 1942, 25.

22. The first survey was on "The Alien Problem," "Special Services Division Report no. 1," April 17, 1942, NA 44–171–1843. For a survey that solicited case studies, see "Special Service Report # 29: Impact of War on the American Family," September 16, 1942, NA 44–171–1844.

23. Seymour Morris to R. D. Boss, P & G, October 14, 1942. Apparently Boss channeled the request to his superior, as the response came from William B. Ramsey, general manager of P & G: Ramsey to Morris, October 21, 1942, NA 208–103–645, folder "Policy."

24. L. Menkin to G. Zachary, November 6, 1942, NA 208–93–602, folder "Pedlar and Ryan."

25. Nat Wolff to William B. Lewis, August 18, 1942, NA 208–93–604, folder "Nat Wolff."

26. "Jack Benny Show," October 18, 1942, UCLA, Special Collections, Jack Benny Collection, Box 26.

27. Fred Allen is quoted in Milt Josefsberg, *The Jack Benny Show* (New Rochelle, N.Y., 1977), 60; for Benny's comment, see Wertheim, *Radio Comedy,* 131.

28. Josefsberg, *The Jack Benny Show,* 54. On the popularity of his greeting, "Jell-O Again," see Jim Harmon, *The Great Radio Comedians* (New York, 1970), 156.

29. Straight appeal read at the end of "The Jack Benny Show." This appeal was closely tailored along the lines of information given by the OWI *Radio War Guide,* which many other shows frequently copied in their straight messages.

30. "Surfeit with War on the Radio," Surveys Division Memorandum No. 47, January 13, 1943, NA 208–103–643, folder "Meetings."

31. Ibid., 16.

32. "Surfeit with Government War Messages," Report by the Bureau of Special Services in connection with the Denver National Opinion Research Center, December 6, 1943, NA 44–164–1799, "Surveys Division Memo #71," 1, 9.

33. Ibid., 15.

34. "The Jack Benny Show," April 4, 1943, UCLA, Special Collections, Jack Benny Collection, Box 27.

35. "The Jack Benny Show," February 8, 1942, UCLA, Special Collections, Box 25.

36. "The Jack Benny Show," November 29, 1942, UCLA, Special Collections, Jack Benny Collection, Box 26.

37. Larry Wilde, *The Great Comedians Talk about Comedy* (New York, 1967), 41.

38. I found the following studies particularly helpful for understanding the role of humor and comedy: Jesse Bier, *The Rise and Fall of American Humor* (New York, 1968); John Morreall, *Taking Laughter Seriously* (Albany, N.Y., 1983); Stephanie Koziski, "The Standup Comedian as Anthropologist: Intentional Culture Critic," *Journal of Popular Culture* 18 (fall 1984): 57–76; Lawrence W. Levine, "American Culture and the Great Depression," *Yale Review* 74 (winter 1985); Arthur Power Dudden, ed., *American Humor* (New York, 1987); T. G. A. Nelson, *Comedy: An Introduction to Comedy in Literature, Drama and Cinema* (Oxford, 1990); and Mary Douglas, "Jokes," in *Rethinking Popular Culture: Contemporary Perspectives in Cultural Studies,* ed. Chandra Mukerji and Mi-

chael Schudson (Berkeley and Los Angeles, 1991), 291–310. Morreall discusses most of the theories I cite in his book; see especially for superiority theory. For a convincing analysis of Freud and Bergson, see Douglas, "Jokes."

39.   Morreall, *Taking Laughter Seriously,* 114. Bier and Nelson have also commented on this unifying function of laughter.

40.   Quinn, "Situation Comedy: 'Tis Funny, McGee!'" 37.

41.   "The Jack Benny Show," May 23, 1943, UCLA, Special Collections, Jack Benny Collection, Box 27.

42.   Josefsberg, *The Jack Benny Show,* 94.

43.   "The Pepsodent Show," February 3, 1942, broadcast from March Field, California, LC, Manuscript Division, 79271.

44.   *Newsweek,* January 5, 1942, 48.

45.   See Wertheim, *Radio Comedy,* 295.

46.   *Variety,* March 1, 1944, 36:1.

47.   "The Pepsodent Show," February 3, 1942, LC, Manuscript Division, 79271.

48.   For a good overview of Bob Hope's career and comedy style, see William Robert Faith, *Bob Hope: A Life in Comedy* (New York, 1982).

49.   Lewis Gannett, "Books," in *While You Were Gone,* ed. Jack Goodman, 451.

50.   See *Variety,* February 11, 1942, 32:1.

51.   *Variety,* April 22, 1942, 27:2.

52.   *Variety,* October 4, 1944, 25:2.

53.   "The Pepsodent Show," March 24, 1942, LC, Manuscript Division, 79862.

54.   Bob Hope with Meville Shavelson, *Don't Shoot, It's Only Me: Bob Hope's Comedy History of the United States* (New York, 1990), 54.

55.   Mikhail Bakhtin, *Rabelais and His World,* trans. Hélène Iswolsky (Bloomington, Ind., 1984), 10. For an insightful discussion on applying Bakhtin's approach to television, see Fiske, *Television Culture,* chap. 13.

56.   "Texaco Star Theater," January 3, 1943; quoted in Havig, *Fred Allen's Radio Comedy,* 208. For discussions of the frequent censorship of Allen's comedy and his cooperation with the OWI, see chapters 5 and 8. See also the intriguing discussion of this satirical side of Allen's broadcasts in Hilmes, *Radio Voices,* 200–212.

57.   Fred Allen, *Treadmill to Oblivion* (Boston, 1954), 212.

58.   "The Pepsodent Show," May 25, 1943, LC, Manuscript Division, 84576.

59.   Interview with Sherwood Schwartz by author, July 28, 1992.

60.   "The Pepsodent Show," March 3, 1942, LC, Manuscript Division, 79559.

61.   "The Pepsodent Show," February 9, 1943, LC, Manuscript Division, 83494.

62.   *Variety,* August 19, 1942, 1:1; *Variety,* December 22, 1943, 1:1.

63.   See Faith, *Bob Hope,* 161, 183.

64.   Memorandum by Douglas Meservey to Archibald MacLeish, May 7, 1942, NA 208–120–707, folder "Treasury Department."

65. Letters by Jack Meakin of Foote, Cone & Belding, dated April 25, 1944, and Robert P. Burrows of the G.E. Company, May 4, 1944, NA 208–1–3, folder "Organization 1–2, Radio Bureau, 1942–1944."

6. Wartime Soap Operas

1. The information on the number of shows and the percentage of daytime broadcasting comes from a report of the Cooperative Analysis of Broadcasting entitled "Radio Program Audiences, October 1941–April 1942," CAB Reports Collection, Box 12, SHSW.

2. For a discussion of the "Berg debate," see *New York Times,* December 6, 1942, VIII, 12:2; and Maurice Zolotow, "Washboard Weepers," *Saturday Evening Post,* May 29, 1943, 16–17f. This episode is also discussed in most of the important general histories of soap operas to date: Raymond William Stedman's book *The Serials: Suspense and Drama by Installment* (Norman, Okla., 1971), the first general history of daytime serials, which evolved out of his dissertation, "A History of Broadcasting of Daytime Serial Dramas in the United States" (Ph.D. diss., University of Southern California, 1959); Madeline Edmondson and David Rounds, *From Mary Noble to Mary Hartman: The Complete Soap Opera Book* (New York, 1976); Muriel G. Cantor and Suzanne Pingree, *The Soap Opera* (Beverly Hills, 1983); and Robert C. Allen, *Speaking of Soap Operas* (Chapel Hill, N.C., 1985), which is an intriguing study informed by reader-oriented literary criticism.

Additional studies that helped me understand soap operas focus largely on television serials: Tania Modleski, *Loving with a Vengeance: Mass-Produced Fantasies for Women* (Hamden, Conn., 1982); Mary Cassatra and Thomas Skill, eds., *Life on Daytime Television: Tuning-In American Serial Drama* (Norwood, N.J., 1983); Peter Buckman, *All for Love: A Study in Soap Opera* (Salem, N.H., 1984); Ien Ang, *Watching Dallas: Soap Opera and the Melodramatic Imagination* (London, 1985); Marilyn J. Matelski, *The Soap Opera Evolution: America's Enduring Romance with Daytime Drama* (Jefferson, N.C., 1988); Mary Ellen Brown, "Motley Moments: Soap Operas, Carnival, Gossip and the Power of the Utterance," in *Television and Women's Culture: The Politics of the Popular,* ed. Mary Ellen Brown (London, 1990); Christine Geraghty, *Women and Soap Opera: A Study of Prime Time Soaps* (Cambridge, England, 1991); and Suzanne Frentz, ed., *Staying Tuned: Contemporary Soap Opera Criticism* (Bowling Green, Ohio, 1992).

3. *New York Times,* December 6, 1942, VIII, 12:2; James Thurber, *The Beast in Me and Other Animals* (New York, 1948), 252.

4. Stedman, *The Serials,* 342.

5. For more analysis, see also Hilmes's intriguing analysis of soap operas, *Radio Voices,* chap. 6.

6. Stedman, *The Serials,* 234–40.

7. Irna Phillips, "Every Woman's Life Is a Soap Opera," *McCall's,* March 1965, 116–17f.

8. Ibid.; Stedman, *The Serials,* chaps. 12 through 15.

9. Katherine Best, "'Literature' of the Air," *Saturday Review of Literature,* April 20, 1940, 11–13; Edmondson, *From Mary Noble to Mary Hartman,* chap. 3, "Soaperstars," 37–47.

10. See "The Right to Happiness," August 14, 1941, Irna Phillips Collection, Box 48, SHSW. On the war-related loss of characters, see letter by Irna Phillips to John Taylor, Pedlar & Ryan, Inc., December 13, 1941, Phillips Collection, Box 62, SHSW. Arthur Peterson, who played Dr. Ruthledge on *The Guiding Light* in the early war years, repeatedly referred to Phillips's emphasis on the theme of racial harmony in an interview with the author, July 27, 1992.

11. Letter to John Taylor, Pedlar & Ryan, Inc., December 13, 1941, Phillips Collection, Box 62, SHSW.

12. George A. Wiley, "The Soap Operas and the War," *Journal of Broadcasting* 7 (fall 1963): 348.

13. "Report on the Present Use of War Themes in Network Daytime Programs," March 2, 1942, NA 208–93–598, folder "Allocation."

14. Ibid., 8.

15. Letter by the OWI Radio Bureau to all sponsors of radio serials, September 19, 1942, NA 208–93–614, folder "Victory Parade."

16. Irna Phillips to Storrs Haynes, Compton Advertising, Inc., September 30, 1942, Phillips Collection, Box 62, SHSW.

17. For an extended theoretical discussion of some of the aspects I have summarized in this paragraph, see Allen's *Speaking of Soap Operas,* chap. 3, "The Soap Opera as Commodity and Commodifier."

18. As Hilmes has argued, because of their inexpensive production costs and their "feminine base," daytime serials never achieved the same status as the evening shows. See Hilmes, *Radio Voices,* 160.

19. *New York Times,* November 29, 1942, VIII, 12:2; Stedman, *The Serials,* 332–33.

20. "A Survey of CBS and NBC Daytime Serials," September 15, 1942; NA 208–93–614, folder "Allocation."

21. "The Guiding Light," October 2, 1942, Phillips Collection, Box 30, SHSW.

22. Maureen Honey, *Creating Rosie the Riveter: Class, Gender, and Propaganda during World War II* (Amherst, Mass., 1984), 48–51.

23. In her chapter "Heroines on the Homefront," D'Ann Campbell argued that housewives were critical to the successful implementation of the wartime rationing measures. These issues were also frequently intertwined in daytime serials, highlighting housewives' important contributions during the war. D'Ann Campbell, *Women at War with America: Private Lives in a Patriotic Era* (Cambridge, Mass., 1984), chap. 6.

24. "Lonely Women," Script no. 1, July 2, 1942, Phillips Collection, Box 50, SHSW.

25. See "Ideas, Characterizations and Projections for Lonely Women," by Irna Phillips, as well as the first several scripts, Phillips Collection, Box 50, SHSW.

26. "Lonely Women," September 2, 1942, Phillips Collection, Box 50, SHSW.

27. Campbell, *Women at War with America*, 107–8.

28. "Lonely Women," November 19, 1943, Phillips Collection, Box 50, SHSW.

29. "Lonely Women," November 23, 1943, Phillips Collection, Box 50, SHSW.

30. Exchange of letters, July 5 and 11, 1945, Phillips Collection, Box 62, SHSW.

31. Letter by Mildred Oldenburg to General Mills, Inc., November 15, 1943, Phillips Collection, Box 50, SHSW.

32. Letters by King Painter (November 11, 1943) and Carl Wester (November 22, 1943), Phillips Collection, Box 50, SHSW.

33. For a discussion of the change in OWI policy, see Maureen Honey, "Remembering Rosie: Advertising Images of Women in World War II," in *The Home-Front War: World War II and American Society*, ed. Kenneth Paul O'Brien and Lynn Hudson Parsons (Westport, Conn., 1995), 97; "Lonely Women," October 9, 1944, Phillips Collection, Box 50, SHSW.

34. Letter by King Painter to Irna Phillips, September 18, 1944, Phillips Collection, Box 62, folder "Knox Reeves Advertising, Correspondence 1943–1946," SHSW.

35. "Lonely Women," October 31, 1944, Phillips Collection, Box 50, SHSW.

36. Eleanor Ferguson Straub, "Government Policy toward Civilian Women during World War II" (Ph.D. diss., Emery University, 1973), 1–4. See also Honey, *Creating Rosie the Riveter*, esp. chap. 1.

37. Geraghty, *Women and Soap Opera*, 46–47, 56–58.

38. Hilmes, *Radio Voices*, 174.

39. "The Pepsodent Show," March 24, 1942, LC, Manuscript Division, 79862.

40. "Jack Benny Show," November 1, 1942, UCLA, Special Collections, Jack Benny Collection, Box 26.

41. Margaret T. McFadden, "'America's Boy Friend Who Can't Get a Date': Gender, Race, and the Cultural Work of the Jack Benny Program, 1932–1946," *Journal of American History* 80 (June 1993): 118, 126–29.

42. "Jack Benny Show," November 8, 1942, UCLA, Special Collections, Jack Benny Collection, Box 26.

43. Tyler May, *Homeward Bound*, 58–68, 140; and Elaine Tyler May, "Rosie the Riveter Gets Married," *Mid-America: An Historical Review* 75 (October 1993): 269–82.

44. Ibid.; see also letter by Irna Phillips to Corlis Wilbur, November 17, 1942, Phillips Collection, Box 62, folder "Compton Advertising, Inc.," SHSW.

45. Irna Phillips to Robert Ross, October 15, 1941, Box 62, folder "P&G, Co.—Correspondence, 1941–47"; and "The Guiding Light," September 3, 1943, Box 31; both in Phillips Collection, SHSW.

46. Irna Phillips to William Ramsey, March 3, 1942, Phillips Collection, Box 62, folder "P&G, Co.—Correspondence, 1941–47," SHSW.

47. Quoted in Zolotow, "Washboard Weepers," 16.

48. Herta Herzog, "What Do We Really Know about Daytime Serial Listeners," *Radio Research, 1942–43,* ed. Paul F. Lazarsfeld and Frank N. Stanton (New York, 1944), 23–33.

49. For a good summary of this debate, see Eleanor S. Boll, "The Child," in "The American Family in World War II," ed. Ray H. Abrams, *Annals of the American Academy of Political and Social Science* 229 (September 1943): 69–78; also Anna W. M. Wolf and Irma Simonton Black, "What Happened to the Younger People?" in *While You Were Gone,* ed. Jack Goodman.

50. Letters by King Painter to Irna Phillips, November 18 and November 23, 1943, Phillips Collection, Box 62, folder "Knox Reeves Advertising, Correspondence 1943–1946," SHSW.

51. "The Guiding Light," May 15, 1944, Phillips Collection, Box 32, SHSW.

52. "The Guiding Light," June 13, 1944, Phillips Collection, Box 32, SHSW.

53. "The Guiding Light," May 23, 1944, Phillips Collection, Box 32, SHSW.

54. The letter that mentioned an "impressive" listener response came from King Painter, June 2, 1944, folder "Knox Reeves Advertising—Correspondence 1943–1946." James M. Gaines, Assistant Director, Advertising and Promotion of NBC, October 11, 1944, folder "NBC correspondence," referred to her Legion citation in a congratulatory letter. Both are from the Phillips Collection, Box 62, SHSW.

55. Letter by Irna Phillips to King Painter, November 26, 1943, Phillips Collection, Box 62, folder "Knox Reeves Advertising—Correspondence 1943–1946," SHSW.

56. Letter by Irna Phillips to King Painter, December 23, 1943, ibid.

57. "Woman in White," June–July 1944; for the breakup between Bill and Alice, see July 11, 1944, Phillips Collection, Box 16, SHSW.

58. "The Woman in White," July 31, 1944, Phillips Collection, Box 16, SHSW.

59. Letter by King Painter to Irna Phillips, July 6, 1944, Phillips Collection, Box 62, SHSW.

60. These sequences in Phillips's soap operas also closely resembled other "prescriptive" advice to women. See Susan Hartmann, "Prescriptions for Penelope: Literature on Women's Obligations to Returning World War II Veterans," *Women's Studies* 5 (1978): 223–39.

61. "Today's Children," September 11, 1945, Phillips Collection, Box 52, SHSW.

62. Irna Phillips mentioned these citations, plus short excerpts from the actual letters of commendations, in her letter to Doris Pullen, the research associate of *Fortune* magazine, January 5, 1946, Phillips Collection, Box 63, folder "Miscellaneous Correspondence," SHSW.

63. "NBC Press Conference, New York, May 29, 1945," Phillips Collection, Box 63, folder "Miscellaneous Correspondence," SHSW.

64. The first instance mentioned is referred to in a letter by John Taylor to Irna Phillips, October 27, 1941, Phillips Collection, Box 62, folder "Pedlar & Ryan, Inc.—Correspondence, 1941." On the deletion of the social drinking

scene, see letter by King Painter to Carl Wester, December 7, 1945, Phillips Collection, Box 62, folder "Knox Reeves Advertising—Correspondence 1943–1946," SHSW.

Epilogue

1. The key studies that have influenced my understanding of this transformation are Daniel J. Czitrom, *Media and the American Mind: From Morse to McLuhan* (Chapel Hill, N.C., 1982); Lary May, *Screening Out the Past: The Birth of Mass Culture and the Motion Picture Industry* (Chicago, 1983); Roy Rosenzweig, *Eight Hours for What We Will: Workers and Leisure in an Industrial City, 1870–1920* (Cambridge, Mass., 1983); Larry Levine, *Highbrow/Lowbrow: The Emergence of Cultural Hierarchy in America* (Cambridge, Mass., 1988); William Leach, *Land of Desire: Merchants, Power, and the Rise of a New American Culture* (New York, 1993), quotation on page 5; and Lears, *Fables of Abundance: A Cultural History of Advertising in America* (New York, 1994). See also the literature on advertising history, which I quoted in chapter 4, and William Leiss, Stephen Kline, and Sut Jhally, eds., *Social Communication in Advertising: Persons, Products and Images of Well-Being* (London, 1990), especially chaps. 4 and 5.

2. Charles McGovern, "Consumption and Citizenship in the United States, 1900–1940," in *Getting and Spending: European and American Consumer Societies in the Twentieth Century,* ed. Susan Strasser, Charles McGovern, and Matthias Judt (Washington, D.C., 1998), 50.

3. Marchand, *Creating the Corporate Soul;* and Lizabeth Cohen, "The New Deal and the Making of Citizen Consumers," in *Getting and Spending,* ed. Susan Strasser, Charles McGovern, and Matthias Judt, 111.

4. As I mentioned in the introduction, George Lipsitz's studies considerably advanced my understanding of this shift. So did the theoretical work by the British cultural studies tradition. But the first book that impressed this transition upon me was the anthology of essays edited by Lary May, *Recasting America: Culture and Politics in the Age of Cold War* (Chicago, 1989); see especially May's introduction and the article "Movie Star Politics: The Screen Actors' Guild, Cultural Conversion, and the Hollywood Red Scare," as well as Jackson Lears's essay in the same volume: "A Matter of Taste: Corporate Cultural Hegemony in a Mass-Consumption Age."

5. Robert Griffith, "The Selling of America: The Advertising Council and American Politics, 1942–1960," *Business History Review* 62 (autumn 1983): 398, 406. See also Marchand, "The Fitful Career of Advocacy Advertising"; and Tedlow, *Keeping the Corporate Image,* chap. 6.

6. Nelson Lichtenstein, "Labor in the Truman Era: Origins of the 'Private Welfare State,'" in *The Truman Presidency,* ed. Michael J. Lacey (Cambridge, 1989), chap. 4; and, in the same anthology, Robert Griffith, "Forging America's Postwar Order: Domestic Politics and Political Economy in the Age of Truman," chap. 2. See also Fones-Wolf, *Selling Free Enterprise.*

7. Lipsitz, *Rainbow at Midnight*, 255, 258.

8. For a revisionist angle on the postwar period, see the collection of articles on the oppositional culture in *Prospects* 20 (1995): 451–509; on the resistant currents in popular music and film in the postwar period, see Lipsitz, *Time Passages*, chaps. 5–8. For a discussion of the ambivalent attitude in the 1940s, see William Graebner, *The Age of Doubt: American Thought and Culture in the 1940s* (Boston, 1991), 119; and, on the impact of the A-bomb, Paul Boyer, *By the Bomb's Early Light: American Thought and Culture at the Dawn of the Atomic Age* (New York, 1985).

9. William Boddy, *Fifties Television: The Industry and Its Critics* (Urbana, Ill., 1993), chap. 3; the Denny episode is recounted on p. 48; and J. Fred MacDonald, *One Nation under Television: The Rise and Decline of Network TV* (Chicago, 1994), 25–37.

10. Charles A. Siepmann, *Radio's Second Chance* (Boston, 1947), 25, 186–87. On the issue of the FCC license freeze, see Boddy, *Fifties Television*, 50–57.

11. Lipsitz discusses the ideological reworking of urban, ethnic sitcoms of the early postwar period in *Time Passages*, chap. 3. For an intriguing discussion of the positioning of women and gender in these emerging television discourses, see Lynn Spigel, *Make Room for TV: Television and the Family Ideal in Postwar America* (Chicago, 1992) especially chaps. 2 and 3.

12. Stephen Whitfield, *The Culture of the Cold War* (Baltimore, 1991), especially chaps. 1, 3, and 7, quotation on p. 155. On the impact of the HUAC witch-hunt on Hollywood and films, see Lary May, "Movie Star Politics: The Screen Actors' Guild, Cultural Conversion, and the Hollywood Red Scare," in *Recasting America: Culture and Politics in the Age of the Cold War*, ed. Lary May, chap. 7.

13. Lizabeth Cohen, "From Town Center to Shopping Center: The Reconfiguration of Community Marketplaces in Postwar America," *American Historical Review* 101 (October 1996): 1050–81. See also the two responses to her essay: Thomas W. Hanchett, "U.S. Tax Policy and the Shopping-Center Boom of the 1950s and 1960s," and Kenneth T. Jackson, "All the World's a Mall: Reflections on the Social and Economic Consequences of the American Shopping Center," in the same issue, pp. 1082–121.

Index

Compositor:	Binghamton Valley Composition, LLC
Text:	10/13 Galliard
Display:	Galliard
Printer and Binder:	Thomson-Shore, Inc.